➤➤➤

PHONOLOGICAL AWARENESS AND PRIMARY PHONICS

THOMAS G. GUNNING

Professor Emeritus, Southern Connecticut State University
Adjunct Professor, Central Connecticut State University

Illustrated by
Norma Kable

Allyn and Bacon

Boston ➤ London ➤ Toronto ➤ Sydney ➤ Tokyo ➤ Singapore

For my children, with love—
Thomas Gerard Gunning
Joy Gunning Pizzuto
Timothy Stephen Gunning
Faith Gunning Dixon

and their spouses
Jay Pizzuto
Joseph Dixon

Vice President: Paul A. Smith
Senior Editor: Arnis Burvikovs
Editorial Assistant: Bridget Keane
Executive Marketing Manager: Lisa Kimball
Editorial Production Service: Marbern House
Manufacturing Buyer: Megan Cochran
Cover Administrator: Linda Knowles

Internet: www.abacon.com

ISBN: 0-205-32323-5

Printed in the United States of America

10 9 8 7 6 5 4 3 2 1   05 04 03 02 01 00

➤➤➤

CONTENTS

➤➤➤

PREFACE

Phonological Awareness and Primary Phonics is a resource manual designed to provide step-by-step suggestions for assessing and instructing children in kindergarten and grades 1 and 2 in phonological awareness and basic phonics. Phonological awareness and phonics are presented as reciprocal, interrelated skills. Phonological skills are presented in such a way that they build a foundation for phonics. Those phonological skills that best prepare students for phonics are stressed. Phonics is presented in such a way that it fosters continued development of phonological skills, which, in turn, makes it easier to learn and apply phonics skills.

Major phonological awareness skills include rhyming, blending, identifying initial consonant sounds, and noting individual sounds (phonemes) in words. Phonics skills include consonants, consonant clusters, consonant digraphs, short-vowel (*-at, -en*), long-vowel (*-ake, -oat*), r-vowel (*-ird, -orn*), and other vowel (*-oy, -ool*) patterns. Emphasis throughout is on presenting phonics as a functional, practical skill. From the beginning, students are taught to apply the skills they have learned by using pronounceable word part, analogy, context, and other powerful decoding strategies. After learning the *-ack* pattern, for example, they use the pronounceable word part *-ack* to decode unfamiliar words such as *tack* or *attack*.

In addition to providing an overview of phonological analysis and phonics, the text presents virtually everything—except actual books—that a teacher might need in order to implement a high-quality, phonological skills program. Major elements include:

➤ Instructions for quickly and efficiently assessing students in phonological awareness and phonics. All assessment devices are available on reproducible masters.

➤ Sample lessons for teaching key skills and strategies.

➤ A carefully sequenced presentation of essential phonological awareness skills: rhyming, blending, initial sounds, and separate sounds in words. Instructional resources include alliterative and rhyming tales, songs, rhyming and initial sound picture sorts, and lots of word games.

➤ Special resource sections for consonants, consonant digraphs and clusters, and vowel patterns (rimes). For each phonics pattern there is a listing of words to be presented, related spelling words, possible writing topics, and reinforcement and application activities. These activities include games, puzzles, riddles, songs, rhymes, real-world materials, and children's books that contain the pattern.

➤ Illustrations that can be duplicated by the teacher and used for sorting, bingo, concentration, or other activities.

➤ More than 140 copyright-free verses, songs, and poems that the teacher can use to reinforce patterns.

➤ A collection of more than 20 fold-and-read books that can be used to reinforce most of the major vowel patterns. These fold-and-read books contain brief stories, information about interesting animals and insects, and nursery rhymes.

Phonological Awareness and Primary Phonics can be used to strengthen the phonological component of your literacy program. It can also be used as the foundation for a program of prevention or intervention. Struggling readers and writers need a firm foundation in phonological awareness and systematic instruction in phonics. They also need lots of reinforcement and the opportunity to read a wide variety of materials on their level. All of these are emphasized in *Phonological Awareness and Primary Phonics*. In addition, Chapter 5 contains suggestions for setting up a program of prevention or intervention.

➤➤Acknowledgments

My sincere appreciation to Arnis Burvikovs of Allyn and Bacon for his encouragement and support of this project. My thanks also to Bridget Keane, editorial assistant, for her gracious assistance in completing the myriad tasks involved in shepherding a manuscript through the production process. I would also like to express my appreciation to Norma Kable, the artist who created most of the illustrations for the text. Her illustrations have added greatly to the appeal of the text's suggested activities and fold-and-read booklets.

►►►Chapter One

PHONOLOGICAL AWARENESS

Looking at the word *man*, Charles said "mmmmmmmmm" for what seemed to be a full minute. His face was turning red. It was obvious that he was making every effort to decode the word but was struggling. Then, much to the teacher's surprise, he said "dog." Charles also recited a rhyme about Mack the magic man. Charles was making some connection between the letter that he saw and the sound that it represents. Unfortunately, the connection was on an associative and not a conceptual level. Charles had memorized some letter–sound relationships before he was aware of separate sounds in words, before he was able to abstract sounds from words. Charles was lacking adequate phonological awareness. He was unable to deal with sounds within the context of words and so was unable to apply the phonics that he had memorized. After several months of instruction that emphasized changing words by changing their beginning sounds, something clicked. Charles began to realize that if you add /m/ to /an/, you create the word *man*, and if you add /p/ to /an/, you get *pan*. Having achieved this fundamental understanding of the sound system of English, Charles was then able to apply his knowledge of initial consonants and began making encouraging progress.

Charles demonstrates both how important phonological awareness is and how difficult it can be to learn. For instance, consider how many sounds the word *cat* has. When spoken words were analyzed in a language lab by a machine, the spectographs created could identify syllables but not individual sounds in a word (Liberman & Shankweiler, 1991). In physical reality, *cat* and other single-syllable words have just one pulse of sound. And indeed that is what we say and hear. We do not say /k/-/a/-/t/ as separate sounds, and we do not hear separate sounds in *cat*. Rather, the sounds are coarticulated. The sounds overlap so that as we say /k/ we also articulate /a/ and say /t/. Coarticulation makes speaking and listening easy, but it makes reading and writing hard (Liberman & Shankweiler, 1991). Because of coarticulation, novice readers and writers must learn to analyze words into their component sounds. Accustomed to using language to communicate, they must now learn to listen to language in an abstract way. They must develop phonological awareness.

In addition to being the most complex skill that novice readers must learn, phonological awareness also is probably the most essential. The prestigious Committee on the Prevention of Reading Difficulties in Young Children declared that phonemic awareness is the "key to understanding the logic of the alphabetic principle and thus to the learnability of phonics and spelling" (Snow, Burns, & Griffin, 1998). Earlier Savin (1972) stated: "In the present author's experience everyone who has failed to learn to read even the simplest prose by the end of first grade has been unable to analyze syllables into phonemes" (p. 321). Savin's assertion was echoed by Elkonin (1973), a Russian psychologist, who maintained that being able to analyze the sounds of words "is the most important prerequisite for the successful learning of reading and writing" (p. 571).

In their everyday lives, children do not have to deal with individual sounds. They deal with language on a meaning level and do not look beyond its meaning to its form. Reading specialists are fond of telling the story of the child who was asked to tell what sound the word *cat* begins with. The child responded, "Meow." However, the ability to deal with the sounds of words on an abstract level is the basis for literacy development. Without the ability to abstract separate sounds, children will not be able to understand, for example, that the letter *d* stands for the sound /d/ heard at the beginning of *dog.* They will not even be able to consider a beginning sound because they will not be able to abstract it from the word itself. These children will also have difficulty with rhyme because of their inability to abstract ending sounds. Their writing will not evolve beyond the early phonemic stage because they will be unable to isolate the sounds of words and so will not be able to represent them with letters. Students may be able to memorize a few words, but apart from recognizing these few words, they will not be able to read.

►►A RECIPROCAL RELATIONSHIP

As a practical matter, the relationship between reading and writing and phonological awareness is reciprocal. Being able to detect and manipulate sounds makes it possible for students to learn phonics and spelling. As they learn phonics and spelling and so acquire more experience with sounds and letters, their reading and writing improve.

Students do not need an advanced knowledge of phonological awareness before beginning to learn to read. They do not need to be able to detect the separate sounds in a cluster, such as the /st/ in *stop.* Detecting the /s/ and /t/ in the cluster is a difficult task, but it is one that students will be better able to learn once they have a grasp of initial consonants. Keys skills required for developing phonological awareness for reading and spelling include: rhyming, blending onsets and rimes, noting beginning sounds, and segmenting sounds in words. Once students can detect beginning sounds, they are prepared to learn initial consonant letter–sound relationships (Stahl, Stahl, & McKenna, 1998). Rhyming and blending onsets and rimes provide preparation for detecting beginning sounds, which, in turn, helps students segment words into individual sounds. Being able to detect individual sounds in words is an important skill, but this can be developed as students begin to learn initial consonant sounds and the letters that represent them. Instruction in phonics should build on the phonemic awareness that has been developed and should extend it. With instruction that combines phonics and phonemic awareness and includes experience with reading and writing, the ability to detect all the sounds in a word should develop. To make sure this happens, fostering phonological awareness should be an integral part of phonics and spelling instruction. In this text, phonics lessons have a phonological awareness component so that, as student learn phonics, their phonological awareness improves.

►►PHONOLOGICAL AWARENESS AND COGNITIVE DEVELOPMENT

Phonemic awareness requires that a child be able to deal with two aspects of language at the same time. The child must be able to put aside the content of the language and pay attention to its form. As Harris and Sipay (1990) comment: "The ability to abstract a beginning sound from a spoken word and compare it with the beginning sound of another word is a cognitive ability that many 5- and 6-year-olds have not yet developed. In Piaget's terms, it requires decentration" (p. 42). Decentration, which is a hallmark of the stage of concrete operations, means that a child must be able to consider two aspects of a situation at that same time. In language, the child must realize that *cat* represents an animal and is a word composed of sounds. Watson (1984) believes that there may be a decentration lag for those who have difficulty noting sounds in words. Some students who perform normally on general language measures are slow to develop decentration ability, which, in turn, slows down development of phonemic awareness, which, in turn, blocks progress in reading. These students will need additional experience with phonemic awareness activities, especially those activities that help the student to think about the form of language.

➤➤STAGES OF PHONOLOGICAL KNOWLEDGE

Children as young as three can be taught nursery rhymes. Experience with nursery rhymes provides an excellent foundation for developing the concept of rhyme (Maclean, Bryant, & Bradley, 1987). Of all the phonological awareness tasks, detecting rhyme is the easiest. Rhyming does not require the student to manipulate sounds (Yopp, 1988). However, rhyming does require a level of abstraction. In order to be able to tell whether the words *man* and *ran* rhyme, the child must be able to abstract *an* from both words, compare them, and note that they are the same. Rhyming continues to pose problems for some kindergarten students and even a few students in first grade. The next easiest task is blending, in which students are required to synthesize a series of speech sounds into words. Hearing /r/, /e/, /d/, the student blends it into the word *red*. Blending words can be good preparation for noting whether two words begin in the same way. Blending onsets and rimes (*r + ed = red*) is easier than blending all the sounds in a word but still provides preparation for detecting initial consonant sounds. Segmenting words is a more advanced task. When segmenting words, students break down a word into its component sounds. Given the word *mouse*, they say, /m/, /ow/, /s/. Segmenting words into syllables, into onset and rime, or simply isolating the first consonant is easier than segmenting words into individual sounds. Segmenting a word into individual sounds is a struggle for many kindergarten children. (Liberman, Shankweiler, Fischer, & Carter, 1974; Yopp, 1995). By age 6, one child in six still had difficulty segmenting a word into its individual phonemes (Sawyer, 1987). The ability to segment words into individual phonemes develops last.

About one of every four middle-class children will have difficulty with phonological awareness unless he or she is given a program of systematic instruction. The proportion is even higher for poor children. As a group, poor children come to school with fewer literacy experiences. They usually are not read to as frequently as middle-class children, and they don't engage in as much word play or know as many nursery rhymes. Fortunately, they do benefit from programs designed to foster phonological awareness. However, students with very low levels of phonemic awareness may need extended periods of instruction (Nicholson, 1999). To be successful, instruction in phonemic awareness should also demonstrate how these skills are related to reading and writing words.

➤➤PHONOLOGICAL AWARENESS AS PART OF A LANGUAGE PROGRAM

Developing phonological awareness should be seen as part of a broader program of overall language development. In fact, some language development specialists now believe that phonological awareness grows out of vocabulary knowledge. The more words children know, the easier it will be for them to develop phonemic awareness. According to current theories, children first learn words holistically.

Because they know few words, it is relatively easy to distinguish them from each other. However, as children's vocabularies grow, they acquire more and more words that have similar sounds, so that they have to distinguish between words such as *big, bit, dig, pig, bag, beg,* and so on (Metsala, 1999). As their vocabularies grow, children develop the ability to make fine discriminations and begin processing words on a phonemic rather than a holistic level. Because they have more experience with everyday words, students are better able to discriminate between familiar, everyday words with similar sounds than they are between unfamiliar or infrequently heard words that have similar sounds.

Students' knowledge of letters should also be developed so that they can use their knowledge of letter forms and phonological awareness to begin to learn phonics. At the same time, students should become acquainted with the conventions and purposes of print so that they come to understand how and why people read and write and so have a reason for developing phonological awareness. A program of phonological awareness should include reading to children, share reading books with them, and encouraging them to draw and write.

►►ASSESSING PHONOLOGICAL AWARENESS

Children vary greatly in their phonological awareness. A program of phonological awareness should be based on a careful assessment of students' development in this area. Phonological awareness can be assessed in a variety of ways. It can be assessed informally by noting whether students are able to tell when two words rhyme or begin with the same sound or whether students can blend or segment words. Phonological awareness can also be assessed using group or individual tests. Although individual tests are time consuming, they yield more valid results. Three individual and one group measure are presented that may be used to assess students' phonological awareness. If necessary, the Beginning Sounds Survey and the Consonant Correspondences Survey can be adapted for group administration.

►►RHYMING SOUNDS SURVEY

The ability to detect rhyme is an indicator of phonological awareness. Distribute copies of the Rhyming Sounds Survey, shown in Figure 1.1, to students. Explain to students the purpose of the measure and give them directions. Say: "I want to see if you can tell when words rhyme. Words rhyme if they have the same ending sound. For example, *Bill* and *Jill* rhyme because they both have an 'ill' sound. *Book* and *look* rhyme because they both have an 'ook' sound. I'm going to point to three pictures. Here are pictures of a pan, a man, and a shoe. Now say the name of each picture. Which two rhyme? Which two have the same sounds at the end?" (If students are unable to answer or give an incorrect response, say: "If you listen carefully, you can tell that *pan* and *man* rhyme. They both have an 'an' sound.") Now say: "Draw a ring around the picture of the pan and the picture of the man to show that they rhyme." Administer the remaining practice sets of pictures in the same way: cake, rake, bus; fish, bee, tree. Then administer the eight test items. An adequate performance would be six out of eight. Record students' performance on the Assessment Survey, which can be found in Figure 1.2.

Scores lower than the criterion suggest a need for additional work in this area. Students may do poorly due to limited experience with rhyme, or they may find the terminology confusing. You might try working on rhyme with the lowest-scoring youngsters to determine how readily they learn this concept. Although most youngsters will learn rhyme naturally through listening to nursery rhymes and participating in shared reading, some will need direct instruction.

FIGURE 1.1   Illustrations for Rhyming Sounds Survey

Assessment Survey

Student's Name _____   Age _____   Grade _____

Date _____

Phonological Awareness

    Rhyming Survey   /8

    Beginning Sounds Survey   /8

    Segmentation Survey   /10

Phonics

    Beginning Consonant Correspondences Survey   /20

    Word Pattern Survey   /80

Observations

Put a plus in the blank if the student has achieved mastery, a check if the student is making satisfactory progress, and a minus if the student has a need in that area. Comments may also be written in the blanks.

Concepts about Print

    Can name letters of alphabet _____

    Can point to each word as line of print is read _____

    Recognizes own name in print_____

Writing

    Can write own name _____

    Writes or draws stories, letters, or lists _____

    Uses invented spelling _____

    Uses conventional spelling_____

Decoding

    Uses initial letters to decode words_____

    Uses consonants and vowels to decode words _____

    Uses short-vowel patterns to decode words _____

    Uses long-vowel patterns to decode words _____

    Uses other-vowel patterns to decode words _____

    Uses r-vowel patterns to decode words _____

    Uses pronounceable word-part strategy to decode words _____

    Uses analogy strategy to decode words _____

    Uses context to decode words _____

FIGURE 1.2   Assessment Survey

▶▶BEGINNING SOUNDS SURVEY

The ability to detect beginning sounds, which is also a measure of phonemic awareness, is a prerequisite for beginning reading. Distribute the Beginning Sounds Survey, shown in Figure 1.3. Explain to students the purpose of the survey and then give them directions. Say: "I want to see if you can tell whether two words begin alike. Words begin alike if they begin with the same sound. The words

FIGURE 1.3   Illustrations for Beginning Sounds Survey

tie and *ten* begin alike because they begin with the same sound, /t/. The words *pen* and *pet* begin alike because they begin with the same sound, /p/. Look at these pictures: saw, cake, sun. Say the name of each picture. See if you can tell which two pictures have names that begin with the same sound: *saw, cake, sun.* Which two begin with the same sound: *saw, cake, sun*?" (If students are unable to answer or give an incorrect response, say: "If you listen carefully, you can tell that *saw* and *sun* both begin with the same sound. The sound they both begin with is /s/.") Administer the remaining sets of pictures in the same way: deer, fork, fish; man, monkey, star; hat, bus, horse; dog, bell, boat; ring, nail, rake; goat, cat, car; lion, shoe, lock.

Record students' performance on the Assessment Survey. A score of six out of eight generally indicates adequate grasp of beginning sounds. Scores lower than that suggest the need for additional work in this area. Students may do poorly because they have little experience with beginning sounds, or they may find the terminology unfamiliar. You might further probe low scores in this area by teaching beginning sounds to low-scoring youngsters and noting how they respond to instruction. Also, check the performance of low-scoring students in the rhyming subtest. Low scores in both Rhyming and Beginning Sounds indicate a need for intensive work in phonological awareness.

➤➤SEGMENTATION SURVEY

The Segmentation Survey (Figure 1.4) measures the student's ability to identify individual phonemes in a word. The Segmentation Survey consists of thirteen illustrations: three practice items and ten test items. The teacher says the name of each picture aloud and then asks the student to say each of the word's sounds. Say: "Today we are going to take words apart. I am going to say the word that tells about each picture. After I say the word, I want you to say it in parts. If I say "hat," you say /h/, /a/, /t/. Let's look at this first picture. It shows a bee. Say *bee* in parts." If the answer is correct, say: "Yes, that's right. *Bee* has two parts: /b/, /ē/." If the answer is not correct, say: "Bee has two parts: /b/, /ē/." Then say: "Now let's try the next picture. It shows a goat. Say *goat* in parts." If the answer is correct, say: "Yes, that's right. Goat has three parts: /g/, /ō/, /t/." If the answer is not correct, say: "Goat has three parts: /g/, /ō/, /t/." Then say: "Now let's try this one. It shows a cat. Say *cat* in parts." If the answer is correct, say: "Yes, that's right. *Cat* has three parts: /k/, /a/, /t/." If the answer is not correct, say, "*Cat* has three parts: /k/, /a/, /t/." After presenting the three sample items, present the remaining ten items in this same manner, including affirming correct responses and correcting erroneous ones. Only responses in which the student provides all the word's sounds are scored as correct. However, the student's attempts should be recorded, as these may provide insight into his or her performance. A partially correct answer, for instance, shows that the student has some segmenting ability. Record students' performance on the Assessment Survey. An adequate performance is seven out of ten.

Students need not get an adequate score on the Segmentation Survey in order to start work on initial consonants, but they should perform adequately on the Beginning Sounds Survey. However, a low score on the Segmentation Survey is a sign that students need continued work on phonemic awareness.

➤➤BEGINNING CONSONANT CORRESPONDENCES SURVEY

Growing out of letter knowledge and phonemic awareness is the ability to match letters and sounds. If students have done poorly on the previous subtests, omit this assessment, since it will most likely be too difficult for them.

FIGURE 1.4　Illustrations for Segmentation Survey

FIGURE 1.5   Illustrations for Beginning Consonant Correspondences Survey

To administer the Beginning Consonant Correspondences Survey (Figure 1.5), copy and cut out the consonant correspondence pictures from the survey shown in Figure 1.3. Explain to the students the purpose of the measure and then give them directions. Say: "I want to see if you can tell which letters are used to spell the beginning sounds of words. I'm going to show you some pictures. I want you to say the name of the picture and then tell me what letter the name of the picture begins with. For instance, this is a picture of a fish. The letter *f* is used to spell the sound /f/ that you hear at the beginning of *fish*. This is a picture of a horse. The letter *h* is used to spell /h/, the sound that you hear at the beginning of *horse*. Now say the name of this picture (*sun*). What letter does *sun* begin with?" (If students are unable to answer or give an incorrect response, say, "If you listen carefully, you can tell that *sun* begins with /s/. The sound /s/ that you hear at the beginning of *sun* is made with the letter *s*.") Administer the remaining sets of pictures in the same way: man, ring, dog, hat, nail, goat, fork, zebra, watch, lion, bus, jar, key, pen, queen, table, violin, car, saw, Yo-Yo.

A score of ten out of twenty indicates that students have begun to master initial consonant correspondences. Record students' performance on the Assessment Survey. Ultimately, of course, they will need to know all of the initial consonant correspondences. However, if students know at least half of the beginning consonant correspondences, they are ready for instruction with short-vowel patterns.

▶▶INSTRUCTIONAL PROGRAM FOR PHONOLOGICAL AWARENESS

A program of phonemic awareness should be flexible. Even at age 4 or 5, children vary greatly in their ability to detect rhyme or sounds in words. Even so, reading rhyming tales, reciting nursery rhymes, and engaging in word play are appropriate for the whole class. Both the least advanced and most advanced pupils will benefit from these activities at some level. However, you may want to group children for some of the more demanding tasks, such as detecting initial sounds in words or segmenting words into their individual sounds. Suggestions for activities to develop phonological awareness are presented below. The activities are listed in approximate order of difficulty.

▶▶RHYME

Rhyming is a natural way to initiate instruction in phonological awareness. One of the most effective ways to teach rhyming is to recite or read aloud nursery rhymes, verses, and rhyming tales, as well as jump-rope and counting-out rhymes. At first, just read or recite the rhymes. Focus on providing students with an enjoyable experience. This should be a nonthreatening activity that builds a base for phonological awareness. In a study in England, students who came to school knowing more nursery rhymes did better in reading than those whose knowledge of nursery rhymes was limited (Maclean, Bryant, & Bradley, 1987).This was true even when such factors as social class and ability were factored out. Recite the rhymes a number of times, so that students begin to memorize them. Send a booklet of rhymes home and encourage parents to read or recite them to the children. Also encourage parents to send in rhymes that are popular in their cultures. Share these with the class or invite parents to share them. Some rhymes that you might use are presented in Appendix A.

As students become familiar with rhyming pieces, begin to build the concept of rhyme. Every once in a while, stop before the last word in a rhyming line and have students supply the rhyming word. Also, call attention to the rhyming words.

As you develop a concept of rhyme, build the language used to talk about rhyme: *same, sounds, rhyme, words*. Stress the concept that rhyming words end with the same sound(s). Also encourage students to think of other words that might have the same sound(s) as the rhyming pair. For instance, lead them to see that there are many words that rhyme with *hat* and *cat*: *bat, mat, sat, fat, that*. Books that might be read aloud to reinforce rhyme include the following:

Cameron, P. (1961). *"I can't," said the ant*. New York: Coward. With the help of some other crea-
   tures, an ant repairs a broken teapot: " 'Push her up,' said the cup. 'You can,' said the pan.
   'You must,' said the crust."
Fox, M. (1993). *Time for bed*. San Diego: Harcourt. Mother animals and a human mother put their
   babies to sleep.
Hague, M. (1993). *Teddy bear, teddy bear*. New York: Morrow. In this action rhyme, Teddy Bear is
   asked to do such things as turn around, touch the ground, and show your shoe.
Hutchins, P. (1976). *Don't forget the bacon*. New York: Greenwillow. Distracted as he heads toward
   the grocery store, a boy distorts his memorized grocery list, with humorous results. Can be
   read aloud to illustrate rhyme and substitution of sounds.
Lobel, A. (1986). *The Random House book of Mother Goose*. New York: Random House. Features
   more than 300 traditional rhymes.
McMillan, B. (1991). *Play day, A book of terse verse*. New York: Holiday House. With color photos
   and two-word verses, depicts children at play: bear chair, fat bat.
Raffi. (1989). *Down by the bay*. New York: Crown. Celebrates silly rhymes: "Did you ever see a
   whale with a polka-dot tail, Down by the bay?"
Shaw, N. (1986). *Sheep in a jeep*. Boston: Houghton Mifflin. Sheep have a series of misadventures.
   Part of a series.

Adding Rhyming Verses.   Sing open-ended songs that lend themselves to having verses added. Some possibilities include the following:

My Aunt Came Back
My aunt came back from old Japan,
And she brought with her a big hand fan.
My aunt came back from Holland, too
And she brought with her a wooden shoe.
My aunt came back from the New York Fair
And she brought with her a rocking chair.
My aunt came back from Kalamazoo
And she brought with her some gum to chew.
My aunt came back from Timbuktu
And she brought with her some clowns like you.

Students can also add verses to "Down by the Bay":

Down by the Bay
Down by the bay, where the watermelons grow
Back to my home I dare not go.
For if I do my mother will say,
Did you ever see a bear combing his hair down by the bay.

Did you ever see a bee with a sunburned knee down by the bay?

Did you ever see a moose kissing a goose down by the bay?

Did you ever see a whale with a polka-dot tail down by the bay?

Did you ever see a fish sailing in a dish down by the bay?

Did you ever see a cat in a tall black hat down by the bay?

What could a bee see sitting in a tree down by the bay?

Building Rhymes.   To extend the concept of rhyme, build rhymes with the students. Using the element *an,* here is how a rhyme might be built. Say *an.* Have students say *an.* Tell students that you are going to make words that have *an* in them. Say *c-an,* emphasizing the *an* portion of the word. Ask students if they can hear the *an* in *c-an.* Holding up a picture of a can, have them say *can* and listen to the *an* in *c-an.* (By using pictures, you are reducing the burden on students' memories.) Hold up a picture of a pan. Have students tell what it is. Tell students that *p-an* has an *an* in it. Ask them if they can hear the *an* in *p-an.* Introduce *man, fan,* and *van* in the same way. Ask students if they can tell what sound is the same in *can, pan, man, fan,* and *van.* Stress the *an* in each of these words. Explain that *can, pan, man, fan,* and *van* rhyme because they all have *an* at the end. Invite students to suggest other words that rhyme with *can: tan, Dan, Jan, plan, ran.*

Ask students if *hat* rhymes with *can.* Discuss the fact that *hat* ends with *at* and *can* ends with *an,* so they don't rhyme. Ask if *Dan* rhymes with *can.* Discuss why these two words rhyme. Emphasize that they both end with *an,* so they rhyme. Other groups of words that might be used to build rhymes are listed below. Illustrations for most of the words can be found at the end of this chapter and the ends of Chapters 3 and 4.

➤ bag, rag, tag, flag
➤ bat, cat, hat, mat, rat
➤ hay, clay, tray
➤ mail, nail, pail, sail, snail, tail
➤ cape, tape, grape
➤ gate, plate, skate
➤ cake, rake, snake
➤ car, jar, star
➤ bed, red, sled, bread, thread
➤ men, pen, ten

➤ bear, pear, chair
➤ king, ring, wing, string, swing
➤ dice, mice, rice
➤ sock, block, clock, lock, rock
➤ bone, cone, phone, stone
➤ boat, coat, goat
➤ hose, nose, rose
➤ bug, jug, mug, plug, rug
➤ gum, drum, plum

Identifying Rhymes.   Ask the students to tell whether word pairs such as the following rhyme: *cat–hat, hat–pan, mat–rat, can–man.* If students give a correct response, affirm their answers and explain why the answers are correct. "Yes, *cat* and *hat* do rhyme. They both end with an *at* sound." If students offer an incorrect response, gently supply the correct response and an explanation, or rephrase the question so the students have a better chance of getting it right: "Do you hear the same sound at the end of *hat* that you hear at the end of *pan*? No, *hat* and *pan* do not rhyme. *Hat* ends with an *at* sound and pan has an *an* sound. *An* and *at* are different sounds." To make the task more concrete and to aid students' memories, show pictures of word pairs as you say them. From time to time, explain again what a rhyme is. Some possible pairs of words that might be used in this activity are listed below.

➤ bag–rag
➤ rag–bat
➤ lamp–stamp
➤ cat–hat
➤ can–mat
➤ clay–tray
➤ nail–sail
➤ grape–tape
➤ cake–man
➤ car–star

➤ ball–net
➤ bell–shell
➤ men–pen
➤ bread–sled
➤ seal–jeep
➤ bee–tree
➤ king–ring
➤ fish–dish
➤ mice–bike
➤ pie–tie

➤ lock–sock
➤ mop–pot
➤ boat–goat
➤ hose–rose
➤ mouse–house
➤ cow–moose
➤ book–hook
➤ boy–toy
➤ bird–sun
➤ bus–skunk

Grab Bag.   For a game, gather objects or toys whose names rhyme. Place the objects in a cloth bag. Have each student pick an object from the bag and then take turns picking a second object, without looking. Have the students name the second object and tell whether it rhymes with the name of the first object. When students locate and name a rhyming object, they should set the pair aside and choose another target object from the bag. The winner is the one who accumulates the most pairs. Some objects that might be used are: car–star, lock–sock, mop–top, book–coat hook, boat–goat, king–ring, bell–shell, cat–hat.

Picture Rhymes.   Supply students with three pictures—a cat, a nail, and a ring, for instance. Discuss the names of the three objects. Then hold up pictures that rhyme with one of the students' three pictures. Say the picture's name and have students say it. Have them hold up the picture that rhymes with the one you are holding up. For instance, holding up a picture of a king, ask: "Which one of your pictures, the cat, the nail, or the ring, rhymes with *king*?" The students should hold up the picture showing a ring. After students have held up their pictures, affirm their responses. Say: "Yes, you are right, *ring* and *king* do rhyme. They both have an *ing* sound." Note which children can do this fairly easily and which seem to be unsure or look to see which picture the other students are holding up. These students may need additional instruction. If students have difficulty, give them just two pictures to select from. Sample illustrations for this activity are found at the end of this chapter.

Sorting Objects and Pictures.   Sorting is also an effective way to teach and practice rhyming. In sorting, students group objects or pictures whose names rhyme. Start with objects, if you can. Objects are more concrete than pictures and less likely to be misinterpreted. Display two boxes, one with a toy cat in front of it and one with a toy goat in front of it. Tell students that they will be putting the objects that rhyme with *cat* in the "cat" box, and those that rhyme with *goat* in the "goat" box. Sort one or two objects as examples. Holding up a hat, say its name, emphasizing the *at* portion. Then say: "*Hat* rhymes with *cat*. Both have an *at* sound, so I'll put it in the 'cat' box." Once students understand what they are to do, have them sort the objects. Have them name the object, tell which of the two boxes it should be placed in, and why. After all the objects have been sorted, have students name the objects in each box and note that all the objects rhyme.

Also have students sort pictures. Some pictures that might be used in sorting rhymes include: bat, cat, hat, rat; can, fan, man, pan, van; nail, sail, tail; cake, rake, snake; pen, hen, men, ten; car, jar, star; king, ring, wing; clock, lock, sock. (These illustrations can be found at the end of this chapter. Additional illustrations for rhymes may be found at the end of Chapter 4.) Pictures are sorted in much the same way as are objects. Select a picture to serve as a model for each rhyming pattern and have students place rhyming pictures underneath them as shown in Figure 1.6. Or have students sort piles of pictures that contain two or three sets of rhyming words. For instance, students might sort *at* and *ing* pictures. Each time a student sorts a picture she should say the name of the picture and the name of the model picture, so that she has a better chance of detecting rhyme.

Students can work individually, in pairs, or in small groups. After a sort has been completed, have students say the name of each picture in a category. Emphasize the rhyming element in each. If students are slow or hesitant, discuss any questions they have and then ask them to sort again. They might also sort the items a second time for additional practice. Sorting cards or objects several times fosters mastery.

Extension and Application.   Since rhyme is a concept that may take a while to develop, continue reading rhyming tales to the students and conducting other activities that will help develop their ability to detect rhyme. Additional reinforcement activities include the following.

FIGURE 1.6   Sorting Rhymes

➤ While reading a rhyming couplet, read all but the last word and have students supply the missing word.

He was so tall, He tripped and had a long _____.
Hurry up, Kate, Or you will be _____.
Sitting in my chair, Was a big, furry _____.
Dad said that he would bake, A very big chocolate _____.
Do not stay in the park, After it gets _____.
A cat with a hat, Is swinging a baseball _____.
I see a man, He is in a tan _____.
There goes Dave, Give him a big _____.
Here is Pam, She likes bread and _____.
Don't be bad, Or Dad will be _____.
Have no fear, I am right _____.
Into my tea, Flew a little _____.
In my dream, I heard a _____.
Who made this mess? Can you _____?
Did you see my sled? It is bright _____.

➤ Using pairs of rhyming cards, have students play go fish or concentration. To play rhyming concentration, place twelve cards (six pairs of rhymes) face down. The student turns over a card, says its name, and then attempts to locate a picture that rhymes with it. Turning over another card, the player says its name, says the name of the card originally turned over, and tells whether they rhyme. If the player succeeds in making a match, he says the name of each card and says that they rhyme. If the player fails to locate a rhyme, he turns the cards face down, and the next player takes his turn. The game ends when all the cards have been picked up. The winner is the person with the most rhyming pairs. The illustrations at the end of this chapter and Chapter 4 may be used to make rhyming cards.

➤ After reading one of Bruce McMillan's terse verse books, help the class create a book of terse verses: fat cat, goat boat, school pool, rag bag, nail pail.

➤ Have students create rhyming books. Each page contains drawings of two items that rhyme, for example: bat, hat; man, fan.

➤ Have students produce rhyming words. Announce a target word and have students supply as many rhyming words as they can. Words that have a large number of rhyming words include: *cat, ham, dad, day, bake, feet, bill, ring, Jack, map, nail, bear.*

➤ Read rhyming riddles to students. The answer to the riddle is two rhyming words. Some riddles that you might read to the class include the following. Provide hints as needed.

What do you call a pot that keeps food hot? (hot pot)
What is the best dad called? (top pop)
What do you call a hen that is not well? (sick chick)
Where do hens live? (hen pen)
What do you call a vet who takes care of cats and dogs? (pet vet)

➤ Have students draw rhyming pictures. For example, provide students with a paper that has a drawing of a cat at the top. Have students draw objects whose names rhyme with *cat.*

➤ Create a sock puppet, Rhymin' Simon. Whenever anyone says a word, Rhymin' Simon says a word that rhymes with it. Have students say a word and have Simon say a rhyming word. Once they catch onto the idea, give each of them a Rhymin' Simon puppet. You say a word and have their puppets supply a rhyme. Students might also do this with partners.

➤ Have students carry out the actions in action rhymes.

➤ Have children extend a rhyming sentence by adding other rhyming words: I see a fat cat. I see a fat cat sleeping in a hat. I see a fat cat sleeping in a hat on a mat. I see a rat looking at the fat cat sleeping in a hat on a mat.

➤➤BLENDING

Blending activities build on students' growing awareness, gained through rhyming, of word parts. In blending activities, students create words by combining word parts. In the activities below, students combine onsets and rimes. The onset is the consonant or consonant cluster preceding the rime: *f-, pl-, scr-.* The rime is the pattern's vowel and any consonants that follow it: *-o, -at, -ot, -een.* Onsets and rimes are felt to be the natural units of words. Using a puppet troll, explain to students that the troll says its words in parts. Instead of saying *man* the way we do, it says *m-an,* so we have to help him by putting the parts of the word together. Have students help put the following words together: *b-ee, tr-ee, c-ow, r-at, h-ouse, r-ug.* Present the words in groups of five. In order to involve all students, provide each student with a set of five pictures showing the five words. When you say the word to be blended, they choose the picture that shows the word and hold it up. By observing the students carefully, you can tell who is catching on and who is struggling. Be sure to discuss the names of the pictures before beginning the activity, so that the students know the names of the pictures. The semantic and phonological systems are related. Students do best when working with words that are familiar.

cat, hat, mat, bat, rat
can, man, pan, van, fan
mail, nail, pail, sail, tail
king, ring, wing, cake, rake
lock, rock, sock, mop, boy
pie, tie, bike, bus, net
boat, coat, goat, dog, saw
bee, jeep, feet, leaf, key

pig, milk, dish, fish, bell
cow, house, mouse, moon, moose

After students have shown the picture for the word being blended, have them say the word. Affirm students' efforts but correct wrong responses. For a correct response, you might say: "Cat. That's correct. When you put /k/ and /at/ together, you get *cat*." For an incorrect response, you might say: "That was a good try. But when I put /b/ and /īk/ together, the word is *bike*. You say it, 'b-ike—bike.' " After students have completed a set, go through it again. Challenge them to put the words together faster. If students have difficulty with the activity, provide assistance or go back to rhyming activities.

Create riddles that incorporate both rhyming and blending. Say: "I'm thinking of a word that begins with /m/ and rhymes with *house*."

> . . . begins with /h/ and rhymes with *cat*
> . . . begins with /s/ and rhymes with *fun*
> . . . begins with /m/ and rhymes with *fan*
> . . . begins with /f/ and rhymes with *dish*
> . . . begins with /z/ and rhymes with *moo*
> . . . begins with /k/ and rhymes with *how*
> . . . begins with /b/ and rhymes with *look*
> . . . begins with /f/ and rhymes with *meet*

➤➤BEGINNING SOUNDS

Rhyming and blending onsets and rimes prepares students for the perception of beginning consonant sounds. If students can't perceive beginning consonant sounds, they will have difficulty learning letter–sound relationships. A fun way to introduce beginning consonant sounds is to read and discuss Dr. Seuss's *There's a Wocket in My Pocket* (New York: Beginner, 1974). In this rhyming tale, Dr. Seuss uses a number of nonsense words that were created by changing the beginning sounds of real words. Playing with words in this way calls students' attention to beginning sounds in a very natural fashion. Since students will probably enjoy this tale, it can be read to them several times.

Alphabet Books.   To develop the concept of beginning sounds further, read and discuss alphabet books with youngsters. Focus on the sounds rather than the letters. As you read a book such as P. D. Eastman's *The Alphabet Book,* discuss how *bird* and *bike* or *cow* and *car* are alike. Lead students to see that the words begin in the same way. Some alphabet books that might be used to reinforce initial consonant sounds include the following:

Base, G. (1987). *Animalia*. New York: Abrams. Each letter is accompanied by a highly alliterative phrase using the target letter.
Chess, V. (1979). *Alfred's alphabet walk*. New York: Greenwillow. Scenes are described with alliterative phrases.
Eastman, P. D. (1974). *The alphabet book*. New York: Random House. Each letter is accompanied by alliterative phrases.
Geisel, T. S. (1973). *Dr. Seuss's ABC*. New York: Beginner. Each letter is accompanied by a humorous alliterative story.
Kellogg, S. (1987). *Aster aardvark's alphabet adventures*. New York: Morrow. Each letter is accompanied by an alliterative story.

In addition to alphabet books, many other books highlight beginning sounds. These offer excellent opportunities for discussing beginning sounds. For instance, when the Hungry Thing in books by Slepian and Seidler asks for foods such as bellyjeans and hookies, you can ask students to guess what foods the Hungry

Thing means and then encourage the class to listen as one of the characters in the book translates the Hungry Thing's requests. Some books that call attention to sounds in words include the following:

Koch, M. (1991). *Hoot howl hiss.* New York: Greenwillow. In words and illustrations, depicts sounds that animals make. Highlights initial /h/.

Noll, S. (1992). *I have a loose tooth.* New York: Greenwillow. People misinterpret what Molly is saying because her speech is distorted by her loose tooth.

Ogburn, J. K. (1995). *The noise lullaby.* New York: Lothrop, Lee & Shepard. Little girl hears all sorts of noises just before she falls to sleep.

Slepian, J. & Seidler, A. (1967). *The hungry thing.* New York: Scholastic. One morning the Hungry Thing appears in town with a sign that says, "Feed me." The creature demands shmancakes, tickles, and hookies. The townspeople and the reader have to figure out what the Hungry Thing really wants.

Slepian, J & Seidler, A. (1990). *The hungry thing returns.* New York: Scholastic. One morning the Hungry Thing and a small Hungry Thing appear in the school yard with signs that say, "Feed Me." and "Me Too." The creatures ask for flamburger, bellyjeans, and crackeroni and sneeze. The headmaster, cook, students, and the reader have to figure out what the Hungry Thing and the Small Hungry Thing really want.

Slepian, J. & Seidler, A. (1992). *The hungry thing goes to a restaurant.* New York: Scholastic. When the Hungry Thing goes to a restaurant and orders a meal, the staff can't understand what it wants when he orders things like bapple moose and spoonadish. Two children translate the Hungry Thing's requests.

Alliterative Tongue Twisters.   Use alliterative tongue twisters such as the ones below to introduce and reinforce the concept of beginning sounds. Recite the tongue twisters to the students and invite them to repeat some of the lines. Discuss the tongue twisters' beginning sounds. Since meaning is important even when your emphasis is on sounds, discuss the meanings of the tongue twisters. For the first, you might bring in a green pepper. For the second, you might bring in cake batter.

Peter Piper
Peter Piper picked a peck of pickled peppers;
Did Peter Piper pick a peck of pickled peppers?
If Peter Piper picked a peck of pickled peppers,
Where's the peck of pickled peppers Peter Piper picked?

Betty Botter
Betty Botter bought some butter,
But, she said, this butter's bitter;
If I put it in my batter,
It will make my batter bitter,
But a bit of better butter will make my batter better.
So she bought a bit of butter
Better than her bitter butter,
And she put it in her batter,
And it made her batter better,
So 'twas a better Betty Botter
Bought a bit of better butter.

Hillary Hume
Hillary Hume has a hundred hamsters.
A hundred hamsters has Hillary Hume.
If Hillary Hume has a hundred hamsters,
Will you share a room with Hillary Hume?

John Jacob Jingleheimer Schmidt
John Jacob Jingleheimer Schmidt, that's my name, too!
Whenever I go out, the people always shout, "John Jacob Jingleheimer Schmidt!"

The Ragged Rascal
Round and round
The rugged rock
The ragged rascal ran.

Sister Sally
My sister Sally is sitting by the sea singing songs.

Birthday
Apples, peaches, pears, and plums,
Tell me when your birthday comes.

A Sailor Went to Sea
A sailor went to sea
To see what he could see,
And all that he could see,
Was the sea, sea, sea.

Dickery, Dickery, Dare
Dickery, dickery, dare,
The pig flew up in the air;
The man in brown
Soon brought him down,
Dickery, dickery, dare.

Students' Names
➤ Call attention to students' names that begin with the same sound. Have the class tell how Tara, Thomas, and Timothy's names are alike.
➤ Have students guess whose name you are saying. Tell them that you are starting to say a name. "Guess whose name it is: SSSSSSaaaammmm."
➤ Say a name but omit the initial sound. Have students say what the name is and what sound is missing. "Is this am? What's missing?"

Names of Objects.   Say the name of an object, but omit the initial sound. Have students say what the object is and tell what sound is missing. Holding up a pen, say "Is this an en?" Holding up a book, say "Is this an ook?" Holding up a toy car, say "Is this an ar?" Holding up a toy tiger, say "Is this an iger?"

Songs.   Sing songs such as "Willoughby Wallaby," in which the sounds of the words are changed so that the last word in the first line begins with a /w/ but rhymes with the last word in the second line:

Willoughby Wallaby Wason,
An elephant sat on Jason
Willoughby Wallaby Wobert
An elephant sat on Robert.

Which Picture?   Because the student only has to choose between two items, this is a relatively easy task, but it provides valuable practice with noting beginning consonant sounds. Hold up two pictures and ask which one begins with a particular sound. Holding up a picture of a saw and a man, ask: "Which picture, the man or the saw, begins with /s/ as in *sun*?" Other items that might be used for this activity include the following. Illustrations for these items can be found at the end of Chapter 3.

/s/	sun	pig
/s/	rabbit	saw
/m/	man	turtle
/m/	rabbit	monkey
/f/	boy	fish
/f/	fan	hammer
/h/	horse	goat
/k/	camel	bat
/k/	bird	cat
/h/	house	nine
/g/	pan	goat
/g/	girl	hat
/d/	dog	car
/t/	tent	door
/t/	horse	turtle
/r/	pig	rabbit
/r/	ring	monkey
/b/	bus	fan
/b/	bear	fish
/j/	man	jacket
/j/	jet	tie
/l/	king	lion
/l/	leaf	wagon
/n/	net	cat
/n/	nest	boy
/p/	pen	bird
/p/	key	pan
/w/	wagon	tent
/w/	watch	pen
/y/	Yo-Yo	dog
/y/	cat	yard
/z/	zebra	rabbit
/z/	king	zipper

Sorting by Initial Sound.   Just as sorting can be used to reinforce rhyming, it can also be used to foster awareness of beginning sounds in words. If possible, start with objects. Sort items whose names begin with /s/, /m/, and /f/, or other sounds, such as /h/, /l/, /n/, /r/, that are relatively easy to distinguish and articulate. Display two boxes, one with a moon pasted on it and one with a sun attached to it. Tell students that they will be putting the objects that begin with /s/ as in *sssun* in the "sun" box and those that begin with /m/ as in *mmmoon* in the "moon" box. Sort one or two objects as examples. Holding up a sock, say its name, emphasizing the initial sound. Then say "*Sock* begins with /s/, the same sound that *sun* begins with, so I put *sssock* in the *sssun* box."

Once students understand what they are to do, have them sort the objects. Have them name the object, tell which of the two boxes it should be placed in, and why. After all the objects have been sorted, have students name the objects in each box and note that all the objects begin with the same sound.

Also have students sort pictures. Some pictures that might be used in sorting beginning sounds can be found at the end of Chapter 3. Pictures are sorted in much the same way as are objects. Select a picture to serve as a model for each beginning sound and have students place pictures that have that same beginning sound underneath the model picture. Before students begin to sort, it is important to discuss the names of the pictures or objects, to make sure that these items are familiar. As students sort, it is also important that they say the model word and the word they are sorting. This helps them focus on the word's initial sound. After they sort, it is important that they tell why they sorted as they did and that they note what sound all the items had in common.

Students can work individually, in pairs, or in small groups. After a sort has been completed, have students say the name of each picture in a category. If students are slow or hesitant, discuss any questions they might have. Have students sort the items a second time for additional practice. A sample sort is shown in Figure 1.7.

Mystery Bag. Place a mystery object in a bag. Mark the bag with an illustration that begins with the same sound as the name of the object. For the /f/ *fish* bag, for example, you can place a feather inside. Give clues. After each clue, encourage the students to guess what is in the bag. Tell them that the name of the object begins with /f/ as in *fish*. When the students respond, tell them whether their response begins with the /f/ sound as in *fish*. You might say, "*Fan* is a good answer because it begins with /f/ as in *fish*, but it is not a fan. Or, if the response does not begin with the right sound, say, "*Ball* is a good try. But *ball* begins with a /b/. It does not begin with /f/ as in *fish*. Try to think of something that might be in the bag that begins like /f/ in *fish*." Clues might include: It is very light. It is white. It is sometimes put in pillows. It came from a bird.

Games. Games add interest to practice activities. One game that students enjoy playing is I Spy. To play I Spy, you provide one or more clues and the students guess the item that you spy. If the object you spy is a mirror, you might say, "I spy something on the wall that begins with *mmm*," or "I spy something on the wall that shows how you look and begins with *mmm*."

Books. Have students create sound booklets. A sound booklet contains drawings or pictures of items that begin with the same sound. An /m/ booklet might contain drawings of a man, a monkey, a moose, the moon, a mouse, and a mop.

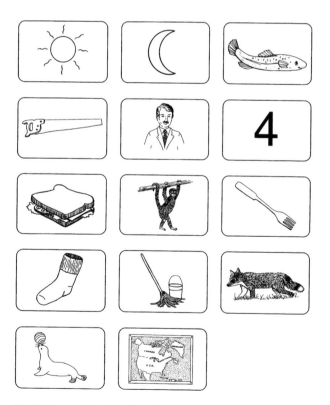

FIGURE 1.7   Sorting by Initial Sound

Forming Sounds.   If students are having difficulty perceiving sounds, you might help them explore the formation of sounds. Sounds differ according to where they are formed, how they are formed, and whether they are voiced or unvoiced. For instance, for a sound such as /b/ or /p/, tell the students to note how their lips make a popping sound. For a sound like /t/ or /d/, ask them to notice how they use their tongues to make the sound. For a sound like /f/ or /v/, they might note the use of teeth and lips. For /th/, they might note the use of teeth and tongue. For /n/, they might note the use of tongue and nose. For /m/, they might note how their lips come and stay together to make the sound and how the nose is used. They could see what happens when they hold their noses and try to articulate one of the nasals: /m/, /n/, or /ng/. The sound /h/ is formed by forcing air through an opening in the larynx, the glottis. Students might note, too, that some sounds—the stops—pop out: /b/, /d/, /k/, /g/, /p/, /t/, but the continuants are articulated with a continuous stream of breath: /f/, /h/, /l/, /m/, /n/, /w/, /r/, /s/, /sh/, /th/, /th̲/, /v/, /s/. Students might note that /p/ and /b/ are both produced in the same way and in the same part of the mouth. However, *b* is voiced—the larynx vibrates when it is articulated—and *p* is not. Most consonants occur in voiced and unvoiced pairs, /d/–/t/, /g/–/k/, /z/–/s/, /v/–/f/, /zh/ (as in *pleasure*)–/sh/, /j/–/ch/, /th/ (as in *think*)–/th̲/ (as in *that*), with the first sound in each pair being the voiced one.

SOUNDS IN WORDS

Introducing the Concept of Sounds in Words.   To introduce the concept of sounds in words or segmentation, play this game with students. Pointing to a picture of a goat, ask, "Is this a /g/?" When the class says no, agree and explain, "That's right. I didn't say all of the word's sounds. I said, 'Is this a /g/?'" Then say, "Is this a /go/?" (emphasize each sound). Explain that no, this is not a /gō/. It doesn't have enough sounds.

Next ask, "Is this a *goat*?" Again, carefully enunciate all three sounds /g/, /ō/, /t/. When the class says yes, say that they are right. *Goat* has three sounds and you said all three of them: /g/, /ō/, /t/. Present *sun* and *cat* in this same way.

To help students become aware of the individual sounds in words, use Elkonin blocks. Blocks are drawn under an illustration of a word (see the practice Elkonin boxes in Figures 1.8a and 1.8b). One block is drawn for each sound. For the word *cat*, three blocks are drawn under the illustration of the cat, one each for /k/, /a/, /t/. Three boxes are also drawn for the word *goat*. Although *goat* has four letters, it has only three sounds: /g/, /ō/, /t/. Students indicate the number of sounds in a word by placing a marker in a box for each sound they hear. Demonstrate the procedure. Say the word, emphasizing each sound. As you say a sound, place a marker in the box. After demonstrating the procedure, walk students through it.

Duplicate the practice exercises in Figure 1.8. Direct students to the drawing of the sun at the top of the page. Ask them to say the name of the picture. Urge them to stretch out each of the word's sounds so they can hear the separate sounds. If students have difficulty, provide additional demonstrations. Explain that they are to put a marker in a box as they say each sound. As the students say /s/, they put a marker in the first box. As they say /u/, they put a marker in the second box; saying /n/, they place a marker in the final box and then say the whole word. Do several items cooperatively. Once the students seem able to apply the procedure, let them finish the exercise independently, but check their responses.

At this level, the emphasis is on detecting sounds in words. That's why students put markers rather than letters in the boxes. Later, as students learn letter–sound relationships, they can put letters rather than markers in the boxes. (When a sound is represented by two letters, then both letters are placed in one box.) As students learn to read and spell words, you might use the Elkonin boxes

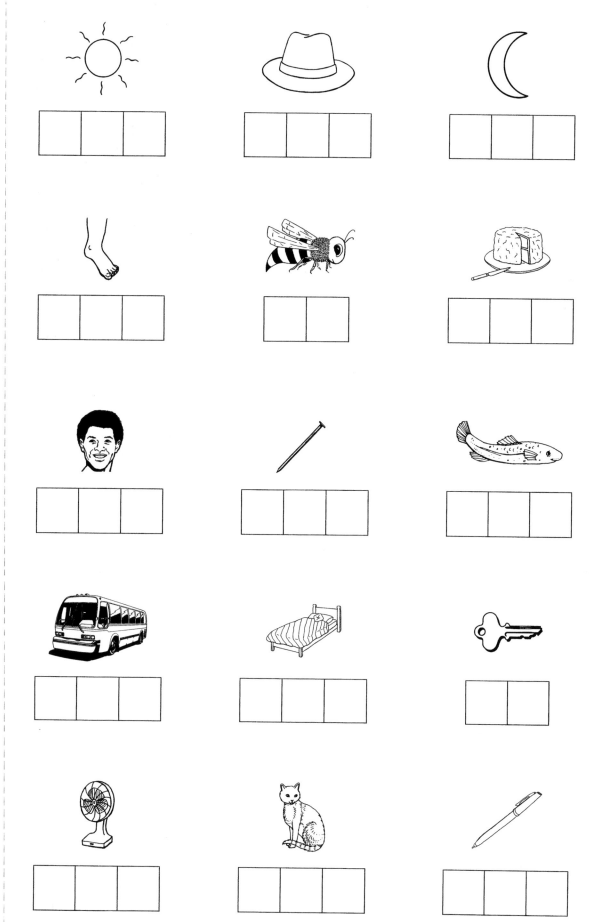

FIGURE 1.8   Elkonin Boxes

FIGURE 1.8   Continued

to aid them. If you are helping a student spell the word *can,* for instance, draw three boxes and fill in the letters that he would most likely be unable to supply. If he knows only initial consonants, fill in the *a* and *n* and encourage him to supply the initial consonant. If he knows initial and final consonants, fill in only the vowel, say the sound it represents, and have him complete the word. Along with or instead of using Elkonin boxes, model how you might stretch out a word so that you can hear how many sounds it has, Encourage students to do the same. For instance, if a student has difficulty spelling *sun,* encourage him to stretch it out—*s-u-n*—and to write a letter for each sound that he hears.

Not all sounds can be stretched. Stops, which include /p/, /t/, /d/, /b/, /k/, and /g/, cannot be stretched without significant distortion. With sounds such as these, you might try iteration, which is saying the sound several times, as in *p-p-p-pig.*

As an alternative to putting tokens in boxes to represent sounds, cut up illustrations of items. Each item should be cut up into as many pieces as it has sounds. For instance, an illustration of a cat would be cut up into three pieces. Have students put the illustrations together, just as they would a picture puzzle. Then have them take the picture pieces apart and put them back together again, saying a sound for each piece. As they place the first piece, they say the first sound of the item. As they place the second piece, they say the second sound. As they say the last piece, they say the third sound.

Extension and Application

➤ Because the ability to detect separate sounds in words may develop slowly and over an extended period of time, continue to present Elkonin boxes and other segmentation activities. Use naturally occurring opportunities to point out the sounds of words. As you write the day's date, messages, or students' names on the chalkboard, say each sound as you write the letter(s) that represents it. As you write the name *Bob,* for instance, say /b/, /o/, /b/. Then discuss the number of sounds in *Bob.*

➤ Read books to students that focus on the sounds of language. Some possible titles include:

Degen, B. (1983). *Jamberry.* New York: Harper. Humorous poem features a number of words that end in *berry.*

Geisel, T. S. (1965). *Fox in socks.* New York: Random House. Uses rhyming words to create a humorous, tongue-twisting tale.

Geisel, T. S. (1979). *Oh say can you say?* New York: Random House. Features a series of humorous tongue twisters.

➤ Deleting sounds. Tell students that you will be making a new word by taking a sound away from a word. Say *f-f-f-fear.* Then say *ear.* Ask children what sound you have taken away. Create other words in this same way. Some possibilities include:

can't–ant	cage–age	pin–in
jam–am	hair–air	pitch–itch
bat–at	part–art	mice–ice
fan–an	farm–arm	cold–old
tape–ape	send–end	sour–our
gate–ate	meat–eat	

➤ Adding sounds. Say *at* and tell children that you will be making a new word. Say *h-h-hat.* Discuss what sound you added to make *hat.* Create other words in this same way. Some possibilities include:

it–sit	old–hold	each–peach
ice–rice	ink–sink	art–part

Illustrations for Rhymes

Illustrations for Rhymes

oil–boil   in–tin   ate–late
owl–howl   eat–seat   an–can
or–sore   ear–hear   am–ham

➤ Completing words. Say sentences in which the beginning sounds of some of the words have been deleted. Have students complete the words and tell what sounds were missing and had to be added.

I had a piece of apple __ie.
I read a big __ook.
Did the bad dog __ark at you?
Song birds like to __ing.
Would you like more __ilk in your glass?

►►►Chapter Two

TEACHING PHONICS

Created in the classroom and refined over a period of two decades, primary phonics is a functional word analysis program that presents basic phonological awareness and phonics skills but stresses strategies that will enable students to decode words independently. A functional, strategic program, it is based on the premise that students should be taught concepts, skills, and strategies that will enable them to become better readers such that if they encounter words that are in their listening vocabularies but unknown in print, they will be able to decode them. Along with being taught the sounds that consonant letters and vowel patterns such as *-at* and *-en* represent, students are also taught strategies that enable them to use their knowledge of phonics to decode unfamiliar words. After learning the *-am* pattern, for instance, students are shown how to use this pattern to read words such as *scram* and *lamp* that they may not have seen in print before but that contain the *-am* pattern.

Primary phonics is a functional program. Instruction in a pattern is followed by many opportunities to meet that pattern in real reading and to write words using that pattern. Primary phonics is also systematic. Although some children may pick up phonics through informal contacts with print, many students need a carefully planned, well-implemented program. The key is to create a balanced program that is reinforced by numerous opportunities to read and write. It is also essential that instruction be provided in the context of real reading and writing. Students should be taught the *-ake* pattern, for instance, in preparation for reading or writing about snakes. The best way to reinforce the *-ake* pattern is to have students read *The Cake That Mack Ate* (Robart, 1986), or another selection that contains *-ake* words.

►►HOW WORDS ARE READ

• When students decode words, four processors are at work: orthographic, phonological, meaning, and context (Adams, 1990, 1994). The orthographic processor is responsible for perceiving the sequences of letters in text. The phonological processor is responsible for translating the letters into their spoken equivalents. The meaning processor contains one's knowledge of word meanings, and the context processor is in charge of constructing a continuing understanding of the text (Stahl, Osborne, & Lehr, 1990, p. 21). The processors work simultaneously, and they both receive information and send it to the other processors; however, the orthographic and phonological processors are always essential participants. Context may speed and/or assist the interpretation of orthographic and phonological information but does not take its place (see Figure 2.1). When information from one processor is weak, another may be called upon to give assistance. For instance, when a word such as *lead* is encountered, the context processor provides extra help to the meaning and phonological processors in assigning the correct meaning and pronunciation.

Although we use our eyes to read, reading is primarily phonological. In the beginning stages of reading, letters are linked to the sounds they represent. Students learn through instruction and experience with reading and writing that letters represent sounds; thus, for instance, young Timothy understands that *t* stands for

29

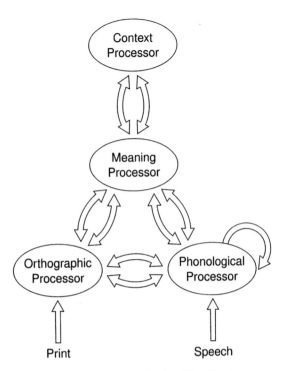

FIGURE 2.1   Modeling the Reading System: The Four Processors

Source: Adams, M. J. (1990). *Beginning to read: Thinking and learning about print. A summary.* Prepared by S. A. Stahl, J. Osborn, & F. Lehr. Champaign, IL: Center for the Study of Reading, University of Illinois.

the first sound in his name. Encountering the word *cat,* students apply their awareness that letters represent sounds and assign each letter its pronunciation: /k/, /a/, /t/. Over time they learn to read chunks of words, so cat is read /k/, /at/. Ultimately, words are stored in memory, so that seeing the letters *c-a-t* enables the student to retrieve the word /kat/. However, in order to bond words in memory, it is important that students be able to analyze the whole word, both fully and accurately. The pronunciation and the meaning of the word are then easier to retrieve. It is important, therefore, that novice readers note every sound in a word and match up those sounds with the letters that represent them. The word *know,* for instance, can be represented as kn = /n/, ow = /ō/. As readers become more experienced, they make connections between groups of letters and groups of sounds so that the word *chunks* is probably recognized as *ch* = /ch/ and *unks* = /ungkz/. Adept readers have met some words so often that they recognize them just about as soon as they see them (Ehri & McCormick, 1998). Although students may process every letter or every chunk, it is done at such lightning speed that it seems to be instantaneous (Juel, 1991). Even irregular words are bonded in memory through matching their spellings and sounds. A word such as *through* might be bonded as *thr* = /thr/ and *ough* = /o͞o/. As Ehri & McCormick (1998) comment: "Knowledge of letter–sound relations provides a powerful mnemonic system that bonds the written forms of specific words to their pronunciations in memory (p. 142)."

▶▶STAGES OF LITERACY

The way students learn words and the strategies they use change as their knowledge of phonics develops. Instructional techniques and elements being taught should match the students' stages.

▶▶EARLY EMERGENT STAGE

The emergent stage includes all those behaviors that lead up to conventional reading. Children learn to handle books, learn that one reads print and not pictures, and that one reads from left to right and from top to bottom. Students also begin to learn where printed words begin and end. When they "read" a book, children at this stage are usually constructing meaning from pictures. When students do learn to read a few words, their reading is generally logographic (Ehri, 1994). They make associations between a nonverbal visual aspect of a word and the spoken equivalent of that word. The visual aspect is not a letter–sound relationship. For instance, to identify a McDonald's sign, they don't sound out the *M*: they use the golden arches. To identify Crest toothpaste, they use the overall design of the label and their knowledge of what is in the tube. However, since they are not reading letter–sound cues, they may "read" a Crest label as "toothpaste." Sometimes, they seem to be using letter–sound cues although they are not. Samantha may recognize her name when she sees it because it starts with an *S*. Although Samantha knows that her name starts with an *S*, she is not aware that *S* represents the sound /s/. If she encountered the word *see* or *seal,* she would not be able to sound out the first letter. Unable to use letter–sound relationships, students in this stage are limited to the use of picture clues, context, or memory of word forms. This stage is also known as the prephonemic stage because it precedes the use of letter–sound relationships.

In writing, Samatha may draw pictures, scribble, use wordlike figures, or use actual letters, but again, the letters do not represent sounds. Samatha may even spell her name and a few other words correctly, but this will be because she has memorized the spellings of the words. The emergent stage flows into the alphabetic stage as children discover and begin to use the alphabetic principle.

➤➤ALPHABETIC STAGE

The hallmark of the alphabetic or letter-name stage is the realization that letters represent sounds. Given this understanding, students begin to use letter–sound relationships to read and write words. Most students first use initial consonants, then initial and final consonants, and finally all the elements in a word. Since decoding skills are limited at this stage, students rely heavily on picture clues or picture clues in combination with the initial consonant. Reading a story that has an illustration of a duck and a fox and encountering the word *fox,* the students can use their knowledge of initial *f* to figure that the word is *fox* and not *duck.*

As students progress through this stage, they use more parts of the word to decode it. Students also begin to notice patterns in words. They begin to notice that an *e* at the end of words like *can* changes the vowel sound so the word is *cane,* not *can.* At some point, students begin using elements longer than a single letter or sound. Instead of decoding *can,* /k/, /a/, /n/, they see natural patterns and decode the word /k/, /an/. As students begin using chunks of words rather than individual letters, they move into the word pattern stage.

Students' progression through the alphabetic stage is often reflected in their writing, especially if they use invented (developmental) spelling. Increasingly, the child's writing incorporates the alphabetic principle (Bear, Invernizzi, Johnston, & Templeton, 1996). In the earliest stages, a single letter may represent a whole word: K for *car.* Later, the child represents the first and last consonant sounds: KR for *car.* As the child progresses, she or he begins using vowels. Long vowels are spelled with letter names: FET for *feet.* Fortunately for the inventive speller, the names of the long vowels incorporate their sounds. Because short vowels do not have letter names, many inventive spellers use the long-vowel letter name that is made in approximately the same place in the mouth as the short vowel they are attempting to spell. Thus, short *e* is articulated in the same place as long *a,* so a student spells *bed* as BAD. This is known as the "close to" tactic. Other "close to" spellings include spelling short *i* with an E (HEM for *him*), short *o* with an I (HIP for *hop*), and short *u* with an O (MOD for *mud*) (Read, 1971). Short *a* is generally spelled with an *a.*

For some consonant spellings, the spelling–sound connection is not apparent at first glance. For instance, *tr* is frequently spelled *ch* as in CHAN for *train* and *dr* may be spelled JR as in JROM for *drum.* To see why these spellings are logical from the child's point of view, listen carefully as you say *chain* and *train.* Did you notice that the beginning sound of *train* is very similar to the beginning sound of *chain?* (Temple, Nathan, Temple, & Burris, 1993). In similar fashion, the *d* in *dr* has a /j/ sound, so *drop* may be spelled JRUP or simply JUP. During this stage, spellings with nasal sounds such as *m* and *n* are often omitted when they occur before a consonant, so *bump* may be spelled BUP and *bunk* might be spelled BUK. In general, students have difficulty with both initial and final clusters. The major characteristic of this stage is that students write what they hear (Gentry, 1997). As students master the spelling of short-vowel words, they move into the word pattern stage.

▶▶WORD PATTERN STAGE

In the word pattern stage, which is generally reached by the end of first or beginning of second grade, students begin using final *e* markers (*hope*) and vowel digraphs (*goat*) to decode words. They realize that *hop*, because it has a (CVC) pattern, is a physical action, and that *e* at the end of *hope* marks its pronunciation as a mental action. They also use patterns such as -*an*, -*op*, -*ine* to decode words. Instead of decoding *shop* as "sh-o-p—shop," they use the word's pattern and decode it "sh-op—shop." Having mastered most short vowels in the alphabetic stage (*hut, top*), students learn short-vowel patterns with clusters or digraphs (*shut, stop*), final-*e* long-vowel patterns (*ride, hope*), digraph and cluster long-vowel patterns (*wheel, steam*), *r*- vowel patterns (*fear, chair, store*), and other-vowel patterns (*coin, hour, soon*).

Through encountering standard spelling in books and environmental print, children begin to notice certain spelling conventions: *train* is spelled with *tr*, the *ai* in *train* and *e* at the end of a word is a marker for a long vowel (*rake*). They begin to use visual features in addition to sound features to spell words. Although their spelling is not always correct—in the early stages *rain* might be spelled *RANE* and *rake* might be spelled *RAIK*—spelling is becoming more standard and incorporates such features as final-*e* markers and double vowel letters to spell long-vowel sounds. They are also able to spell *r*-vowel (*chair, here, bear, fir, turn*) and other-vowel patterns (*tall, claw, caught, fruit, boot, noise, brook*). The major characteristic of this stage is that students visualize spellings rather than relying strictly on what they hear (Gentry, 1997). By the end of this stage, they are able to spell most single-syllable words correctly. As they master single-syllable patterns, students begin encountering a greater proportion of multisyllabic words that incorporate these patterns and move into the multisyllabic or syllable juncture stage. Although students show increasing ability to write single-syllable words, they experience difficulty with multisyllabic words, especially those that drop final *e* (*hoping*) or double final consonants (*stopping*).

Children's spellings can offer insight into their understanding of phonics. To determine students' spelling stage, analyze samples of their writing. See Table 2.1. You might also use the *Elementary Spelling Inventory* (Bear & Barone, 1989), presented in Table 2.2. The inventory presents twenty-five words that increase in difficulty and embody key elements of the stages. Start with the first word and continue testing until the words become too difficult. Ask the students to spell as best they can, because even partially spelled words reveal important information about the students' spelling. Before administering the inventory, explain to the students that you want to see how they spell words. Tell them that some of the words may be hard, but they should do the best they can. Say each word, use it in a sentence, and say the word once more.

Using the error guide, carefully analyze the students' performance. Most novice readers will be in the early letter name stage. However, a few might be in a

TABLE 2.1   Spelling Stages

Age	Stage	Example
18 months	Random scribbling	↻↝↺
3 years	Wordlike scribbling	∿∿⌐
4–5 years	Early emergent (prephonemic)	SVB
4–6+	Early alphabetic (early letter name)	NT
5–7+	Alphabetic (letter name)	NIT
6–7	Word pattern (within-word)	NITE, NIGT, NIGHT
8–10+	Syllabic (syllable juncture)	STOPPING

TABLE 2.2 The Elementary Spelling Inventory (with Error Guide)

Stages	Early Letter Name	Letter Name	Within-Word Pattern	Syllable Juncture	Derivational Constancy
1. bed	b bd	bad	bed		
2. ship	s sp shp	sep shep	sip ship		
3. drive	jrv drv	griv driv	drieve draive drive		
4. bump	b bp bmp	bop bomp bup	bump		
5. when	w yn wn	wan whan	wen when		
6. train	j t trn	jran chran tan tran	teran traen trane train		
7. closet	k cs kt clst	clast clost clozt	clozit closit		
8. chase	j jass cs	tas cas chas chass	case chais chase		
9. float	f vt ft flt	fot flot flott	flowt floaut flote float		
10. beaches	b bs bcs	bechs becis behis	bechise beches beeches beaches		

Stages	Within-Word Pattern	Syllable Juncture	Derivational Constancy
11. preparing	preparng preypering	preparing prepairing preparing	
12. popping	popin poping	popping	
13. cattle	catl cadol	catel catle cattel cattle	
14. caught	cot cote cout cought caught		
15. inspection	inspshn inspechin	inspecshum inspecsion inspection	
16. puncture	pucshr pungchr puncker	punksher punture puncturec	
17. cellar	salr selr celr seler	seller sellar celler cellar	
18. pleasure	plasr plager plejer plesher	plesour plesure	pleasure
19. squirrel	scrl skwel skwerl	scqoril sqrarel squirle squirrel	
20. fortunate	forhnat frehnit foohinit	forchenut fochininte fortunet	fortunate

Stages	Within-Word Pattern	Syllable Juncture	Derivational Constancy
21. confident		confedent confedint confedent confadent conphident confiadent confident confendent confodent confident	
22. civilize		sivils sevelies sivilicse cifillazas sivelize sivalize civalise civilise civilize	
23. flexible		flecksibl flexobil fleckable flexible flexeble flexibel flaxable flexibal flexable	flexible
24. opposition	opasion opasishan opozcison opishien opasitian	opasition oppasishion oppisition	oposision oposition opposition
25. emphasize		infaside infacize emfsize emfisize imfasize ephacise empasize emphasise	emphisize emphasize

Note: The Preliterate Stage is not presented here.

Adapted from *Reading Psychology 10* (3), 1989, pp. 275–292, by Donald Bear and Diane Barone. Reproduced with permission. All rights reserved.

33

more advanced stage, and some may be in the prephonemic stage. Often, students move back and forth between adjacent stages.

➤➤THE CONTENT OF PHONICS

The American English sound system is composed of approximately forty-one sounds: twenty-five consonant and sixteen vowel sounds. When discussing consonants and vowels, it is important to distinguish between sounds and spellings. For instance, the statement that "*y* is sometimes a vowel" is confusing. A more precise way to describe *y* is to say that the letter *y* is sometimes used to spell a vowel sound or phoneme, as in *why*. To prevent confusion, vowel and consonant sounds will be presented between slashes (/b/). Vowels and consonants referred to as letters will be italicized.

➤➤CONSONANTS

Consonant spellings are more regular than those of vowels. The sound /d/, for instance, is almost always spelled *d* (**dad**). Some consonants are spelled with two letters (**sh**oes, chur**ch**). These are known as digraphs. A list of consonant correspondences frequently taught to emergent readers is presented in Table 2.3. The last four correspondences, *c* = /s/, *g* = /j/, *qu* = /kw/, and *x* = /ks/, are usually taught after the preceding correspondences have been introduced. A list of consonant digraph correspondences frequently taught to beginning readers is presented in Table 2.4.

Variable Consonant Correspondences.   The letters *c* and *g* can each represent two sounds. The letter *c* represents both /k/ and /s/, as in *cup* and *city*; the letter *g* represents /g/ and /j/, as in *go* and *giant*. The letter *c* represents /k/ far more often than it stands for /s/ (Gunning, 1975), and this is the sound students usually attach to it (Venezky, 1965); the letter *g* more often represents /g/. In teaching the consonant letters *c* and *g*, the more frequent sounds (*c* = /k/, *g* = /g/) should be presented first. The other sound represented by each letter (*c* = /s/, *g* = /j/) should be taught some time later. At that point, you might want to teach the following generalizations:

➤ The letter *g* usually stands for /j/ when it is followed by *e*, *i*, or *y*, as in *gem*, *giant*, and *gym*. (There are a number of exceptions: *geese*, *get*, *girl*, *give*.)
➤ The letter *c* usually stands for /k/ when it is followed by *a*, *o*, or *u*, as in *can*, *cold*, or *cup*.
➤ The letter *c* usually stands for /s/ when it is followed by *e*, *i*, or *y*, as in *cent*, *circus*, or *cycle*.

TABLE 2.3   Consonant Correspondences Taught to Beginning Readers

b = /b/	ball	*p* = /p/	pen
c = /k/	cat	*r* = /r/	ring
d = /d/	dog	*s* = /s/	sun
f = /f/	fish	*t* = /t/	ten
g = /g/	goat	*v* = /v/	vase
h = /h/	hat	*w* = /w/	wagon
j = /j/	jar	*y* = /y/	yo-yo
k = /k/	king	*z* = /z/	zebra
l = /l/	lion	*c* = /s/	city
m = /m/	man	*g* = /j/	giraffe
n = /n/	nail	*x* = /ks/	fox

TABLE 2.4 Digraph Correspondences Taught to Beginning Readers

ch = /ch/	**ch**air
sh = /sh/	**sh**oe
th = /th/	**th**umb
th = /<u>th</u>/	**<u>th</u>**e
wh = /w/	**wh**eel

➤ The letter *g* usually stands for /g/ when it is followed by *a, o,* or *u,* as in *gave, got,* or *guppy.*

When teaching the *c* and *g* generalizations, have students sort *c* = /k/ and *c* = /s/ words and, later, *g* = /g/ and *g* = /j/ words and discover the generalizations for themselves. An alternative to presenting the *c* and *g* generalizations is to teach students to be prepared to deal with the variability of the spelling of certain sounds. Students need to learn that, in English, letters can often stand for more than one sound. After learning the two sounds for *c* and *g*, students should be taught to use the following variability strategy when they are unsure how to read a word that begins with *c* or *g*.

1. Try the main pronunciation—the one the letter usually stands for.
2. If the main pronunciation gives a word that is not a real one or does not make sense in the sentence, try the other pronunciation.
3. If you still get a word that is not a real word or does not make sense in the sentence, try using context clues, skip it, or ask for help.

➤➤CONSONANT CLUSTERS

Consonants often appear in clusters. Consonant clusters (*stop*, be*st*, *str*ap), which are sometimes known as blends, are spelled with two letters or more and consist of two or more sounds. Because their separate sounds are difficult to distinguish, clusters pose special decoding problems for struggling readers. Major clusters are presented in Table 2.5.

➤➤VOWELS

In reading programs, twenty-one vowels are taught. These include short vowels (*cat, pet, hit, hot, but*), long vowels (*late, meet, life, hope, use*), other vowels (*paw, cow, boy, book, moon*), *r*-vowels (*her, hear, fire, where, four*), and schwa (*sofa*). Technically, there are only sixteen vowels. Linguistically, *r*- vowels are not a separate category. However, in reading instruction, *r*- vowels are traditionally listed separately. Vowels and their major spellings are presented in Table 2.6.

➤➤ONSET AND RIMES

Vowel correspondences may be taught in isolation, but in primary phonics they are taught as part of rimes. Words are composed of two parts: the onset and the rime.

TABLE 2.5 Consonant Clusters

L clusters

bl (**bl**anket), *cl* (**cl**oud), *fl* (**fl**ower), *gl* (**gl**ass), *pl* (**pl**ane), *sl* (**sl**ed)

R clusters

br (**br**ead), *cr* (**cr**ab), *dr* (**dr**um), *fr* (**fr**og), *gr* (**gr**apes), *pr* (**pr**etzel), *tr* (**tr**ee)

S clusters

sc (**sc**arecrow), *sch* (**sch**ool), *scr* (**scr**eam), *shr* (**shr**ink), *sk* (**sk**unk), *sl* (**sl**ed), *sm* (**sm**ile), *sn* (**sn**ake), *sp* (**sp**oon), *spl* (**spl**ash), *spr* (**spr**ing), *st* (**st**ar), *str* (**str**ing), *squ* (**squ**irrel), *sw* (**sw**ing)

Other clusters

tw (**tw**elve), *qu* (**qu**een)

TABLE 2.6   Vowel Spellings

Vowels	Examples	Model Word
Short vowels		
/a/	hat, batter, have	cat
/e/	ten, better, bread	bed
/i/	fit, little, remain	hit
/o/	hot, bottle, father	mop
/u/	cup, butter	bus
Long Vowels		
/ā/	made, nail, radio, hay, flavor	cake
/ē/	he, see, seal, sunny, turkey, these, neither	tree
/ī/	smile, night, pie, spider	bike
/ō/	no, hope, grow, toad, gold, roll, local	goat
/ū/	use, music	mule
Other vowels		
/aw/	ball, walk, paw, song, caught, thought, off	saw
/oi/	joy, join	boy
/ōō/	zoo, blue, grew, fruit, group, two	moon
/oo/	took, could push	book
/ow/	owl, south	cow
/ə/	ago, telephone, similar, opinion, upon	banana
R-vowels		
/ar/	car, charge, heart	star
/air/	fair, bear, care, there	chair
/eer/	ear, cheer, here	deer
/ir/	sir, her, earth, turn	bird
/or/	for, four, store, floor	door

The onset is the initial consonant, digraph, or cluster (*s, sh, st*). The rime is the rhyming part of the word, the vowel or the vowel plus consonant(s) coming after the vowel (*-o, -ag, -eet*). Rimes, which are also referred to as word patterns, word families, and phonograms, are more stable than vowels appearing alone. Theoretically, the letter *a* can represent more than a dozen sounds. However, in the following rimes the sound of *a* is highly predictable: *-at, -an, -ap, -ain, -ay, -ate*. Because rimes or patterns are highly predictable, they are the core of primary phonics instruction. Rimes that appear with a high degree of frequency and which are presented in this program are listed in Table 2.7.

Vowel Generalizations.   Although vowels can be spelled in many ways, their spellings generally fall into one of four patterns. The most frequent pattern is the vowel–consonant–vowel or closed syllable pattern (*sat, sit, set, set-tle*), in which the word or syllable ends in a vowel and the vowel is short. Long vowels have three major patterns: open syllable, digraph, and final *e*. In an open syllable, the syllable or word ends with a vowel and is usually long (*no, he, o-pen*). A final *e* frequently indicates that the preceding vowel is long: *pane, hope*. Long vowels can also be spelled with digraphs: *pain, sheep, goat*. However, digraphs are also used to spell other vowel sounds: *paw, boil*; and a few digraphs represent a number of pronunciations: *beat, steak, bread*.

Since none of the vowel patterns applies all the time, students should be introduced to the variability principle. They need to learn that digraphs and single

TABLE 2.7 High-Frequency Rimes

Short Vowels		Long Vowels		R-Vowels		Other Vowels	
-ack	tack	-ace	race	-air	hair	-al(l)	ball
-ad	sad	-ade	made	-are	square	-alk	walk
-ag	bag	-age	page	-art	cart	-aught	caught
-am	ham	-aid	paid	-ear	bear	-aw	saw
-an	pan	-ail	nail	-ar	star	-ew	new
-ap	map	-ain	train	-ard	card	-ong	song
-at	cat	-ait	wait	-ark	shark	-oss	boss
-ed	bed	-ake	cake	-arm	arm	-ost	lost
-ell	bell	-ale	whale	-art	chart	-ought	bought
-en	ten	-ame	name	-ear	ear	-oice	voice
-end	send	-ane	plane	-eer	deer	-oil	boil
-ent	went	-ate	gate	-er	her	-ong	song
-est	nest	-ave	wave	-ir	stir	-oin	coin
-et	net	-ay	hay	-ird	bird	-oo	zoo
-ick	stick	-e	me	-ire	tire	-oon	moon
-id	lid	-ea	sea	-oor	door	-oy	toy
-ig	pig	-ead	bead	-or	for	-ound	round
-in	pin	-eak	beak	-ore	score	-our	hour
-ing	ring	-eal	seal	-orn	corn	-ouse	house
-ip	ship	-eam	dream	-ort	fort	-out	shout
-ish	fish	-ean	bean	-ur	fur	-ow	cow
-it	hit	-eat	eat	-urn	burn	-own	clown
-ob	Bob	-ee	bee			-ood	wood
-ock	lock	-eed	seed			-ould	could
-op	mop	-eel	wheel			-ook	book
-ot	pot	-een	green			-ool	school
-ub	tub	-eep	jeep			-oom	broom
-uck	duck	-eet	feet			-oon	spoon
-ug	rug	-ice	mice			-oot	boot
-um	gum	-ide	ride			-oud	cloud
-ump	jump	-ie	tie			-ound	round
-unk	skunk	-ife	knife			-ull	pull
-up	cup	-ike	bike			-ue	blue
-us(s)	bus	-ile	smile				
-ut	cut	-ime	dime				
		-igh	high				
		-ight	night				
		-ine	nine				
		-ite	kite				
		-o	no				
		-oad	road				
		-oak	oak				
		-oat	goat				
		-oke	smoke				
		-old	gold				
		-ole	mole				
		-oll	roll				
		-one	bone				
		-ope	rope				
		-ote	note				
		-ose	rose				
		-ow	crow				
		-y	cry				

vowels can represent a variety of sounds. If they try one pronunciation and it is not a real word or does not make sense in context, then they must try another. A student who read "steek" for *steak* would have to try another pronunciation, because *steek* is not a real word. A student who read "braid" for *bread* would need to check to see if that pronunciation fits the context of the sentence in which the word was used. Although *braid* is a real word, it does not make sense in the sentence, "The store had no rye bread," so the student would need to try another pronunciation. Students should use the same variability strategy that was presented earlier for decoding words such as those containing initial *c* or *g*.

1. Try the main pronunciation—the one the letter(s) usually stand for.
2. If the main pronunciation gives a word that is not a real one or does not make sense in the sentence, try the other pronunciation. (If a chart of spellings is available, students can use it as a source of other pronunciations.)
3. If you still get a word that is not a real word or does not make sense in the sentence, try using context clues, skip it, or ask for help.

The variability strategy is a simpler procedure than the application of rules. Rather than trying to remember a rule, all the student has to do is try the major pronunciation, and, if that pronunciation does not work out, try another.

▶▶GUIDELINES FOR TEACHING PHONICS

First and foremost, phonics should be functional. The sole reason for teaching phonics is to provide students with tools so that they can decode words. Phonics elements taught should be those that students need in order to read and spell. Students need to be able to read short-vowel and long-vowel patterns. However, they do not need to be able to classify patterns as being long or short. Exercises in which students tell which vowels are long and which are short should be replaced by activities in which students read words that contain long vowels and words that contain short vowels, preferably in the context of an interesting story or informative article. Time spent learning rules, such as "when two vowels go walking, the first one does the talking," should be replaced by activities in which students build vowel–digraph patterns and read stories containing these patterns.

Phonics should also be closely related to the reading and writing that students are doing. One way of deciding which phonics element to present is to survey the selection students are about to read and note a dominant phonic pattern, which might be the *-ice* pattern in a book such as *Mrs. Brice's Mice* (Hoff, 1988), and present that pattern if it is one that is likely to pose problems for the students.

Time spent on phonics instruction should be limited. Most of the time should be spent with actual reading and writing. Time spent on phonics instruction should be only a small proportion of the time set aside for literacy instruction. As a rule of thumb, 10 to 15 minutes of phonics instruction a day should be sufficient. The rest of the time should be spent applying skills.

►►►Chapter Three

PHONEMIC AWARENESS AND BEGINNING CONSONANT CORRESPONDENCES

The most effective phonological awareness programs are those that combine phonemic awareness and letter–sound relationships or beginning phonics. Once students are able to detect initial sounds and can identify most of the letters of the alphabet, they are able to learn the relationship between sounds and letters. They are able to learn that b = /b/ and t = /t/. They are ready to go beyond merely memorizing that b = /b/, so that when they see the letter b, they associate the sound /b/ with it. Building on a base of phonemic awareness, they also realize that /b/ is the sound heard at the beginning of *boy* and *bicycle*. Students without adequate phonemic awareness might learn the b = /b/ correspondence by rote, but they would have difficulty applying it.

Beginning consonants can be taught in a number of ways. They can be presented analytically, synthetically, or through a combination approach. In an analytic approach, elements are taught within the context of a whole word. For instance, the correspondence b = /b/ is presented as the sound heard at the beginning of *ball*. Since the element is not isolated, the student must abstract it from the word. In the synthetic approach, elements are presented in isolated fashion; that is, the student is told, for instance, that b makes a "buh" sound. Saying speech sounds in isolation distorts them. However, struggling readers may find it difficult to abstract sounds from words, so sounds presented in isolation are easier for them. When teaching initial consonants, use a combination of the analytic and synthetic approaches. Novice readers need to have the target sound emphasized by hearing it in isolation, which is what the synthetic approach does. And they need to hear it in the context of a real word, which is what the analytic approach does.

The first correspondences recommended for presentation are s = /s/, m = /m/, and f = /f/. These correspondences are continuants: they are articulated with a continuous stream of breath and so are relatively easy to perceive. Although they are very different from each other, they also are among the most frequently occurring correspondences. They have very different pronunciations and their letters have very different shapes, so students are not likely to confuse them.

Presented below is a sample lesson for introducing the consonant correspondence s = /s/. The lesson starts with auditory perception, an aspect of phonemic awareness, to make sure students can perceive the sound of the element, and proceeds to the visual level, when the children integrate sound and letter knowledge. The lesson assumes that the students have an awareness of beginning sounds and realize that sounds are represented by letters. If possible, relate your presentation to a story, song, or rhyme that you have read aloud or share-read. This helps students relate the phonics they are learning to real reading.

➤➤SAMPLE LESSON 3.1: CONSONANT CORRESPONDENCE

Step 1: Auditory Perception.   In teaching the correspondence (letter–sound relationship) *s* = /s/, read a story such as "Six-Dinner Sid" (Moore, 1991) that contains a number of *s* words. Call the students' attention to the *s* words in the book: *six, sick, said, Sid.* Stressing the initial sound as you say each word, ask the students to tell what is the same about the words: *sssix, sssick, sssaid,* and *SSSid.* Help students note that the words all begin with the same sound. Present the sound /s/ both in isolation and within the context of a word. Although saying the sound in isolation distorts it, some students may have difficulty perceiving a sound in the context of a word. Explain that *six, sick, said,* and *Sid* begin with the sound /s/ as in *sun.* Ask the class if there are students whose first names begin with /s/—Sam, Sandra, Samantha, for example. Help the class determine whether or not the names do actually begin with /s/ and write them on the board. Note that the names begin with an uppercase *s.* If students volunteer names such as *Cecil* or *Cicely* that begin with an /s/ sound but are spelled with a *C,* explain that the sound /s/ can sometimes be spelled with a *C.*

If students experience difficulty perceiving initial sounds, ask silly questions that focus on /s/. Holding up a toy saw, ask, "Is this a paw? Is this a law?" Lead students to see that *paw* and *law* begin with the wrong sound and must be changed to /s/ to make *saw.* Other silly questions might include: "Is this a lock? (holding up a picture of a sock). Is this a meal?" (holding up a picture of a seal).

Step 2: Letter–Sound Integration.   Write each of the *s* words from Step 1 on the board: *six, sick, said,* and *Sid.* Read each word and have students tell which letter each of the words begins with. Lead the students to see that the letter *s* stands for the sound /s/ heard at the beginning of *six, sick, said,* and *Sid.* Compose a consonant chart, like the one shown in Figure 3.1. On this chart include a model word for *s* = /s/ and a picture to illustrate the key word. A model word is one that would most likely be a part of the students' listening vocabulary and that is easy to illustrate. An appropriate model word for *s* = /s/ is *sun.* If students forget the sound that a letter represents, the model word accompanied by its picture can be used as a reminder. Tell students that if they forget what sound *s* stands for, they can use the consonant chart to help them.

Step 3: Guided Practice.   Have students read signs or labels containing /s/ words: salt, syrup, soap. Holding up a bottle of syrup, ask them to tell what is in the bottle and then to find the word *syrup* on the bottle. Do the same for salt and soap. You might also conduct a shared reading of a big book that contains a number of words beginning with *s* and conduct a sorting exercise as explained in the Additional Application and Reinforcement section that follows, or you might create an interactive story that contains *s* words. You might also share-read the following verse or another one that contains a number of *s* words.

> **Sing, Sing**
> Sing, sing,
>   What shall I sing?
> The cat's run away
>   With the pudding string!

Step 4: Writing.   Review or introduce the formation of capital and lowercase *s.* Show the students how to form the word *see* by adding *s* to *ee.* To introduce *ee* = /ē/, write *ee* on the board. Ask students to name the letters. Explain that the

Bb	**b**all	
Cc	**c**at	
Cc	**c**ity	
Ch ch	**ch**air	
Dd	**d**og	
Ff	**f**ish	
Gg	**g**oat	
Gg	**g**iraffe	
Hh	**h**at	
Jj	**j**ar	
Kk	**k**ing	
Ll	**l**ion	
Mm	**m**an	
Nn	**n**ail	
Pp	**p**en	
Qu qu	**qu**een	
Rr	**r**ing	
Ss	**s**un	
Sh sh	**sh**oe	
Tt	**t**en	
Th th	**th**umb	
Vv	**v**ase	
Ww	**w**agon	
Wh wh	**w**hale	
Xx	fo**x**	
Yy	**y**o-yo	
Zz	**z**ebra	

FIGURE 3.1   Consonant Chart

letters *ee* make the sound /ē/ as in *see* and *tree*. Ask students to tell what letter they would add to *ee* to make the word *see*. After the word *see* has been formed, ask volunteers to read it. Then write *I* in front of it. Ask students if they know the name of the letter that you have written. Explain that this is also the word *I*. Read the two words with the students. Then cooperatively compose " I see" sentences that tell what the students see. To provide additional practice with *s* = /s/, you might encourage students to tell what they see that begins with /s/: I see Sue. I see a seven. I see socks. I see a sandwich. Using an interactive or shared writing approach as explained later in this chapter, begin composing a class alphabet book. Start with the *s* page. Encourage students to draw or paste in pictures of items whose names begins with *s*. Help the students label these items and encourage them to read the page.

Step 5: Application.   Students apply their skill by looking at the *s* pages in alphabet books. You might also share-read books that contain words that begin with *s*, or you might create experience stories that contain *s* words. Also encourage students to use *s* as they compose stories.

➤➤ADDITIONAL APPLICATION AND REINFORCEMENT

➤   Help students create individual alphabet books. Show the students how you want them to set up their books. One possibility is to distribute thirty sheets, one for each letter of the alphabet and one for *ch, sh, th,* and *wh* (later you might add pages for *c* = /s/ and *g* = /j/). Each sheet should be marked with a letter (or letters) in both upper- and lowercase. Students might create covers for the books, which could then be stapled or stitched together. Once students have studied a letter, they can draw illustrations or paste in pictures whose names begin with the sound represented by that letter.

➤   Create highly predictable stories in which students use their knowledge of initial consonants. This shows students the purpose of learning initial consonants and gives them a sense of what reading is, so that they feel like readers. As students read these highly predictable stories, encourage them to point to each word as they read it, so they match up print with what they are saying. Appendix B provides several highly predictable fold-and-read books designed to reinforce initial consonants. Three of the books use the "I see ___" pattern. In presenting the books, teach the words *I, see, a* and show students how to use picture clues and initial consonants to figure out the ending word in each pattern. Each ending word will begin with a recently presented consonant. Follow the same procedure with the "I am ___" and "I like ___" predictable books. Read the books with your students and encourage them to read them with partners, with family members, and on their own.

➤   Conduct every-pupil response activities. In every-pupil response activities, students hold up cards to respond. That way all can respond at the same time. Say a series of words, some of which begin with the target letter. Have students hold up the letter card when words beginning with that letter are called out. If students know several correspondences, give them several letters (but not more than three or four) and ask them to hold up the letter that represents the beginning sound of the word being spoken. For example, you might say, "Which of these begins with the letter *s*? Seal, dog, sun." Students should hold up the *s* card when you say *seal* and *sun*.

➤   Continue to share-read books with students. As you encounter *s* words, point them out and have the students tell you what sound the words begin with. Continue to read and discuss alphabet books and environmental print. Also share-read rhymes that illustrate the correspondence.

➤ Have students conduct a word search. Ask them to search classroom walls and their books for words that begin with the correspondence being taught.

➤ Have students create a word bank of words that they can read and words that they are learning to read. Have them locate and read words in their word bank that begin with the target letter.

➤ If students continue having difficulty grasping the concept of consonant correspondences, try the partial-word technique. Holding up a picture of the sun, ask, "Is this the *un*?" Note that a sound is missing. Ask students to tell what the word should be and what sound is missing. Stress the fact that you need to add /s/ to /un/ to make *sun*. Write *un* on the board, explaining that this stands for /un/. Then add *s*, explaining as you do so that this letter stands for /s/. Then say the word, emphasizing /s/. Follow the same procedure with other *s* words: *saw, seal*. Avoid initial clusters, as in *snake*, since it is harder to isolate a single consonant sound in a cluster.

Sorting.   Sorting is also a highly effective way to reinforce letter–sound correspondences. After at least two correspondences have been introduced, students can sort them. When supplying correspondences for students to sort, choose ones that are distinctively different. For instance, students might sort *f* and *h* because they are formed in different parts of the mouth and the letters that represent them are very different from each other. Pairs such as *m* and *n* or *p* and *b* would not be good candidates for sorting, especially for students in the beginning stage of learning letter–sound relationships. Create letter cards for the sounds to be sorted and assemble pictures that begin with the target sounds: illustrations for initial consonant sounds can be found at the end of this chapter. To make the cards more durable, copy them onto card stock, which is available at most stationery stores. You might also laminate the cards.

Place each letter card at the head of a column, say the sound each represents, and then place under it an illustration of the sound's model word. For *f*, place an *Ff* card at the head of the column and say *f* stands for /f/, the sound that you hear at the beginning of *fish*. Place a picture of a fish under *f* and say, "*Fish* is the model word for /f/." Follow this same procedure for the correspondence *h* = /h/ as in Figure 3.2.

Point to a stack of cards containing objects whose names begin with /f/ or /h/ and tell the students, "We're going to sort these picture cards. If the name of the picture begins with /f/ as in *fish*, we're going to put it in the *fish* column. If the name of the picture begins with /h/ as in *hat*, we'll put it in the *hat* column." Holding up a picture of the number 4, ask, "What is this? What sound does it begin with? What column should we put it in?" Affirm or correct students' responses. "Yes, *four* begins with the sound /f/ that we hear in the beginning of *fffish*, so we put it in the *fish* column." Go through the rest of the cards in this fashion. Once all the cards have been categorized, ask volunteers to say the names of all the cards in a column and note that they all begin with either /f/ or /h/. Encourage students to suggest other words that might fit into the columns. Also have them re-sort the pictures on their own to promote speed of response. You might also add a third item to be sorted.

If students seem to be using a picture card as a basis for sorting—they put *fan* under *fish* because they both begin the same way—remove the picture cards as soon as they have been sorted so that they are matching the cards to the letter: *fan* is placed under the letter *f* because it begins with the sound represented by *f* (Morris, 1999).

Students should be asked to sort no more than three correspondences at a time. After students have mastered a group of three correspondences, you might drop the best-known correspondence and add a new one.

Sorting activities are very effective, and they can be made more advanced as students' knowledge of phonics elements becomes more advanced. Through sorting, students make discoveries about the spelling system. Because sorting is active

FIGURE 3.2   Sorting by Initial Consonant Sound

and challenging, students also enjoy sorting. Best of all, research supports sorting as being a highly effective activity (Santa & Høien, 1999).

Shared Reading.   Shared reading is also an excellent device for fostering literacy development. Through shared reading, using enlarged text can convey initial concepts of print, letter knowledge, phonological awareness, consonant correspondences, and other phonic elements. Enlarged text may take the form of commercially produced big books, big books that you create yourself, poems or songs written on the chalkboard, or experience stories written on large sheets of paper or on the chalkboard. Because the text is enlarged, the class can follow along as you read a selection. If you are working with just one student, you can use a regular-size text. This procedure can be used to introduce or reinforce nearly any skill or understanding in early reading, from the concept of going from left to right to the reading of words, phrases, and sentences or the reinforcement of initial consonant correspondences or vowel patterns. A good time to introduce shared reading is while students are learning initial consonant correspondences. Knowing initial consonants helps students to track print, because the consonants mark where words begin. The following sample lesson illustrates how to conduct a shared reading activity.

➤➤SAMPLE LESSON 3.2: SHARED READING

Step 1: Preparing for the Reading.   Prepare students for a shared reading by discussing the cover illustration and the title and, if you wish, some illustrations from the text. Based on the discussion of the cover and the title, ask them to predict what the selection might be about. Establish a purpose for reading. If students have made predictions about the content, the purpose might be to compare their predictions to what actually happens in the text.

Step 2: Reading the Selection.   As you read the selection, point to each word as you say it, so students get the idea of going from left to right and that there is a one-to-one match between the spoken and the printed word. Stop and clarify difficult words and concepts. Discuss interesting parts and have students evaluate their predictions, revising them if they wish.

Step 3: Discussing the Selection.   After students have read the selection, discuss it with them. Begin by talking about their predictions. Also try to relate the selection to experiences the students may have had. Try to elicit responses to the characters and situations portrayed, asking such questions as: "Do you know anyone like the main character? Has anything like this happened to you?"

Step 4: Rereading the Selection.   During subsequent readings of the text, point out one or two concepts of print, such as words, letters, or a phonics element such as initial consonants. For instance, if you are working on the consonant correspondence *m* = /m/, emphasize words that begin with *m*. Discuss the fact that the words begin with the same sound and the same letter. During subsequent readings, pause before the *m* words and invite students to read them. Give help as needed. During these subsequent readings, also encourage students to join in and read other parts that they can handle. This may be a repeated word or phrase or a whole sentence. If the book is a popular one, schedule several rereadings. Each time, the students should take more responsibility for the reading. As a follow-up, students may want to listen to taped versions of the big book, or read regular-size versions to a partner.

➤➤THE ROLE OF INVENTED SPELLING

Daily writing activities in which invented spelling is encouraged foster development in both reading and writing. Through their attempts to write, students make discoveries about the sounds of language and how these sounds might be spelled.

As they gain experience with writing, children develop a deeper understanding of the spelling system. They begin to use visual and meaning features to spell words, instead of relying just on sound characteristics. Instruction is most effective when it matches the student's stage of development. For instance, a student in the early alphabetic or letter name stage may have difficulty with final-*e* words. She or he might be able to memorize the spelling of *note* but would not understand the final-*e* principle and so would not apply it to other words.

Regardless of where students are on the path to conventional writing, encourage them to write and draw. If young students are reluctant to write because they feel they don't know how, encourage them to write as best they can. Show samples of other students' writing that includes drawing, scribbling, random letters, invented spelling, and conventional spelling.

➤➤LANGUAGE EXPERIENCE

Students' writing may be assisted using the language experience approach. In this approach, students discuss an experience they have had. This might be an account of a visit to a pumpkin farm, a description of a new classroom pet, or a piece about the seasons of the year. With the teacher providing guidance, the students dictate a story, which the teacher scribes and then reads back to the students. The story is then read again in shared-reading fashion. The teacher can focus on the concept of separate words in a sentence, beginning sounds, the sound that a particular letter makes, or any other skill or concept of print. Experience stories can be created by a small group, the whole class, or an individual student.

➤➤SHARED WRITING

In shared writing, students and teacher collaborate in the writing of a story. Instead of functioning merely as a scribe, the teacher adds content to the story and makes suggestions. In a form of shared writing known as interactive writing, students "share the pen" and do some of the actual writing of the selection. Interactive writing begins with the selection of a topic. As with the traditional experience story approach, students can write about a trip they have taken, a classroom pet, a story they have read, or a similar topic. With the teacher's help the students compose their message orally. The teacher writes words that are so difficult that students would not be able to supply any parts. Students are invited to write word parts that they can handle. For instance, after students have learned to write a few consonants, the teacher may invite the class to supply those consonants in a written piece. The teacher provides help by elongating words or relating a word that is being written to a student's name or another familiar word. The teacher can also use prompts to call students' attention to the number of words in the sentence, to reinforce the concept of separate words. Some prompts that might be used include the following (Pinnell & Fountas, 1998):

➤ How many words are there in our sentence?
➤ Can you clap as I say each word?
➤ What is the first word that we want to write?
➤ Say the word slowly. What sounds do you hear?
➤ What sound do you hear at the beginning of the word?
➤ Whose name begins like that word?
➤ What letter stands for that sound?
➤ Can you write the letter that stands for that sound?

Here is how an interactive story might be created. After the teacher reads "Down by the Bay" to the students, the class decides to add a verse of its own: "Did you ever see a pig, Wearing a wig, Down by the bay." The teacher repeats the verse and perhaps has the class clap out the words as she says them. The teacher and the class then write the story. The teacher scaffolds the writing so that students contribute as much as they can. Emphasizing the word's sounds, the teacher says "Did" and asks the class what sounds they hear. She notes that *Did* begins like *Dora*, so she has Dora write the first letter. The story is written on chart paper. Meanwhile, the rest of the class might use white boards to attempt to represent the first sound in *Did*. Using white boards gives each student the opportunity to participate. The teacher then asks the class what other sound they hear in *Did*. When a volunteer responds /i/, the teacher writes *i* and says that *i* in the middle of a word sometimes makes an /i/ sound. The teacher does not call on a student to supply the *i*, because she knows the group does not know how to spell vowels. Meanwhile, students add an *i* to the *D* on their white boards. The teacher reads what is there, "Dih," and asks what sound is missing. A volunteer responds that /d/ is missing. The teacher asks what letter is used to spell /d/. Dora again responds that the letter *d* spells /d/ and adds it to the word. Students also add *d* to the *Di* on their whiteboards. The teacher points to *Did* and the class reads it chorally. The class discusses how many sounds are in *you* and *ever*, but the teacher spells the words because all of the phonics elements in those words are unfamiliar. However, a volunteer is able to write *see*, because this is a word that the class has learned to spell. The class identifies the number of sounds in *pig* and the teacher asks who has a name that begins like *pig*. Paul does, and he writes a *p* on the board. The teacher adds an *i* and asks the class what sound they hear at the end of *pig*. The class responds /g/. The teacher asks what letter is used to spell /g/ as in *goat*. A volunteer says *g* and adds the letter. After each word has been written, the class reads the part that has been written so far chorally. The process continues until the new verse has been written.

The scaffolding and explanations that the teacher offers are geared to the students' level of understanding. Skills and understandings that students are currently working on are the concept of word and beginning sounds. Later, the teacher might focus on ending and then medial sounds or high-frequency words. Stories are posted and students are encouraged to read them from time to time. As a reference, all of the students' first names may be listed in alphabetical order on a chart which is displayed prominently. An alphabet strip may also be available in case students forget how to form a letter. As students learn high-frequency words such as *the,* these are listed on the class's word wall. As students grow in their knowledge of initial consonants, the teacher suggests that they say the word slowly and think of the beginning sound and the letter used to spell it. In time they are asked to represent additional sounds in the word.

After an interactive story has been completed, it is displayed so that it can be share read or read independently. In an activity known as "reading around the room," students read interactive and other experience stories that have been placed on the walls. Here is sample dialog to show how the last part of the verse, "Down by the bay," was written.

TEACHER: "How does *Down* begin? Who besides Dora has a name that begins like *Down*?"

DONALD: "I do."

TEACHER: "How does your name begin?"

DONALD: "With a *D.* My name begins with a *D.*"

TEACHER (POINTING TO DONALD'S NAME ON THE NAME CHART): "Can you write a *D* here?" Judging that /ow/ is too advanced for the class, the teacher says: "I will add the /ow/ sound to /d/. Now we have *Dow.* What sound do we need to add to make the word *Down*?"

MARIA: "/n/."

TEACHER: "Good, Maria. If we add /n/ to *Dow,* we have *Down.* What letter makes the /n/ sound? Who has a name that ends in /n/?"

JAN: "I do. My name ends with an *n.*"

TEACHER (POINTING TO JAN'S NAME ON THE NAME CHART): "Yes you do. Add *n* to *Dow* to make *Down.*"

TEACHER: "Who can read this word for us?"

MAUREEN: "Down."

TEACHER: "Very good. Check your white boards, boys and girls, to make sure that you have written *Down* correctly. What word comes after *Down?*"

JAMES: "By."

TEACHER: "How does *by* begin? Who has a name that begins like *by*?"

BERNARD: "I do."

TEACHER: "How does your name begin?"

BERNARD: " My name begins with a *b.*"

TEACHER (POINTING TO BERNARD'S NAME ON THE NAME CHART): "Can you write a *b* here?" Judging that $y = /\bar{\imath}/$ is too advanced for the class, the teacher says; "I will add the $/\bar{\imath}/$ sound to /b/. Now we have *by.* Who can read what we have written so far?"

GERMAINE: "Down by."

TEACHER: "What is the next word that we want to add?"

TANYA: "The."

TEACHER: "Can you write *the*? *The* is on our Word Wall."

TANYA: "I can write *the*."

TEACHER (POINTING TO THE SPOT ON THE CHART PAPER):   "Tanya, will you write *the* here? Class, you can write *the* on your white boards. Who can point to *the* on our Word Wall?"

TEACHER (POINTING TO *THE* THAT TANYA HAS WRITTEN):   "Very good, Tanya. Check your white boards, boys and girls, to make sure that you have written *the* correctly."

The teacher has a volunteer read what has been written so far. The class continues working until the verse is complete. In addition to the name chart, the class can also refer to the consonant chart for the spelling of consonant sounds. For high-frequency words, the students can refer to the Word Wall. The Word Wall contains high-frequency words such as *the* and *is,* number words, and color words. They are placed on the wall in alphabetical order after they have been introduced to the students.

▶▶USING CHILDREN'S BOOKS

Continue to read alphabet and alliterative books to students and encourage them to read some of the simpler ones on their own. Emphasize consonant letters and the sounds they represent. An excellent series of books for reinforcing initial consonant correspondences is Ray's Readers (Outside the Box Publishing Company). Each eight-page booklet provides practice with a single correspondence. *The Hungry Goat,* for instance, provides practice with *g* = /g/ by telling a story about a goofy goat that gobbles up gold, gifts, gowns, games, and gum. The books are available in both big book and regular formats. Listed below are a number of other alphabet and alliterative books.

Berenstain, S., & Berenstain, J. (1971). *The Berenstains' b book.* New York: Random House. Big brown bear, a blue bull, and a beautiful baboon undertake activities that begin with *b.*

Brown, R. (1994). *What rhymes with snake?* New York: Tambourine. Uses lift-the-flap to foster consonant substitution. For instance, lifting the picture of a hen, the reader finds a picture of a hen. Lifting the *h* from the word *hen,* the reader uncovers the word *pen.*

Dr. Seuss. (1973). *Dr. Seuss's ABC.* New York: Random House. Each letter is accompanied by a humorous alliterative story.

Dr. Seuss. (1979). *Oh say can you say.* New York: Random House. Presents a series of humorous tongue-twisters.

Elting, M., & Folsom, M. (1980). *Q is for duck.* Boston: Houghton Mifflin. Readers are invited to guess why "A is for zoo, B is for dog" (Animals live in the Zoo, Dog Barks, etc.).

Hofbauer, M. P. (1993). *All the letters.* Bridgeport, CT: Green Bark Press. Letters of the alphabet are depicted with objects and labels (Dd: dinosaur, duck, dog).

Le Tord, B. (1981). *An alphabet of sounds.* New York: Scholastic. Each letter of the alphabet is illustrated with sounds spelled with that letter (B = buzz).

Modesitt, J. (1990). *The story of Z.* Saxonville, MA: Picture Book Studios. Z leaves the alphabet, so people must say things such as "ip your ipper."

Pallotta, J. (1987). *The bird alphabet book.* Watertown, MA: Charlesbridge. Each letter of the alphabet is represented by a bird. A brief description of the bird is provided.

Potter, B. (1987). *Peter Rabbit's ABC.* Middlesex, England: Frederick Warne. Old-fashioned illustrations accompany a letter of the alphabet and a word that begins with that letter (*b* is for *butter*).

➤➤USING GAMES AND PLAY RHYMES

A number of traditional children's games and rhymes provide a natural reinforcement for beginning consonant correspondences. Two especially effective ones are described below.

> **A My Name Is Alice**
> A my name is Alice,
> And my husband's name is Alex.
> We come from Alabama,
> And we sell apples.

Players create additional verses, one for each letter of the alphabet. For the next verse the player uses the letter *b*, makes up names, a location, and an item to be sold, all of which begin with *b*. Boys can substitute wife's name for husband's name in line 2.

> B my name is Benjamin,
> And my wife's name is Barbara.
> We come from Boston,
> And we sell boats.

> "Concentate on" is a similar game

> **Concentrate on**
> Concentrate on the letter A.
> Apple begins with the letter A.

The player goes through the letter *B* and then the rest of the alphabet, or players may take turns.

> Concentrate on the letter B.
> Banana begins with B.

➤➤TECHNOLOGY

Use software, such as *Dr. Peet's Talk/Writer* (Edmark) or *Write Out Loud* (Don Johnston), that helps students discover letter–sound relationships. These word-processing programs will say words that have been typed in. *Simon Sounds It Out* (Don Johnston), an award-winning piece of software, pronounces and helps students build words by combining initial consonants (onsets) and word patterns (rimes). Since it pronounces and shows parts of words, it also helps develop phonemic awareness. A demo disk is available.

➤➤FUNCTIONAL READING

Encourage students to read labels, signs, and other real-world materials. Point out both visual and graphic clues that they might use. Food labels and other possible functional reading items are listed for most correspondences in the resources section below.

➤➤HOLISTIC APPLICATION

Whenever possible, present letter–sound relationships and other understandings about reading in a holistic, functional context. Along with alphabet books, use the shared reading of big books and interactive writing to reinforce initial–consonant correspondences and general concepts of print. Most important, surround students with reading materials and the tools of literacy. Set up reading and writing corners and listening centers. Place easy signs and stories on the wall. Set the scene for engaging in a variety of literacy tasks that lend themselves to the exploration of letter–sound relationships.

➤➤RESOURCES FOR TEACHING CONSONANT CORRESPONDENCES

In this section, words that might be used to present consonant correspondences are listed. For the most part, these are words that can be illustrated. Illustrations that have been created for most of these words can be found at the end of this chapter. Also listed are food labels and other possible functional reading items. Presented, too, are references to rhymes, songs, and riddles that might be used to reinforce the target correspondence, and suggestions for sorting and writing. The rhymes and songs referred to can be found in Appendix A. Since students' reading vocabulary is probably very limited at this point, share-read the rhymes with them. Fold-and-read books that incorporate predictable patterns and consonants, so that students can gain some experience with "real" reading, can be found in Appendix B. A suggested sequence for all phonics elements is presented in Table 3.1

It is suggested that you present the correspondences in the order presented. As consonant correspondences are introduced, a limited number of vowels should be introduced so that students can start forming words. This will build additional phonemic awareness as students are provided with the opportunity to consider all the sounds in a word. It also makes it possible for students to read connected text and to write words.

s = /s/ Correspondence.   See Sample Lesson 3.1.

m = /m/ Correspondence

Correspondence words that can be illustrated: man, moon, mop, map, mouse.

*Rhyme: "The Three Little Kittens"

Functional reading: milk, mustard, mayonnaise, muffins, macaroni

Sorting: Have students sort picture cards beginning with /m/ or /s/. Cards should be placed under the *m* or the *s* so that students make the association between the initial sound of the name of the card and the letter that spells that sound. Illustrations for cards can be found at the end of this chapter.

Writing: Review or introduce the formation of capital and lowercase *m*. Students might draw a picture of some things that they see that begin with *m*. Review the "I see _____." pattern that was previously introduced, and model the process of drawing pictures of things that begin with /m/ and writing an "I see ____" caption for them. Also introduce *a*, so that students can write sentences such as "I see a man." Review the *s* page in the class alphabet book and add an *m* page.

*Note: All rhymes and songs referred to can be found in Appendix A.

TABLE 3.1   Sequence for Teaching Consonants and Vowels

Preparatory Level: letter names, phonological awareness

Level 1

    High-frequency initial consonants

s = /s/	r = /r/	n = /n/
m = /m/	g = /g/	h = /h/
b = /b/	l = /I/	t = /t/
f = /f/	c = /k/	d = /d/

    Lower-frequency initial consonants and y

j = /j/	y = /y/	z = /z/
p = /p/	c = /s/	qu = /kw/
w = /w/	g = /j/	x = /ks/
k = /k/	v = /v/	x = /z/

    High-frequency initial consonant digraphs

sh = /sh/	th = /th/
ch = /ch/	wh = /hw/ or /w/

    Short vowel patterns

Level 2

    Final consonants

    High frequency initial consonant clusters

        L clusters: bl, cl, fl, gl, pl, sl
        R clusters: br, cr, dr, fr, gr, pr, tr
        S clusters: sc, sch, scr, sk, sl, sm, sn, sp, spl, st, str, squ, sw
        Other clusters: tw, qu

    Long vowel Patterns

Level 3

    R-vowel patterns

    Other-vowel patterns

    Low-frequency digraphs

    kn = /n/
    ph = /f/
    wr = /r/

Level 4

    Multisyllabic patterns

Note: The teaching of consonant correspondences and vowel patterns should be integrated. After introducing four or five consonant correspondences, introduce a short-vowel pattern such as *am.* As more correspondences are presented, introduce additional short-vowel patterns. After most beginning consonant correspondences have been presented, introduce some high frequency digraphs and clusters.

b = /b/ Correspondence

Correspondence words that can be illustrated: book, bell, bee, boat, bat, ball.

Rhyme: "Baa, Baa, Black Sheep."

Functional reading: baked beans, butter, bacon, beets, biscuits.

Sorting: Have students sort picture cards beginning with /b/, /m/, or /s/. Cards should be placed under the *b, m,* or *s* so that students make the association between the initial sound of the name of the card and the letter that spells that sound.

Writing: Review or introduce the formation of capital and lowercase *b*. Students might draw a picture of some things that they see that begin with /b/. Review the "I see _____" pattern and model the process of drawing pictures of something that begins with /b/ and writing an "I see _____" caption for it. Review the *s* and *m* pages in the class alphabet book and add a *b* page.

f = /f/ Correspondence

Correspondence words that can be illustrated: fish, four, five, fox.

Rhyme: "Fuzzy Wuzzy."

Functional reading: frozen fish.

Sorting: Have students sort picture cards beginning with /b/, /f/, or /m/.

Writing: Review or introduce the formation of capital and lowercase *f*. Review the *m* and *b* pages in the class alphabet book and add an *f* page. As a group, write an experience or interactive story about things that are fun.

r = /r/ Correspondence

Correspondence words that can be illustrated: ring, rabbit, radio, rake, rug, rat.

Rhyme: "Rain, Rain, Go Away."

Functional reading: raisins, raisin bran, rice.

Sorting: Have students sort picture cards beginning with /b/, /f/, or /r/.

Writing: Review or introduce the formation of capital and lowercase *r*. Review the *b* and *f* pages in the class alphabet book and add an *r* page.

g = /g/ Correspondence

Correspondence words that can be illustrated: gum, goat, gorilla, girl, gate.

Rhyme: "A-Hunting We Will Go"; "Gobble, Gobble."

Functional reading: gum.

Sorting: Have students sort picture cards beginning with /f/, /r/, or /g/.

Writing: Review or introduce the formation of capital and lowercase *g*. Review the *f* and *r* pages in the class alphabet book and add a *g* page.

l = /l/ Correspondence

Correspondence words that can be illustrated: lion, lamp, lock, lettuce, leopard, ladder.

Rhyme: "Three Little Bugs;" "Lobby Loo."

Functional reading: lemonade, lima beans.

Reading: Have students read the *I See a Bear* fold-and-read book which can be found in Appendix B. Review the phrase "I see," and model how you would use the initial consonant and illustration to read the last word in each pattern sentence.

Sorting: Have students sort picture cards beginning with /r/, /g/, or /l/.

Writing: Review or introduce the formation of capital and lowercase *l*. Review the *f* and *r* pages in the class alphabet book and add a *g* page. Introduce the word *like* and have students draw pictures or write about some things that they like.

c = /k/ Correspondence

Correspondence words that can be illustrated: can, cat, cup, car, comb.

Rhyme: "What Animals Say."

Functional reading: corn, carrots, cat food, cocoa, cake mix.

Sorting: Have students sort picture cards beginning with /g/, /l/, or c = /k/.

Writing: Review or introduce the formation of capital and lowercase c. Review the g and l pages in the class alphabet book and add a c = /k/ page.

n = /n/ *Correspondence*

Correspondence words that can be illustrated: nine, nail, net, nickel, necklace.

Rhymes: "Engine, Engine, Number Nine"; "It Ain't Going to Rain No More."

Functional reading: box of nails.

Sorting: Have students sort picture cards beginning with /l/, c = /k/, or /n/.

Writing: Review or introduce the formation of capital and lowercase n. Review the l and c = /k/ pages in the class alphabet book and add an n page. Show students how to form the word *can*. First form the word *an*. Say the word *an*, stretching out the sounds as you do so. Have students tell what sounds they hear and then tell what letters spell those sounds. After *an* has been formed, have volunteers read it. Then have students tell what letter would need to be added to *an* to make the word *can*. After *can* has been formed, have volunteers read it. Also have a volunteer add *I* to form the phrase "I can." Have volunteers read the phrase. Then compose sentences telling about something that you can do. Use words that begin with correspondences that have already been introduced, so that students can tell what sound and what letter these words begin with as you write them on the board. Discuss with students some things that they can do. Write the words interactively and add them to the Word Wall. Invite students to create "I can" books in which they tell about some things that they can do.

h = /h/ *Correspondence*

Correspondence words that can be illustrated: hat, ham, hand, hook, horn, horse, house.

Rhyme: "Hiccup, Hiccup."

Functional reading: canned ham.

Sorting: Have students sort picture cards beginning with c = /k/, /n/, or /h/.

Writing: Review or introduce the formation of capital and lowercase h. Review the c = /k/ and n pages in the class alphabet book and add an h page. As part of an interactive writing project, have students write about some things that they have.

t = /t/ *Correspondence*

Correspondence words that can be illustrated: ten, tire, toe, tiger, table, tent, teeth.

Functional reading: tea, toothpaste, tomatoes, tomato juice.

Rhyme: "Little Tommy Tucker."

Sorting: Have students sort picture cards beginning with /n/, /h/, or /t/.

Writing: Review or introduce the formation of capital and lowercase t. Review the h and n pages in the class alphabet book and add a t page.

d = /d/ *Correspondence*

Correspondence words that can be illustrated: dog, desk, dish, deer, door, duck.

Rhyme: "My Son John."

Sorting: Have students sort picture cards beginning with /h/, /t/, or /d/.

Functional reading: donuts, hot dogs.

Reading: Have students read the *I See a Camel* fold-and-read book, which can be found in Appendix B. Review the phrase "I see," and model how you would use the initial consonant and illustration to read the last word in each pattern sentence.

Writing: Review or introduce the formation of capital and lowercase *t*. Review the *h* and *t* pages in the class alphabet book and add a *d* page. In interactive style, create booklets in which drawings of animals are accompanied by captions that tell what the animal is: For instance, drawing of a horse can be accompanied by the caption, "I am a horse."

j = /j/ Correspondence

Correspondence words that can be illustrated: jar, jeep, jet, jeans.

Rhyme: "Jack, Be Nimble."

Functional reading: jam, jelly, tomato juice.

Sorting: Have students sort picture cards beginning with /t/, /d/, or /j/.

Writing: Review or introduce the formation of capital and lowercase *j*. Review the *t* and *d* pages in the class alphabet book and add a *j* page. In interactive style, have students add to the list of things they can do.

p = /p/ Correspondence

Correspondence words that can be illustrated: pen, pie, pencil, pillow, piano, purse.

Rhyme: "Pease Porridge."

Functional reading: jar of peanut butter, bag of peanuts.

Sorting: Have students sort picture cards beginning with /t/, /j/, or /p/.

Writing: Review or introduce the formation of capital and lowercase *p*. Review the *t* and *j* pages in the class alphabet book and add a *p* page.

w = /w/ Correspondence

Correspondence words that can be illustrated: wagon, window, wig, well, web, wallet.

Rhyme: "Fuzzy Wuzzy."

Functional reading: replicas of "Walk" and "Don't Walk" signs, wax beans.

Sorting: Have students sort picture cards beginning with /j/, /p/, or /w/.

Writing: Review or introduce the formation of capital and lowercase *w*. Review the *j* and *p* pages in the class alphabet book and add a *w* page.

k = /k/ Correspondence

Correspondence words that can be illustrated: key, king, kite, kangaroo.

Rhyme: "Polly, Put the Kettle On."

Functional reading: ketchup.

Reading: Review the phrase "I like ___" and introduce the *I Like* fold-and-read book, which can be found in Appendix B.

Sorting: Have students sort picture cards beginning with /p/, /w/, or /k/.

Writing: Review or introduce the formation of capital and lowercase *k*. Review the *p* and *w* pages in the class alphabet book and add a *w* page.

y = /y/ Correspondence

Correspondence words that can be illustrated: Yo-Yo, yarn, yogurt, yawn.

Rhyme: "Clouds"

Functional reading: yogurt.

Sorting: Have students sort picture cards beginning with /w/, /k/, or /y/.

Writing: Review or introduce the formation of capital and lowercase *y*. Review the *w* and *k* pages in the class alphabet book and add a *y* page.

c = /s/ Correspondence

Correspondence words that can be illustrated: circle, cent, city.

Functional reading: apple cider.

Sorting: Have students sort picture cards beginning with /y/, /k/, or *c* = /s/.

Writing: Review or introduce the formation of capital and lowercase *c* = /s/. Review the *y* and *k* pages in the class alphabet book and add a *c* = /s/ page.

Note: When presenting *c* = /s/, teach the variability principle. Tell students that *c* can stand for the sound /k/ as in *can* or the sound /s/ as in *cent*. Tell them to try the /k/ pronunciation first; if that doesn't work, try the /s/ pronunciation.

g = /j/ Correspondence

Correspondence words that can be illustrated: giraffe, giant, gym.

Functional reading: ginger ale, ginger snaps.

Sorting: Have students sort picture cards beginning with /y/, *c* = /s/, or *g* = /j/.

Writing: Review or introduce the formation of capital and lowercase *g* = /j/. Review the *y* and *c* = /s/ pages in the class alphabet book and add a *g* = /j/ page.

Note: When presenting *g* = /j/, teach the variability principle. Tell students that *g* can stand for the sound /g/ as in *girl* or the sound /j/ as in *giraffe*. Tell them to try the /g/ pronunciation first; if that doesn't work, try the /j/ pronunciation.

v = /v/ Correspondence

Correspondence words that can be illustrated: vase, van, violin, vest, vet.

Rhyme: "Our Van."

Functional reading: vegetables, vanilla ice cream.

Sorting: Have students sort picture cards beginning with *c* = /s/, *g* = /j/, or *v*.

Writing: Review or introduce the formation of capital and lowercase *v*. Review the *g* = /j/ and *c* = /s/ pages in the class alphabet book and add a *v* page.

z = /z/ Correspondence

Correspondence words that can be illustrated: zebra, zoo, zipper.

Rhyme: "The Zigzag Boy and Girl."

Functional reading: zucchini.

Reading: Have students read the *I See a Wolf* fold-and-read book, which can be found in Appendix B.

Sorting: Have students sort picture cards beginning *g* = /j/, /v/, or /z/.

Writing: Review or introduce the formation of capital and lowercase *z*. Review the *g* = /j/ and *v* pages in the class alphabet book and add a *z* page. In interactive style, create booklets in which students draw pictures of zoo animals and write captions telling what each animal is and where it is: "I am a tiger. I am in the zoo."

qu = /kw/ Correspondence

Correspondence words that can be illustrated: queen.

Rhyme: "Five Little Ducks."

Sorting: Have students sort picture cards beginning with /v/, /z/, or *qu = /kw/*.

Writing: Review or introduce the formation of capital and lowercase *qu*. Review the *v* and *z* pages in the class alphabet book and add a *qu = /kw/* page.

x = /z/, x = /ks/ Correspondences

Correspondence words that can be illustrated: xylophone, x-ray, box.

The letter *x* rarely appears as an initial consonant, but it should be introduced for the sake of completeness.

➤➤RESOURCES FOR TEACHING CONSONANT DIGRAPHS

Consonant digraphs (*di* = "two," *graphs* = "letters"). are correspondences in which single consonant sounds are represented by two letters, such as *ch* in *church* and *sh* in *ship*. Because they represent just one sound, digraphs are taught in the same way as single consonant–letter correspondences are. However, because digraphs are spelled with two letters, students find them somewhat more difficult to master. Although they are discussed here after single consonants, digraphs may be introduced before all the single consonants have been taught. Introduce digraphs when there is a need—when students are about to read a story that contains digraphs. You might also follow the suggested order of introduction presented in Table 3.1 on page 51.

sh = /sh/ Correspondence

Correspondence words: sheep, shirt, shell, shark, shovel.

Rhyme: "I'm a Little Teapot."

Functional reading: shaving cream, shrimp.

Reading: Rohman, C. (1996). *Sherman shoots*. Thousand Oaks, CA: Outside the Box. Sherman shoots pictures with his camera. Part of Ray's Readers.

Sorting: Have students sort picture cards beginning with *qu = /kw/*, /s/, or /sh/.

Writing: Review or introduce the formation of capital and lowercase *sh*. Review the *qu = /kw/* and *z* pages in the class alphabet book and add a *sh = /sh/* page.

ch = /ch/ Correspondence

Correspondence words: chair, cheese, chain, cherry, chin, church.

Functional reading: cheese, chocolate chip cookies.

Rhyme: "Let's Be Merry."

Functional reading: cheese, Cheerios, chocolate chip cookies.

Reading: Rohman, C. (1996). *Charles*. Thousand Oaks, CA: Outside the Box. Portrays Charles at school. Part of Ray's Readers.

Sorting: Have students sort picture cards beginning with /ch/, /sh/, or *c = /s/*.

Writing: Review or introduce the formation of capital and lowercase *ch*. Review the *qu = /k/* and *sh = /sh/* pages in the class alphabet book and add a *ch = /ch/* page.

th = /**th**/ *Correspondence*

Correspondence words: thumb, thermos, thirteen, thorn.

Reading: Rohman, C. (1996). *Theodore*. Thousand Oaks, CA: Outside the Box. Portrays Theodore the rabbit. Part of Ray's Readers.

Sorting: Have students sort picture cards beginning with /ch/, / sh/, or /th/.

Writing: Review or introduce the formation of capital and lowercase *th*. Review the *sh* = /sh/ and *ch* = /ch/ pages in the class alphabet book and add a *th* = /th/ page.

wh = /**hw**/ *Correspondence*

Correspondence words: whale, wheel, whistle, whip.

Rhyme: "Whistle, Daughter."

Functional reading: wheat bread.

Sorting: Have students sort picture cards beginning with /sh/, /*th*/, or /wh/.

Writing: Review or introduce the formation of capital and lowercase *wh*. Review the *sh* = /sh/ and *th* = /th/ pages in the class alphabet book and add a *wh* = /wh/ page.

Note: When presenting *ch* = /ch, *sh* = /sh/, *th* = /th/, and *wh* = /wh/ stress that the two letters make just one sound.

►►RESOURCES FOR TEACHING ADVANCED CONSONANT DIGRAPHS

kn = /**n**/

Correspondence words: *knee, know, knot, knock.*

Rhyme: "The Zigzag Boy and Girl."

ph = /**f**/

Correspondence words: *phone, phonics, photograph.*

wr = /**r**/

Correspondence words: *wrap, wring, wrist, write, wrong, wrote.*

►►CONSONANT CLUSTERS

Although consonants, consonant clusters, and vowel patterns are presented separately, their introduction should be integrated. Clusters, which are sometimes known as *blends*, are combinations of consonants, as in *spot* or *straw*. Clusters represent two (/s/ + /p/) or more (/s/ + /t/ + /r/) sounds clustered or blended together. They are difficult for novice readers and spellers and should be taught directly and systematically. When teaching clusters, build on the knowledge of initial consonants that students already possess. If possible, show how words with clusters build on known words. For instance, when presenting *stop*, show how it is related to *top*. When presenting *stay*, show how it is related to *say*. When presenting *stand*, show how it can be related to *sand*. Teach *s* clusters first. They occur with high frequency and are easier to discriminate than *l* or *r* clusters.

➤➤SAMPLE LESSON 3.3: CONSONANT CLUSTERS

Step 1: Building Clusters by Adding an Initial Consonant.   Write the following words on the chalkboard: *nail, nap*. Have a volunteer read *nail*. Ask students to tell what letter needs to be added to *nail* to make *snail*. After *snail* has been formed, have students read it. Have students read *nap* and tell what letter needs to be added to *nap* to make the word *snap*. After *snap* has been formed, have students read it. Then have students read both *snap* and *snail*.

Step 2: Building Clusters by Adding a Second Consonant.   Write *sack* and *sake* on the board. Have a volunteer read *sack*. Ask students to tell what letter needs to be added to the *s* in *sack* to make *snack*. After *snack* has been formed, have a volunteer read *sake* (as in "for safety's sake."). Ask students to tell what letter needs to be added to *s* to make the word *snake*. After *snake* has been formed, have students read it. Then have students read both *snack* and *snake*.

Step 3: Letter–Sound Integration.   Have students read all four *sn* words: *snail, snap, snack,* and *snake*. Lead them to see that some words begin with two consonant sounds and that these are known as clusters. Explain that *sn* spells the cluster that appears in *snake*. Create a model word for the *sn* cluster and start a model word chart for clusters.

Step 4: Guided Practice.   Share read a rhyme, song, or other short piece that contains *sn* words.

Step 5: Application.   Have students read stories and real-world materials that contain *sn* words. They might read *Hoorary for Snail* (Stadler, 1984), for instance. Students might also write stories that contain *sn* words. Select additional practice and application exercises from the reinforcement activities listed below.

➤➤REINFORCEMENT ACTIVITIES

➤ To help students distinguish between single consonants and clusters, have them sort stacks of word or picture cards containing single consonants or clusters. For instance, have students sort *s* and *st* words. Because students may have difficulty discriminating between the sound of /s/ and the sound of /st/, begin with picture sorts so the students can focus on sounds. Students might sort the following picture cards: sun, saw, sandwich, socks, six, seal, star, stick, step, and store (see illustrations of words beginning with consonants and clusters at the end of this chapter). Pointing to a stack of cards containing illustrations whose names begin with /s/ or /st/, tell students, "We're going to sort these picture cards. If the name of the picture begins with /s/ as in *sun*, we're going to put it in the sun column. If the name of the picture begins with /st/ as in *star*, we'll put it in the star column. Holding up a picture of a stick, ask, "What is this? What sound does it begin with? What column should we put it in?" Affirm or correct students' responses. "Yes, *stick* begins with the sound /st/ that we hear at the beginning of *ssstttick*, so we put it in the *star* column." Go through the rest of the cards in this fashion. Once all the cards have been categorized, have volunteers say the names of all the cards in a column and note that they all begin with /s/ or /st/. Encourage students to suggest other words that might fit into the columns. Also have them re-sort the pictures on their own to promote speed of response. You might then have them sort /s/ and /sp/ pictures and words and then /s/, /sp/, and /st/ pictures and words.

➤ Use real-world materials to reinforce clusters. When introducing *sp,* for example, have students read food labels for spaghetti and spinach and such brand names as Spam and Spic and Span.

➤ Have students create words by adding newly learned clusters to previously presented word patterns. After being introduced to *st,* for instance, students might add it to short-vowel patterns that they have been taught: *-and, -ill, -ick,* and *-ing.*

➤ To further emphasize the difference between words beginning with a single consonant and those beginning with a cluster, have students spell words containing these elements. For words beginning with *s* or *st,* they might spell the words *sick, stick, sing, sting, sand, stand, sore, store, sad, stop, sit, store.* To make the task easier, you might set up two columns, one for *s* words and one for *st* words.

➤ Secret word, secret message, and other word games described in the next chapter can also be used to provide practice with clusters.

➤➤BOOKS THAT REINFORCE CONSONANT CLUSTERS

The best reinforcement is for students to meet clusters in their reading. Clusters occur naturally in most books, so it is simply a matter of looking over the texts and deciding which clusters you wish to emphasize. However, the following books have a high proportion of clusters or present clusters in such a way as to lend themselves to instruction or reinforcement.

Axworthy, A. (1993). *Along came Toto.* Cambridge, MA: Candlewick Press. Reinforces several major clusters.

Ehlert, L. (1990). *Fish eyes, A book you can count on.* San Diego, CA: Harcourt. Reinforces several major clusters.

Emberley, Ed. (1992). *Go away, Big Green Monster.* Boston: Little, Brown. Reinforces *s* clusters.

Janovitz, M. (1994). *Look out, bird!* New York: North-South. Reinforces a variety of clusters.

Kline, S. (1985). *Don't touch.* Niles, IL: Whitman. Reinforces *fl* cluster.

McMillan, B. (1984). *Kitten can.* New York: Lothrop, Lee & Shepard. Reinforces several clusters.

Miller, J. (1988). *Farm noises.* New York: Simon & Schuster. Reinforces a variety of clusters.

Milstein, L. (1995). *Coconut mon.* New York: Tambourine. Coconut man sells his goods by calling out that his coconuts are "crrr-unchy," "crrr-isp," thus emphasizing sounds of clusters.

O'Brien, J. (1995). *Sam and Spot, A silly story.* Boca Raton, FL: Cool Kids. Good alliterative read-aloud that emphasizes *s* clusters.

Rohman, C. (1996). *Grumpy Grizzly.* Live Oaks, CA: Outside the Box. Grumpy Grizzly growls at grapes and grass and other items beginning with *gr.* Reinforces *gr* cluster.

Rohman, C. (1996). *Stories.* Live Oaks, CA: Outside the Box. Reinforces *st* cluster.

Rohman, C. (1996). *Tricksters.* Live Oaks, CA: Outside the Box. Reinforces *tr* cluster.

Serfozo, M. (1993). *Joe Joe.* New York: Macmillan. Reinforces a variety of clusters.

➤➤RESOURCES FOR TEACHING CONSONANT CLUSTERS

In this section, words that may be used to present consonant clusters are presented. Also listed are food labels and other possible functional reading items. Listed, too, are titles of rhymes and songs that may be used to reinforce the target cluster. The rhymes and songs can be found in Appendix A. Clusters should not be introduced until after most single consonants, digraphs, and a number of short-vowel patterns have been taught. The cluster correspondences are listed in the order in which they might be presented, but feel free to adapt the sequence to meet the specific needs of your class. For instance, if students are about to read a story about how sneakers are made, then introduce the *sn* cluster.

st = /st/ *Correspondence*

Cluster words: star, stand, stay, step, stick, still, stone, stop, stood, store, story.

Rhyme: "The Little Bird."*

Functional reading: stop sign.

str = /str/ *Correspondence*

Cluster words: street, string, strange, stream, straw, strike.

Rhyme: "Sing, Sing."

Functional reading: strawberry ice cream, street sign.

sp = /sp/ *Correspondence*

Cluster words: space, speak, speed, spell, spend, spider, spin, spoke, spoon, spot, sports.

Rhyme: "I'm a Little Teapot."

Functional reading: spinach, spaghetti.

spl = /spl/ *Correspondence*

Cluster words: splash, split.

sn = /sn/ *Correspondence*

Cluster words: snail, snack, snake, snap, sneakers, sneeze, snip, snow.

Rhyme: "The Little Turtle."

br = /br/ *Correspondence*

Cluster words: brush, bread, break, brick, bright, bridge, bring, brother.

Rhyme: "The Mocking Bird."

Functional reading: bread, brown rice.

gr = /gr/ *Correspondence*

Cluster words: grapes, grass, gray, great, green, ground, group, grow.

Rhyme: "Go and Tell Aunt Nancy."

Functional reading: green beans, grape juice, grapefruit.

tr = /tr/ *Correspondence*

Cluster words: trap, train, tree, truck, trunk.

Rhyme: "Twinkle, Twinkle, Little Bat."

bl = /bl/ *Correspondence*

Cluster words: black, blame, blank, blind, blood, blow, blue.

Functional reading: blueberry pie.

cl = /kl/ *Correspondence*

Cluster words: class, clam, clay, clap, claw, click, climb, clock, close, cloth, clothes, cloud, clown.

Rhyme: "The Mulberry Bush."

Functional reading: clam soup label.

*Note: All rhymes and songs referred to can be found in Appendix A.

fl = /fl/ Correspondence

Cluster words: flag, flame, flap, flock, flat, flea, flour, flower, float, floor, flew, fly.

Functional reading: corn flakes, flour.

pl = /pl/ Correspondence

Cluster words: plate, place, plan, plane, plant, play, please, plug, plus.

Rhyme: "A Little Plant."

Functional reading: plums.

sl = /sl/ Correspondence

Cluster words: slap, slid, slide, sled, sleep, sleeve, slip, slipper, slow.

sw = /sw/ Correspondence

Cluster words: swam, swan, swamp, swim, sweater, swing, switch, sweep.

Functional reading: sweet corn, sweet peas.

Rhyme: "Swim, Swan, Swim."

sm = /sm/ Correspondence

Cluster words: small, smart, smash, smile, smell, smoke, smooth.

sk = /sk/ Correspondence

Cluster words: skate, ski, skin, skirt, skunk, sky.

fr = /fr/ Correspondence

Cluster words: free, fresh, Friday, friend, frog, front, from, frozen, fruit, fry.

Functional reading: French fries, fruit cup, Friday.

Rhyme: "Swing, Swing."

pr = /pr/ Correspondence

Cluster words: pray, pretty, price, prince, print, prize, problem, probably, promise.

Functional reading: pretzels, prunes.

cr = /cr/ Correspondence

Cluster words: crab, crack, crash, crawl, crayon, cream, crocodile, crow, crowd, crown, cry.

Rhyme: "If You Should Meet a Crocodile."

Functional reading: crackers, cranberry sauce, cream.

gl = /gl/ Correspondence

Cluster words: glass, glad, glance, globe, glow, glove, glue.

Functional reading: glue.

dr = /dr/ Correspondence

Cluster words: dragon, draw, drum, dream, dress, drink, drip, drive, dry.

Functional reading: French dressing.

sc = /sk/, sch = /sk/ Correspondences

Cluster words: scale, scar, scare, scarecrow, scoop, score, scout; school.

Rhyme: "Mary's Lamb."

scr = /skr/ *Correspondence*

Cluster words: scrap, scrape, scratch, scream, scribble, scrub.

Rhyme: "Ice Cream Rhyme."

squ = /skw/ *Correspondence*

Cluster words: square, squirrel, squeak, squeeze, squawk.

Rhyme: "By Mr. Nobody."

Functional reading: squash.

tw = /tw/ *Correspondence*

Cluster words: twelve, twice, twin, twenty, twig, twist, twinkle.

Functional reading: Twinkies.

Rhyme: "Twinkle, Twinkle, Little Star."

A suggested sequence of introduction is presented in Table 3.1 on page 51.

Consonant Illustrations

Consonant Illustrations

Consonant Illustrations

Consonant Illustrations

Consonant Illustrations

Consonant Illustrations

Consonant Illustrations

Consonant Illustrations

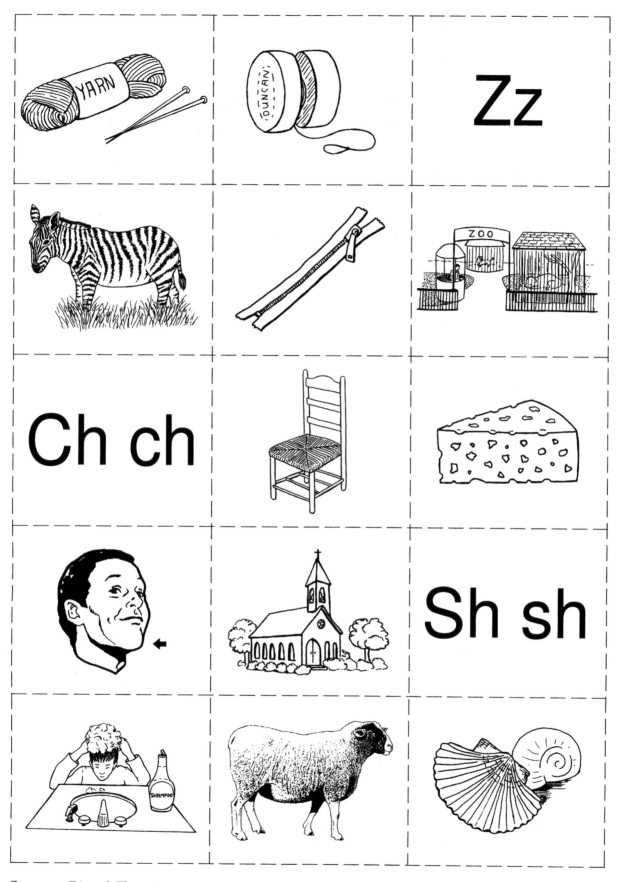

Consonant Digraph Illustrations

Consonant Digraph Illustrations

Consonant Cluster Illustrations

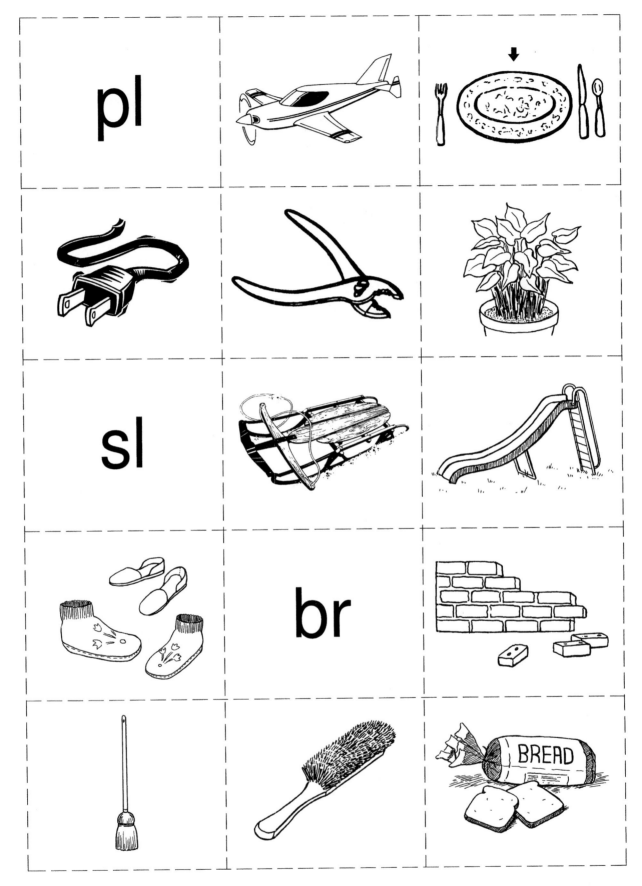

Consonant Cluster Illustrations

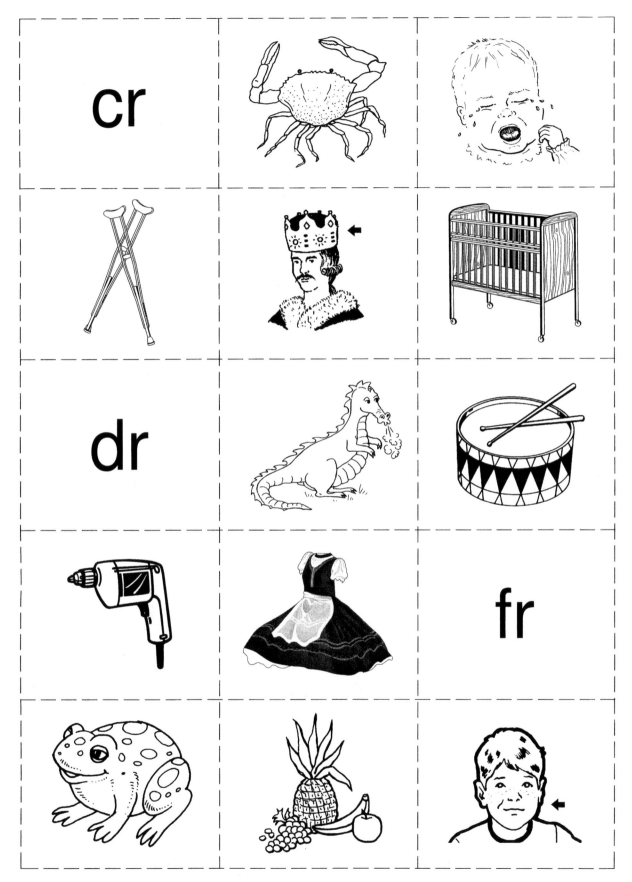

Consonant Cluster Illustrations

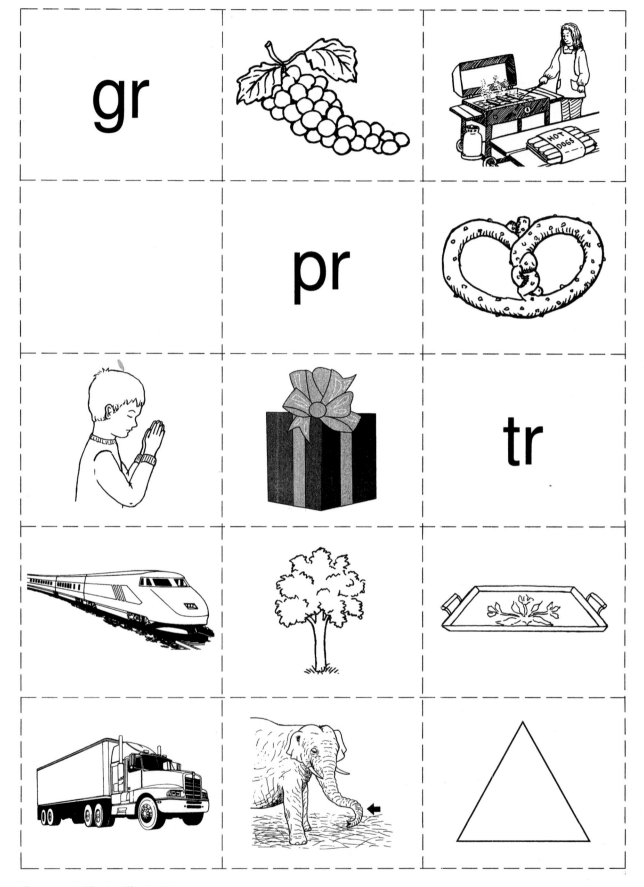

Consonant Cluster Illustrations

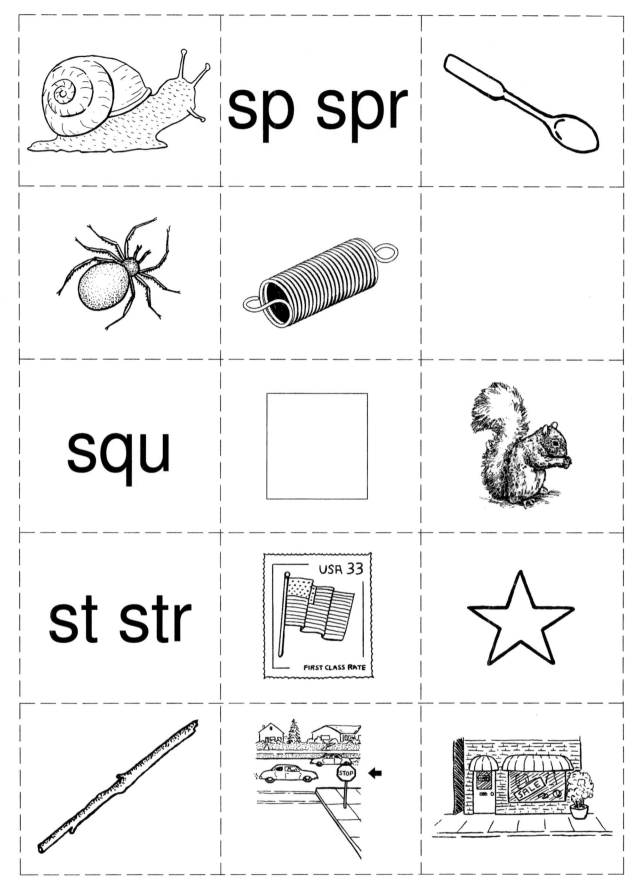

Consonant Cluster Illustrations

Consonant Cluster Illustrations

Chapter Four

TEACHING VOWEL PATTERNS

In primary phonics, vowels are taught through a word-building approach. Word building presents the most basic pronounceable element in the pattern being taught and leads students to build words by adding to that core element. In presenting long *o*, for example, the teacher tells students that *o* represents /ō/ and helps them to build words such as *no, go,* and *so.* Working with a short-vowel pattern, the teacher helps students build words by adding onsets to the rime, adding consonants to -*at* to form *cat, hat, sat, hat,* for instance. Wylie and Durrell (1970) found that students were better able to read the rimes of words than they were the individual sounds that made up the words. Word building also builds on what students know. For instance, students typically know onsets but not rimes, so the teacher introduces the rime and has the students add the onsets.

By showing how phonic elements are used to construct words, students get a more concrete understanding of the alphabetic spelling system. They are then shown how to use this knowledge to decode unfamiliar words independently. When faced with a word that is unfamiliar, students use the strategy of seeking a pronounceable word part and then using that pronounceable word part as the basis for reconstructing the word. A student who is unable to pronounce the printed word *plant* might use the pronounceable word part *an* to reconstruct the word, saying "an," "ant," "plant" or the student might use the rime *ant* as the pronounceable word part and say "ant, plant." If the pronounceable word-part strategy does not work, the student might then try an analogy strategy. Unable to find a pronounceable word part in the unknown word *blank,* the student might compare it to the known word *thank* and work out the pronunciation through analogy. The overall sense of the selection and the immediate context in which the unfamiliar word appears are woven into the pronounceable word-part and analogy strategies. Students check to make sure the word they have constructed is a real one and fits the sense of the selection in which it appears. Context, including picture clues, is also used when neither the pronounceable word-part nor the analogy strategy works.

►►SAMPLE LESSON 4.1: VOWEL PATTERN

The model lesson presented here should be adapted to fit the needs of your students and your personal approach to teaching basic phonics skills. The lesson assumes that students can name most of the letters of the alphabet and know at least ten initial consonant correspondences.

Step 1. Phonemic Awareness and Building the Rime. Read a selection, such as *Green Eggs and Ham* (Dr. Seuss, 1988) or a rhyme in which there are a number of -*am* words. Call the students' attention to the pattern words in the selection: *ham, am, Sam.* Stressing the rhyming element as you say each word, ask students to tell what is the same about the words. Lead students to see that they all have an /am/ sound as in *ham.* Ask the students to listen carefully so they can tell how many sounds the word *am* has. Articulate it slowly, stretching out the sounds as you do so: *aaamm.* Tell the students to say the word *am* and stretch out the sounds as they do so. Discuss how many sounds the word *am* has. Then tell students that you are going to spell the word *am*. Ask students to tell what letter should be used to spell the sound /a/ in *am*. Write *a*, commenting as you do so that it makes an /a/ sound. Have students tell what sound they hear at the end of *am*. Ask them what letter is needed to spell /m/. Add *m*, saying /m/ as you do so. Explain that now you have the word *am*. Run your hand under each letter as you say its sound. Have several students read *am*.

Step 2: Adding the Onset.   Explain to students that you can use *am* to make other words. (Write a second *am* under the first one.) Ask students: What do I need to add to *am* to make the word *hhhham*? As you add *h* to *am*, carefully enunciate the *h* and the *am* and then the whole word. Have several students read the word. Then have students read *am* and *ham*. Then write *am* underneath *ham*. Ask the students: What do I need to add to *am* to make the name *SSSSam*? As you add *S* to *am*, carefully enunciate the *S* and the *am* and then the whole word. Have several students read the word. Then have students read *am*, *ham*, and *Sam*. Form *Pam* and *jam* in this same way and have all the *am* words read. Lead students to see what is the same about the words—that they all end in *am*. Ask the students if they know of any other words that rhyme with *ham*. If so, write these on the board and discuss them.

Step 3: Adding the Rime.   To make sure that students have a thorough grasp of both key parts of the word—the onset, which is the initial consonant or cluster, and the rime, which is the vowel and an ending consonant or cluster—present the onset or initial consonant and have students supply the rime or vowel–consonant element. Writing *h* on the board, have students tell what sound it stands for. Then ask them to tell what you should add to /h/ to make the word *ham*. After adding *-am* to *h*, say the word in parts, /h/—/a/—/m/, and then as a whole. Point to *h* and, say /h/, point to *a* and say /a/, point to *m* and say /m/. Running your hand under the whole word, say "hhhaaammm—ham." Form *Sam*, *Pam*, and *jam* in this way. After all the words have been formed, have students read them.

Step 4: Providing Mixed Practice.   Realizing that they are learning words that all end in the same way, students may focus on the initial letter and fail to take careful note of the rest of the word, the rime, when asked to read a list of pattern words. After presenting a pattern, mix in words from previously presented patterns and have these read. For instance, after presenting the *-at* pattern, present a list of mixed *-at* and *-am* words: *hat, ham, sat, Sam, jam, cat, Pam, pat*. Besides being a good review, this trains students to use all the word's letters in their decoding processes. Otherwise, students might say the first word in a series of pattern words and then just use the initial consonant to say the rest. If students fail to use all the letters when reading on their own, they may misread *Pam* for *Pat*, *ham* for *hat*, etc. Reading mixed patterns fosters accurate reading.

Step 5: Introducing the Model Word.   Choose one of the pattern words to be a model word. Select a word that has a high frequency, is easy, and—if possible—can be depicted. For the *-am* pattern, you might choose *ham*, which is easily illustrated. Create a model words chart for your class. An illustrated chart of model words for short-vowel patterns is presented in Figure 4.1.

After a pattern has been introduced, add its model word to the chart. If students forget the pattern, they can refer to the model words chart. Point out the model word *ham* and explain that it has a picture that shows the word. Tell students that if they forget how to say the model word, the picture will help them. If students encounter difficulty with *am* words, help them to look for a part of the word they can say (*am*) and, if that doesn't work, to use the model word *ham* as an analogy word to help them decipher the unknown word. Also encourage the use

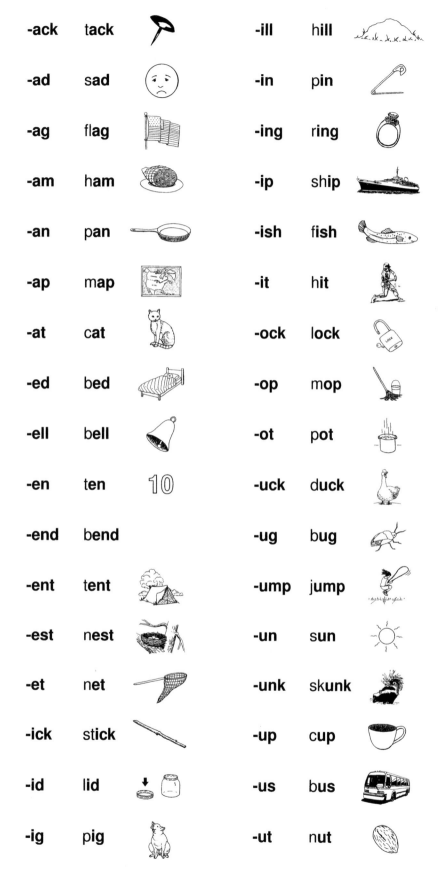

-ack	tack		-ill	hill	
-ad	sad		-in	pin	
-ag	flag		-ing	ring	
-am	ham		-ip	ship	
-an	pan		-ish	fish	
-ap	map		-it	hit	
-at	cat		-ock	lock	
-ed	bed		-op	mop	
-ell	bell		-ot	pot	
-en	ten		-uck	duck	
-end	bend		-ug	bug	
-ent	tent		-ump	jump	
-est	nest		-un	sun	
-et	net		-unk	skunk	
-ick	stick		-up	cup	
-id	lid		-us	bus	
-ig	pig		-ut	nut	

FIGURE 4.1   Model Words

of context. Students should use context to assist in the use of pronounceable word-part or other sounding-out strategies and especially when sounding-out strategies don't work. Context should also be used to make sure that the word decoded is a real word and fits the sense of the selection.

Step 6: Guided Practice. Use functional reading materials to provide practice with the pattern. Holding up a jar of jam, ask the class to tell which word on the jar says *jam*. Do the same with a ham label.

You can also compose a brief experience story using *am*. Say to your students: "I can use *am* to write something about myself. I can write, I am Mr. Thomas. I am a teacher. I am a man." (As you write each word, stretch out the word's sounds.)

Step 7: Application. Have students apply their knowledge of the *am* pattern by reading selections that contain *am* words. If possible, share-read *Green Eggs and Ham* with students. Also have them read the "I am" fold-and-read book in Appendix B. Show them how to fold the booklet and help them with any words that are difficult.

Step 8: Spelling: am, jam. Learning to spell new pattern words is excellent rein-forcement. For the most part, pattern words have been chosen that students will most likely use in their writing. In this lesson, only two pattern words are used. In other lessons, up to five words will be chosen for the spelling lesson. To introduce the spelling lesson, explain to students that they will be learning how to spell words that use the pattern just presented. To introduce the words, give a pretest. Dictate the words and have students attempt to spell them. Say each word, use the word in a sentence, and then say each word: "am. I am a teacher. am. jam. I like jam on my toast. jam." Have students say the word, enunciating it carefully before writing it. This will help them focus on the word's sounds. After the pretest, write the correct spellings on the board, and have students check their attempts, making any corrections necessary. They should focus their studying on words that were difficult for them.

Step 9: Writing. Students compose an illustrated "I am" piece, telling about themselves. They might write a piece similar to the following: "I am Sam. I am a boy. I am 7." Encourage the use of invented spelling. However, students are expected to spell pattern words correctly.

➤➤ADDITIONAL HIGH-PAYOFF REINFORCEMENT ACTIVITIES

There are dozens of ways to reinforce patterns. Some of the most effective of these are described on the following pages. As time allows and as students demonstrate need, provide added practice. Be especially thorough with initial patterns, because these form the foundation for later patterns. However, keep in mind that the best reinforcement activities are real reading and writing. As a rule of thumb, do not spend more than 10 or 15 minutes a session on phonics. Devote most of the time to reading and writing.

➤➤SCRAMBLED SENTENCE

Create or have students compose a sentence that incorporates some of the words that have been taught. Write the words on a strip of tagboard. Have students read the sentence. Then cut up the strip and have the students reassemble it. Sentences can be reassembled by students working alone or in pairs. Cut-up sentences provide excellent reinforcement because they are manipulative and offer contextual reading. Keep cut-up sentences in envelopes. A possible cut-up sentence for the -*am* pattern is: "I am Sam."

➤➤SORTING

Sorting activities also provide excellent reinforcement. After being introduced to the -*am* pattern, students might be asked to sort a group of words composed of -*am* words and other known words into two piles: those that rhyme with *ham* and those that don't. Later, after being introduced to several short-*a* patterns, they might sort words according to whether they fall into the -*at*, -*an*, or -*am* pattern. Sorting helps students to note differences in patterns and to generate their own conclusions about how the patterns are spelled. A sample sort is shown in Figure 4.2. After students have been introduced to several patterns, try a spelling sort. In a spelling sort, students write in the appropriate column words dictated by the teacher. Columns can be created by folding a piece of paper lengthwise into three equal parts. Headings are created for each column, such as -*am*, -*an*, and -*ad*. The teacher then dictates words containing these elements and students write them in the appropriate column. After each word is dictated, the teacher checks to see that the word has been put in the correct column. A sample spelling sort is presented in Figure 4.3.

After students have some experience sorting patterns, they might start sorting the words strictly by looking at the letters, without taking the time to actually say the words and consider which pattern they belong to. To get students to attend to sounds and letters, use a sound or blind sort. Using a pocket chart, set up three columns: *ham, pan, cat*. Having assembled a stack of words to be sorted, read the first word but don't show it to the students. Students take turns telling in which column the word belongs on the basis of its sounds. Place the word in the column mentioned by the student. The other students check the placement of the words to make sure that they are being placed in the appropriate columns.

Working in pairs, students can conduct their own sound sorts. One student reads the word while the other student points to the columns in which the words should be placed. The partner reading the words places each word in the column as directed. The other partner then checks visually to make sure the card has been placed in the appropriate column (Johnston, 1999). Sheets of pattern words can be found at the end of this chapter. Sheets can be duplicated, cut apart, and used to create cards for sorting. To make them more durable, sheets can be printed on card stock and laminated.

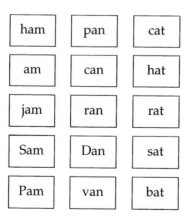

ham	pan	cat
am	can	hat
jam	ran	rat
Sam	Dan	sat
Pam	van	bat

FIGURE 4.2   Word Pattern Sort

-am	-an	-ad
am	pan	sad
ham	man	bad
jam	can	had
	ran	mad

FIGURE 4.3   Spelling Sort

▶▶LITTLE BOOKS

An inexpensive way to obtain easy-to-read books is to create your own fold-and-read books. Sample fold-and-read books are provided in Appendix B. Fold-and-read books can be teacher-created or they can be composed by students, with your help. The books can simply contain words or they can be illustrated with student or teacher drawings, photos or magazine illustrations, or, if you have access to a desktop publishing system, clip art. Fold-and-read books can be helpful devices for reinforcing *-at*, *-am*, *-an*, and other basic patterns. Some patterns that might make effective little books include:

I am _____.
I can _____.
The cat _____.
I like _____.
I play _____.
I help _____.
I saw _____.
Yesterday, I _____.
Saturday, I will _____.

You might also create fold-and-read caption books devoted to a topic: numbers, colors, seasons, pets, dogs, cats, birds, farm animals, cars, trucks, toys, or similar topics.

More than 20 fold-and-read books are shown in Appendix B. They have been created to provide opportunities for students to apply their knowledge of initial consonants and key short-vowel and long-vowel patterns. Insofar as possible, vocabulary in the fold-and-read books has been restricted to words containing the consonant or vowel pattern being reinforced and words previously introduced. However, several of the selections contain a few content words that should be previewed before students read the book. One way of previewing books is to conduct a text-walk. In a text-walk, the teacher provides an overview of the selection, fills in needed background, and goes over any words or expressions that may pose problems for students.

FIGURE 4.4   Rhyming Concentration

➤➤MODIFIED CONCENTRATION

In the traditional game of concentration, pairs of cards are shuffled and placed face down on a table or desk. The first player turns over a card and then tries to guess where its match might be. If the player turns over its match, she removes it and places the pair in front of her. The player then continues to take turns until she fails to make a match. Then the second player attempts to make a match. In modified concentration, the cards used consist of pairs of rhyming words. Students make a match by locating the rhyming partner of the word turned over, as shown in Figure 4.4. When a player turns over a card, she must read it. She then must find its rhyming partner and read it also. Concentration requires keeping the rime in mind as you search for its partner. It fosters focusing on the rime that the two words share (Morris, 1999). Sheets of illustrations that can be used to make short-vowel pattern cards can be found at the end of the chapter. The cards can be used for concentration, bingo, sorting, or other activities.

➤➤MODIFIED BINGO

Modified bingo, which is another sorting activity in a game format, may be played with just three or four columns instead of five. Rather than being a letter, the heading for each column is a pattern word as in Figure 4.5. A row must be filled out with words in the same pattern or with wild cards. Cards are placed in the center of the table and players take turns choosing cards. After selecting a card, the player reads

hat	pot	hit	pet
cat	hot	sit	wet
	not		get
	pot		
	got		

FIGURE 4.5   Sample Bingo Card

it and looks to see if he can place it on one of the squares. After placing a card, he reads the column's heading word and all the words that have been placed in the column. This provides added practice reading pattern words (Morris, 1999). Bingo cards can be created on a variety of levels. An early set might contain only short-*a* patterns. A later set might contain a short-*a*, short-*e*, short-*i*, and short-*o* patterns. A more advanced set might reinforce long-vowel or other-vowel patterns. A blank bingo card that may be duplicated and used is presented in Figure 4.6.

➤➤MAKE-AND-BREAK TECHNIQUE FOR INTRODUCING OR REVIEWING PATTERNS

A technique known as make-and-break is an excellent on-the-spot device for reinforcing a word pattern (Iverson & Tunmer, 1993). Selecting a word such as *am,* the teacher forms it with magnetic or cut-up letters, says the word, and requests that the student say it. The teacher then scrambles the letters and asks the student to re-create the word and say it. Once students are able to do this without hesitation, the teacher forms other words using the rime. Adding an *h,* the teacher now says that the word is *ham* and asks the student to say it. The teacher then scrambles the letters and asks the student to re-create the word and say it. Substituting *j* for *h,* the teacher says that the word is now *jam.* The student says the word. After the student reads it, the teacher scrambles the letters. The student is asked to make the word *jam* and read it. Make-and-break works especially well when students need an on-the-spot review of a pattern or fail to note all the sounds or letters in words.

➤➤WORD WALL

One way to emphasize key printed words is to place them on the wall. There they can be readily reviewed and serve as a handy reference for students who are trying to decode or spell them. Newly learned pattern words can be placed on the wall, as can high-frequency words such as *the, are,* and *where.* Words should be arranged in alphabetical order so they are readily located. Pattern words should be arranged by the first letter in the rime, rather than the initial consonant. Thus, all *-at* words should appear together and after *-am* and *-an* words. Because their vowel spellings

FIGURE 4.6 Word Bingo

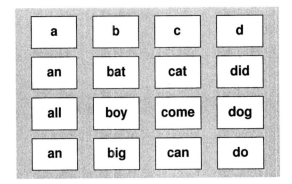

FIGURE 4.7   Word Wall

may be irregular, high-frequency words should be ordered by initial letter. To keep the two systems straight, put them on different walls. To help students further differentiate among words you might use a variety of colors. Short-vowel words might be red, long-vowel words might be blue, and irregular high-frequency words might be yellow. You might also group some words by category—animals, colors, numbers, for example. A sample word wall is shown in Figure 4.7.

Review the wall words periodically. To review -am words, you might have students read all the words that rhyme with *ham*. Or students might read all the number or color words. Students might also be asked to locate opposites. Shown *on*, they must find *off*. Students might also create personal word walls. These might contain words personally important to the students or words that the student needs in his reading or writing. A grid for a personal word wall is presented in Figure 4.8.

➤➤SECRET WORD

Select a familiar pattern word and jot it down on a slip of paper, but don't reveal its identity to your students (Cunningham & Allington,1999). Choose a word that will provide a review or extension of a pattern or other element. Explain to the students that the word is a secret and that you are going to give them a series of clues and see who can guess the word using the fewest number of clues. Ask students to number their papers 1–5. Give a series of five clues as to the identity of the word (number of clues may vary). After each clue, students should write down their guess. Possible clues for the secret word *snack* include:

1. The secret word is in the -*ack* pattern.
2. It has five letters.
3. It is something that you might get after school when you get home.
4. It might be fruit or cookies and milk.
5. When you are hungry, you eat a _____.

After supplying the five clues, show the secret word (*snack*) and discuss students' responses. See who guessed the secret word first. If the word is one that appears in a story students are about to read, have them find it in the selection.

➤➤MAKING WORDS

Making Words is a group activity in which students put letters together to create words. Beginning with two-letter words and extending to five-letter or even longer words, students form as many as a dozen words (Cunningham & Cunningham,

My Word Wall							
a	b	c	d	e	f	g	h
i	j	k	l	m	n	o	p
qu	r	s	t	u	v	w	xyz

FIGURE 4.8   A Personal Word Wall

1992). The last word that the students construct contains all the letters they have been given. Here's how it works. Students are given cut-up or magnetic letters *c, s, u, r, b* and are asked to do the following:

➤ Use two letters to make *us*.
➤ Add a letter to make *bus*.
➤ Change the letters around to make *sub*.
➤ Change a letter to make *rub*.
➤ Change a letter to make *cub*.
➤ Now break up your word and see what word you can make with all the letters (*scrub*).

➤➤SECRET MESSAGES

Secret messages have been created to give students the opportunity to manipulate phonic elements and should be especially helpful for providing practice with onsets and rimes (Education Department of Western Australia, 1994). Secret messages are formed by adding or deleting parts of words and can be geared to virtually any decoding skill at any level of difficulty. At the easiest levels students can manipulate beginning and ending consonants. At more advanced levels they may manipulate vowels, or syllables. Once students become proficient at solving secret messages, they can be challenged to create their own.

Secret messages should be composed in such a way that new elements being substituted for old elements have the same sound as the old elements. For instance, taking the *r* from *raid* and substituting *p* so as to make *paid* is acceptable. But substituting *pl* for *r* in *raid* is not, because the *aid* in *plaid* is not pronounced in the same way as the *aid* in *paid*. Although they are a gamelike activity, secret messages should also meet specific instructional objectives. For example, the sample secret message is designed to provide practice with initial consonant clusters. For your convenience, a secret message has been created for each phonics unit and appears in the Vowel Pattern Resources section.

Secret Message
1. Add a **C** to **rows**. __ __ __ __ __
2. Add a **c** to **an**. __ __ __
3. Put an **l** after the **p** in **pay**. __ __ __ __
4. Put an **r** after the **t** in **ticks**. __ __ __ __ __ __
5. Put an **o** in front of **n**. __ __
6. Take the **b** from **bus**. __ __

__ __ __ __   __ __ __   __ __ __ __   __ __ __ __ __   __ __   __ __.

➤➤FLIP CHARTS

Rimes, such as *-at* or *-oat*, are printed on a piece of card stock. A space is left for placement of the onset. Onsets—initial consonants and clusters—are printed on pieces of card stock. The cards are bound with rings so that the onsets fit directly in front of the rimes. Words are formed when the student moves an onset so that it lines up with the rime, as can be seen in Figure 4.9. By moving the onsets the students form and read a variety of words. Booklets are usually about 4 inches wide and 2 inches tall, but they should be larger if you plan to use them with large groups.

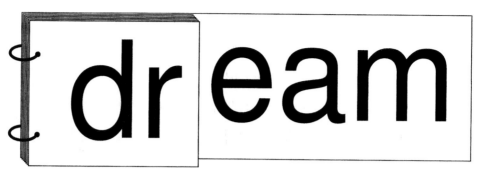

FIGURE 4.9   Flip Book

➤➤USING A SOUND-BY-SOUND APPROACH

Having students build words by adding onsets to rimes is an efficient, effective approach to teach phonics. However, at the earliest stages of learning to read, some students may have difficulty dealing with combinations of sounds. For this reason, Word Building presents rimes as units (*at, eep*) and as individual elements (*a-t, ee-p*). However, some students may still have difficulty with rimes. For these students, modify the approach by placing greater emphasis on the individual sounds in words. Later, as they begin to see patterns in words, place more emphasis on rimes.

➤➤IMPLEMENTING STRATEGIES

The implementation of strategies should be at the center of a word analysis program. It should pervade all reinforcement and application activities, for this step shows students how to use a newly learned pattern to decode words. In this step students are shown how to use the key decoding strategies noted earlier: pronounceable word parts and analogy. To show students how to use the pronounceable word-part strategy, write a series of pattern words on the board that were not presented in the lesson. For instance, after presenting the *-an* pattern, you might write the following on the board: *Dan, fan.* Urge students to find the letters that make the /an/ sound. Then help them use this pronounceable part to reconstruct the whole word. Explain to students that whenever they come across a word that they can't read, they should look to see if there are any parts of the word they can pronounce. Then tell them that if that doesn't work—if they can't find a part that they can say—then they should see if the word is like *pan* or another model word that they might know. Also discuss the use of picture and context clues.

Most children naturally use familiar rimes to help them read unfamiliar words. Encountering the unfamiliar word *screen,* achieving readers would use their knowledge of the rime *-een* in the known word *seen* to read *screen*. However, disabled readers, even those who are familiar with rimes, often fail to use an analogy or similar strategy to decode unfamiliar words that contain familiar rimes. Greaney, Tunmer, & Chapman (1997) hypothesize that disabled readers lack adequate phonological skills when first being taught to read, have difficulty learning phonics, and so overrely on context and initial and final letters instead of processing the whole word. As a result, they don't learn to use analogy or pronounceable word-part strategies. Moustafa (1997) found that the ability to use analogies is related to the number of words that the student can recognize. Students who can read a large number of words are more likely to be able to use analogies to read unfamiliar words than are those who know just a few words. However, the development of this ability varies. Some students need more experience than others.

When taught rimes and strategies directly, disabled readers made encouraging gains and were able to transfer their newly acquired ability to use strategies to read new words. They also outperformed a control group that was trained in the use of a contextual strategy (Tunmer & Chapman, 1999). Pronounceable word-part and analogy strategies work better than do contextual strategies (Tunmer & Chapman, 1999; Gunning, 1988, 1999). However, context should be used along with the pronounceable word part and analogies as a way of checking to make sure that the decoded word is a real word and makes sense in the sentence. Context should also be used in situations where a pronounceable word-part or analogy strategy does not work.

As students encounter difficult words, use a "pause, prompt, praise" approach (Tunmer & Chapman, 1999). At first, say nothing and, if this is during a group activity, do not allow other students to chime in. Give the student the opportunity to work out the word on his own. If the student is not able to decode the word, provide a prompt. Unless the word has an irregular spelling or contains elements that have not been taught, provide a pronounceable word part prompt. Ask: "Is there any part of that word that you can say?" If the student does not respond, provide additional assistance. For instance, if a student who has been taught the -ee pattern has difficulty with a word such as *seem* and is unable to note any known parts in the word, you might cover up all but the middle *ee* and have her say what sound *ee* makes. Uncovering the *s*, have her pronounce *see* and then, uncovering the final *m*, lead her to pronounce *seem*. If the child is unable to pronounce the *ee* in *seem*, use an analogy strategy. Using the model word *bee*, have her compare *seem* with *bee* (cover the *m* in *seem* if necessary, so that she can read *see* and then *seem*).

Some students may be slow detecting patterns in words, such as the -*an* in *man* or the -*in* in *pin*. For these students the pronounceable word part might be the initial consonant, or they may need to say each sound of the word individually. If this is the case, encourage them to do so. In time, perhaps as they approach the word pattern stage, they should be able to detect patterns in words.

If the student is unable to use a pronounceable word-part or analogy strategy or if the word does not lend itself to a sounding-out strategy, prompt the use of context. Urge the student to skip the word and read to the end of the sentence. Ask: "What word would make sense here?" Even when a sounding-out strategy is used, context should be used as a cross-check. After a student has used the pronounceable word part or analogy strategy, prompt to see if the word is a real word and fits the sense of the sentence.

If the student is unable to decode the word, even with the help of prompts, use a starter prompt. A starter prompt supplies the word but does so in the form of a question, so that the student has some input and is asked to think about what the word might be. For instance, if the difficult word is *stand*, you might ask: "Does it look like *stand*?" or "Would *stand* fit here?"

The main goal of reading instruction is for students to read for meaning. After they have decoded a word, students should make sure that it is a real word. They might ask themselves, "Is this a real word? Does it sound right?" They should also make sure that the word they have decoded fits the context. They might ask themselves, "Does this fit? Does this make sense?" In fact, whenever students read, they should be monitoring to make sure that what they are reading makes sense. If students read a passage and the passage doesn't make sense because of a misreading error and they don't notice it, prompt them to check their reading. Ask: "Does that make sense? Does that sound right?"

Ultimately, you want students to be able to select appropriate strategies to use when encountering difficult words. As they grow in their ability to analyze words, occasionally have them decide which strategy they might use to decode an unfamiliar word. Ask: "What might you do to figure that word out?" In addition to nudging them toward independence in the application of strategies, the prompt supplies you with useful information about the student's use of decoding strategies.

After a student has applied a strategy, praise the student's efforts. The praise should be very specific: "I like the way you used the pronounceable word part to figure that word out." Or "I like the way you reread the sentence when you noticed that it didn't make sense." Affirming the students' efforts rewards them and also highlights the use of the particular strategy that they applied. Students may have applied a strategy without realizing its value. Affirming it strengthens their knowledge of the strategy and the likelihood that they will use it in the future.

After students have successfully decoded a difficult word on their own, ask them how they figured out that hard word. Make a note of their response. Their response can shed light on their use of word analysis strategies. As part of your ongoing assessment of students' use of strategies, observe students as they grapple with difficult words. If possible, administer the Student Decoding Interview, which is presented in Figure 4.10.

Make a note of students' attempts to decode a difficult word. Are they using context or sounding-out strategies? Are they analyzing the word sound by sound, or by chunks? A listing of strategies and prompts is presented in Table 4.1.

Give students as much guidance as they need, but gradually lead them to the point where they can decode independently. Listed on the next page are steps that students might take when confronting a word that is unfamiliar in print.

FIGURE 4.10   Student Decoding Interview

Name _____   Date _____

Grade _____   Age _____

Student Decoding Interview

1. What is the hardest thing for you to do in reading?

2. What do you do when you come to a hard word?

3. What makes it hard to figure out words?

4. If someone asked you how to figure out a hard word, what would you tell that person?

5. How do you try to figure out hard words?

Observations while student is reading:

As student is figuring out a hard word, make notes of his attempts.

After student has figured out a hard word, ask: How did you figure out that word?

TABLE 4.1 Word Analysis Prompts

Strategy	When Used	Prompt
Pronounceable word part	Unknown word contains a part student can say: *am* or *amp* in *champ*	Can you say any part of that word?
Analogy	Unknown word is like a word student knows: unknown word *grain* is like known word *rain*.	Is this word like any word that you know?
Sound by sound	Student is unable to chunk word. Works out word sound by sound: /s/-/p/-/e/-/l/: spell.	Can you say the first sound, the next sound, the next sound?
Context	Student is unable to use phonics clues, but the text provides usable context clues.	What would make sense here? Read to the end of the sentence and see what word would fit.
Monitoring	Student checks to see if the word pronounced is a real word and fits the context of the selection (actually, students should monitor for meaning whenever they read)	Is that a real word? Does that make sense? Does that sound right?
Affirmation	Teacher wishes to reinforce the student's correct use of a strategy	I like the way you used a part of the word that you knew to help you say the whole word.
Assessment	Teacher wants to see what strategies the student is using	How did you figure out that word?
Starter	Student is unable to use any of the strategies to decode an unknown word	Could the word be _____?

▶▶STEPS FOR FIGURING OUT HARD WORDS

1. See if there is any part of the word that I can say. (If I can't say any part of the word, go to step 4.)
2. Say the part of the word I know. Then say the rest of the word. (If I can't say the rest of the word, go to step 4.)
3. Ask: "Is the word I said a real word? Does it make sense in the story?" (If not, try again or go to step 4.)
4. Is the word like any word I know? Is it like one of the model words? (If not, go to step 6.)
5. Say the word. Is it a real word? Does it make sense in the story? (If not, try again, or go to step 6.)
6. Say "blank" for the word. Read to the end of the sentence. Ask myself: "What word would make sense here?"

▶▶USING WORD ANALYSIS REFERENCES

At all stages of word analysis development, students should have references that they can use to help them read and spell unfamiliar words (Pinnell & Fountas, 1998). These references could include picture dictionaries, real dictionaries (for older students), illustrated charts of model words, lists of pattern and other words, word walls, a chart listing the steps in decoding a difficult word, and a talking word processor such as *Dr. Peet's Talk Writer* (Edmark) or *Writing Out Loud* (Don Johnston), or a talking electronic dictionary such as those manufactured by Franklin Electronics, so that students can type in an unknown word and have it pronounced.

►►COMMERCIAL MATERIALS

The best way to reinforce phonics skills and strategies is to use the teaching techniques already presented, including: shared reading; language experience stories and especially interactive writing; student-generated writing and spelling; the high-payoff techniques described above; and lots and lots of group and individual reading. Reading children's books on the appropriate level of difficulty is especially effective. Specific titles that might be used to reinforce key vowel patterns are listed in the Vowel Patterns Resources section. In addition, there are kits of books designed to foster word analysis skills. These kits can be classified as sight-word texts or decodable texts.

►►SIGHT-WORD TEXTS

Sight texts are also known as predictable books. They are generally brief books that are heavily illustrated. Students use predictable and repeated words and phrases and picture clues to help them read the books. One problem with some of these books is that they are so predictable and so heavily illustrated that students memorize them or simply use the pictures to "read" them. This, of course, deprives them of the opportunity to apply newly acquired skills. One way of getting around this problem is to have students cover the illustrations as they read the book a second time.

>*Story Box* (The Wright Group) booklets range from beginning reading to about third grade.

>*Sunshine Series* (The Wright Group) features more than a hundred titles ranging in difficulty from beginning reading to third grade.

>*Literacy 2000* (Rigby) includes hundreds of books ranging from beginning reading through grade three.

►►DECODABLE TEXTS

Decodable texts are similar in appearance to sight-word texts. Both are brief and heavily illustrated. However, decodable texts were written to provide practice with a specific phonic element: short-*a* or short-*e* words, for instance. As a result, depending on the skill of the author, the books may seem natural or they may seem contrived and artificial. Some of the story words may not even be in the students' listening vocabularies, but are included simply because they incorporate the pattern being taught. Because the language of decodable texts may be somewhat artificial, these books may actually be more difficult to read. Use of artificial language also makes it more difficult to make use of context clues. However, some decodable texts are well done and can be used effectively. It is suggested that you judge each title for yourself.

>*Let's Read Together Books* (Kane Press) include five 32-page books that focus on short vowels.

>*A First Book* (Barron's) is a series of five 16-page books that provide practice with short vowels.

>*Real Kid Readers* (Millbrook Press) are generously illustrated with full-color photos.

>*Start to Read Books* (School Zone) are 16-page books at three levels.

➤➤SOFTWARE

Because of speech capability and interactive features, phonics software has the potential to provide excellent practice. The best phonics software titles present phonics in a functional way that motivates students. *Simon Sounds It Out* (Don Johnston), an award-winning piece of software, pronounces and helps students build words by combining initial consonants (onsets) and word patterns (rimes). Featuring an electronic tutor, it provides especially effective practice for Word Building. Since it pronounces and shows parts of words, it also helps develop phonemic awareness.

➤➤ASSESSING ABILITY TO READ VOWEL PATTERNS

An essential element in a word analysis program is to find out where students are and begin instruction at that point. To assess students' ability to read basic vowel patterns, administer the Word Pattern Survey, shown in Figure 4.11. The survey consists of 80 words that include most of the major word patterns found in single-syllable words. It is arranged in four levels of difficulty: easy long-vowel and short vowels, long vowels, *r*-vowels and other vowels, and infrequent vowel patterns. There are 20 words at each level. The mastery standard at each level is 80%. If students can read orally 16 out of 20 words at a level, they are judged to be proficient at that level. The first level at which students' performance falls below 80% is the level at which students need instruction. However, if students get fewer than 5 words correct, they should be given the Beginning Consonant Correspondences Survey, if this has not already been administered. If students get 60 or more correct, they have probably mastered primary phonics but may need work with multisyllabic patterns. Record students' performance on the word pattern assessment survey in Figure 4.11.

Before administering the Word Pattern Survey, discuss with the student why she is being tested. Say: "I want to see how well you can read single words, so I'm going to give you a list of words to read. Some of the words may be difficult, but I want you to read as many words as you can."

All students begin with the first word and continue reading until they miss 5 in a row. As the student reads each word, record her performance on your copy of the test with a plus or minus. You may also want to write out incorrect responses. Incorrect responses provide valuable insight into the student's method of approaching words. If the student makes no response, write a 0 in the blank. Be encouraging and supportive. If a student says "I don't know" or gives no response, encourage her to try to read the word or, at least, to read as much as she can.

➤➤VOWEL PATTERN RESOURCES

The Vowel Pattern Resources section provides a listing of possibilities for teaching and reinforcing each of the vowel patterns. Included are some or all of the following: a listing of pattern and mixed practice words with possible model words being starred, scrambled sentences, spelling words, books, titles of songs, sorting activities, riddles, titles of rhymes, and real-world signs or labels that reinforce the element. (Rhymes and songs referred to can be found in Appendix A.) A number of secret-word and making-word activities are also presented, along with writing topics related to the phonic element. For a number of the patterns, there are also fold-and-read books that might be used to reinforce the pattern. The fold-and-read books can be found in Appendix B.

FIGURE 4.11   Word Pattern Survey

Name _____   Total number correct _____

Date _____   Estimated level _____

Word Pattern Survey

1. go _____	21. game _____	41. spark_____	61. through_____
2. me _____	22. tree _____	42. stair_____	62. straight _____
3. see _____	23. wide_____	43. shore _____	63. enough _____
4. I _____	24. road _____	44. curl _____	64. clue_____
5. no _____	25. use_____	45. steer _____	65. edge _____
6. hat _____	26. goat_____	46. park _____	66. strong_____
7. wet _____	27. save _____	47. purse_____	67. suit _____
8. sit _____	28. wheel _____	48. clear _____	68. thought_____
9. hop _____	29. mine_____	49. storm_____	69. flood _____
10. fun_____	30. cute_____	50. charge_____	70. breathe _____
11. ran_____	31. chain _____	51. chalk _____	71. calm _____
12. men_____	32. speak_____	52. brook_____	72. clothes _____
13. win _____	33. slide _____	53. crown_____	73. knock _____
14. got_____	34. toast_____	54. join _____	74. soft _____
15. bug _____	35. blind _____	55. should _____	75. fault _____
16. drop_____	36. plane_____	56. stew _____	76. tough _____
17. jump _____	37. steel _____	57. bounce_____	77. height_____
18. sand_____	38. drive _____	58. crawl_____	78. laugh_____
19. ship_____	39. broke_____	59. broom_____	79. earth _____
20. lunch_____	40. price_____	60. pound _____	80. brought_____

Directions: Give one copy of the survey to the student and keep one for marking. Mark each response + or –. Start with the first item for all pupils. Say to the student, "I am going to ask you to read a list of words to me. Some of the words may be hard for you, but read as many as you can." Stop when the student gets five in a row wrong. The Survey test has four levels. Each level has twenty items as follows: 1–20, easy long-vowel and short-vowel patterns; 21–40: long-vowel patterns; 41–60: *r*-vowel and other-vowel patterns, /aw/, /o͞o/, /oo/, /ow/, /oy/, 61–80: irregular and low-frequency patterns. Students are proficient at a level if they get 80% or more correct at that level. Students should be instructed at a level if they get more than 4 out of 20 wrong at that level.

Patterns are presented in approximate order of difficulty and frequency. The most frequently occurring and easiest-to-learn patterns are introduced first. Short-vowel patterns are introduced first, followed by long-vowel, *r*-vowel, and other-vowel patterns. The first short-vowel pattern is *am*, because the *m* is a continuant and makes the pattern especially easy to perceive. In addition, students can use the word *am* to write brief stories about themselves. The *-at* pattern is introduced next because it also has a high frequency and *at* and *am* are easy to distinguish from each other. Once a second pattern is introduced, the two patterns are contrasted with each other through sorting and other activities. The third pattern to be introduced is *an* because it, too, has a high utility. The *an* pattern is contrasted through sorting with *am* and *at*. Sorting is one way of reviewing previously presented patterns. Sort no more than three patterns at a time. When students encounter a fourth pattern, sort the fourth pattern with the second and third patterns.

➤➤SHORT-*a* PATTERNS

-am Pattern (See Model Lesson)

Pattern words: am, ham*, jam, Sam.

Scrambled sentence: I am Sam.

Shared reading: Dr. Seuss (1988). *Green eggs and ham.*

Functional reading: jar of jam and can of ham labels.

Reading: "I am Sam" fold-and read book.

"I am a bird" fold-and-read book. Text-walk: Show students how to use their knowledge of the *-am* pattern and the illustrations and initial consonants to read the two "I Am" books. For instance, for the sentence, "I am a boy," ask students to look at the picture and tell what word beginning with /b/ would make sense. If students have difficulty, ask if the word *boy* would fit.

Spelling: am, jam.

Writing: Students compose an illustrated "I am" piece telling about themselves: "I am Sam. I am a boy. I am 7."

-at Pattern

Pattern words: at, bat, cat,* fat, hat, mat, rat, sat.

Mixed practice: bat, ham, hat, jam, mat, Sam, sat.

Scrambled sentence: I see a fat cat.

Reading: Carle, E. (1973). *Have you seen my cat?* New York: Scholastic.

Cameron, A. (1994). *The cat sat on the mat.* Boston: Houghton.

Wildsmith, B. (1986). *Cat on a mat.* New York: Oxford.

*Rhyme: "Jack Hall."

Sorting: Students sort a mixed group of *-at* and *-am* words: at, bat, cat, hat, pat, sat; am, ham, jam, Sam.

Spelling: cat, sat, at, that.

Writing: Students draw a picture of a favorite, unusual, or interesting cat and write a caption to go along with the drawing.

-an Pattern

Pattern words: an, can, man, pan,* ran, van.

Mixed practice: man, van, pan, can, cat, ham, hat, jam, am.

*Note: Rhymes and songs referred to can be found in Appendix A.

Scrambled sentence: The man has a van.

Reading: "I can" fold-and-read book. Text-walk: Show students how to use their knowledge of the *-an* pattern and the illustrations and initial consonants to read the "I can" book.

"The rat ran" fold-and-read book. Text-walk: Direct students to the first page of the selection. Explain that the rat ran. Turning to the second page, explain that the cat ran. Turning to the third page, explain that the cat ran after the rat. Have the students find the word *after*. Have students read the rest of the story silently to find out who else ran. After students have read the story silently, discuss it and have them orally read parts to tell which animals ran.

Rhyme: "Higher than a House."

Sorting: Students sort a mixed group of -am, -an, and -at words: at, bat, cat, hat, pat, sat; am, ham, jam, Sam, an, can, man, pan, ran, van.

Bingo: with -am, -at, and -an words.

Riddle: I am a he. I am not a she. My name rhymes with *van*. What am I? (a man)

Spelling: can, man, an, ran.

Writing: Students compose an illustrated booklet telling about things they can do.

-ad Pattern

Pattern words: bad, dad, had, mad, sad.*

Mixed practice: bad, bat, had, hat, mad, mat, sat, sad.

Scrambled sentence: I had a bad cat.

Reading: Antee, N. (1984). *The good bad cat.* Grand Haven, MI: School Zone.

Song: "Old MacDonald."

Sorting: bad, had, mad, sad, sat, can, man, pan, ran, van, Sam, jam, am, ham.

Riddle: I have a little boy. And I have a little girl. But I am not a mom. I rhyme with *sad*. What am I? (a dad)

Spelling: had, bad, mad, sad.

Writing: Students make a list of things that make them mad or sad.

-ag Pattern

Pattern words: bag, flag,* rag, tag, wag.

Mixed practice: bad, bat, rag, rat.

Scrambled sentence: A happy dog wags its tail.

Sorting: bag, flag, tag, wag, bad, had, sad, dad, mad, an, can, man, pan, ran, van.

Riddle: I can be a game or a thing that you put your name on. What am I? (tag)

Spelling: bag, flag.

Writing: Students make up a flag for themselves. The flag shows two or three important things about the student. It might show what students like to do, their favorite colors, and their favorite animals or possessions.

-ap Pattern

Pattern words: cap, map,* nap, tap, snap, trap.

Mixed practice: bad, bat, rag, rat, sat, snap.

Scrambled sentence: The cat naps on my cap.

Reading: Coxe, M. (1996). *Cat traps.* New York: Random House.

Sorting: cap, map, nap, tap, trap, bag, flag, tag, wag, bad, dad, had, mad, sad.

Making words: Distribute the letters: *a, n, p, s.*

➤ Use two letters to make *an.*
➤ Add a letter to make *pan*
➤ Keeping the same letters, make the word *nap.*
➤ Using the letters *a, p, s,* make the word *sap,* like the *sap* that flows in a tree.
➤ Using all the letters, make a word. (*snap* or *pans*).

Spelling: map, snap.

Writing: Students draw and label a map of their neighborhood.

-ack Pattern

Pattern words: back, pack, tack,* black, snack, track.

Mixed practice: back, black, bad, pat, pack, sat, snack.

Scrambled sentence: I have a snack in my back pack.

Sorting: back, pack, black, snack, track, cap, map, nap, tap, trap.

Rhyme riddle: What do you call a backpack that has lots of things to eat? (snack pack)

Spelling: back, black, pack.

Writing: Students make a list of items that they carry in their back packs or might carry if they had back packs.

Short -a Unit Review.   On the chalkboard or an overhead, write the short-*a* vowel pattern words presented in this unit. Mix the patterns so students are not simply using the first word as a clue to the other words in that column: cat, sad, flag, ham, pan, tack, hat, mad, can, bag, back, jam, ran, wag, tack, dad, rat, am, sat, had, tag, Sam, Pam, tan, bat, pack, bad, track, rag, van.

If students aren't able to read 90% of the words, continue to review them until they are able to do so.

Concentration: Pairs of students play Concentration with short-*a* words.

Secret message: Write the words on the lines and read the secret message.

1. Take the **P** off **Pack** and put in **J.** ___ ___ ___ ___
2. Take the **s** off **sand.** ___ ___ ___
3. Take the **S** off **Sam** and put in **P.** ___ ___ ___
4. Take the **b** off **bike** and put in **l.** ___ ___ ___ ___
5. Take the **h** off **ham** and put in **j.** ___ ___ ___

_____ _____ _____ _____ _____ .

➤➤SHORT -*e* PATTERNS

-ed Pattern

Pattern words: bed,* fed, led, red, sled.
Mixed practice: bed, bad, rat, red, fed, fat.

Scrambled sentence: Ted has a red sled.

Reading: "What Is Red?" fold-and-read book. Text-walk: Show students how to use their knowledge of the -*ed* pattern and the illustrations and initial consonants to read the selection.

Shared reading: One of Norman Bridwell's "Big Red Dog" books.

Rhyme: "Bedtime."

Sorting: back, pack, tack, black, snack, track, cap, map, nap, tap, snap, trap bed, fed, led, red, sled.

Rhyme riddle: What do you call a bright place to sleep? (red bed)

Spelling: bed, red.

Writing: Students draw and label objects that are red.

-ell Pattern

Pattern words: bell,* fell, sell, tell, well, yell, shell, smell, spell.

Mixed practice: bell, bed, fat, fell, sell, sad.

Scrambled sentence: The man sells bells.

Song: "The Farmer in the Dell"; "Out."

Sorting: bed, fed, led, red, sled, bell, fell, sell, tell, well, yell, shell, smell.

Spelling: tell, well, yell.

Writing: Students write about bells that they hear: school bells, doorbells, church bells, etc.

-en Pattern.   (In some areas the *e* in *-en* has a short-*i* pronunciation, so that *ten* sounds like *tin*. Adjust your teaching to fit the dialect spoken in your area.)

Pattern words: ten, hen, men, pen,* when, well.

Mixed practice: hen, hat, ten, tell, men, met, pen,* pet, when, wet.

Scrambled sentence: Ten hens are in a pen.

Reading: Gregorich, B. (1984). *Nine men chase a hen.* Grand Haven, MI: School Zone.

Rhyme: "Little Blue Ben."

Song: "Roll Over."

Sorting: ten, hen, men, pen, when, bed, fed, led, red, sled, bell, fell, sell, tell, well, yell, shell, smell.

Bingo: with -ed, -en, -ell words.

Rhyme riddle: Where do hens live? (hen pen)

Spelling: ten, men, when.

Writing: Students list ten things that they like to do.

-et Pattern

Pattern words: get, let, met, net,* pet, set, wet, yet.

Mixed practice: hen, get, ten, net, men, met, pen, pet, when, wet.

Scrambled sentence: Did your pet get wet?

Reading: Snow, P. (1984). *A pet for pat.* Chicago: Children's Press.

Sorting: get, let, met, net, pet, set, wet, yet, fell, sell, tell, well, yell, ten, hen, men, pen, when.

Rhyme riddle: What do you call a vet who helps cats and dogs? (a pet vet)

Spelling: get, let, pet, set, wet, yet.

Writing: Students write about their pets or a pet that they might like to have.

-end Pattern

Pattern words: end, bend,* lend, send, spend.

Mixed practice: bet, bend, let, lend, set, send, spend.

Scrambled sentence: Do not spend the pennies.

Sorting: end, bend, lend, send, spend, ten, hen, men, pen, when, get, let, met, net, pet, set, wet, yet.

Riddle: I am part of a story. I can be happy, or I can be sad. But I am always last. What am I? (the end)

Making words: Distribute the letters: *d, e, n, p, s.*

> ➤ Use three letters to make *pen.*
> ➤ Add a letter to make *pens.*
> ➤ Use three letters to make the word *end.*
> ➤ Add a letter to make the word *send.*
> ➤ Using all the letters, make a word. (*spend*)

Spelling: end, send, bend.

Writing: Students write a piece telling how they might spend ten dollars.

-ent Pattern

Pattern words: cent, lent, sent, spent, tent,* went.

Mixed practice: let, lent, send, sent, tend, tent,* when, went.

Scrambled sentence: We went to our tent.

Reading: Create a pattern book that shows how money was spent: "How I Spent My Money." I went to the zoo. I spent 50 cents. I went to the candy store. I spent 60 cents. I went to the ice cream store. I spent 60 cents. I spent all my money.

Rhyme: "The Bear Went over the Mountain."

Rhyme riddle: What would you call a tent that cost only a penny? (cent tent)

Sorting: cent, lent, sent, tent, went, end, bend, lend, send, spend, spent, get, let, met, net, pet, set, wet, yet.

Spelling: cent, went, sent.

Writing: Students write about a place they went to that was fun or interesting.

-est Pattern

Pattern words: best, nest,* rest, pest, test.

Mixed practice: bend, best, net, nest, pet, pest, ten, test.

Scrambled sentence: Which bird makes the best nest?

Rhymes: "Turn to the East;" "Good, Better, Best."

Sorting: best, nest, rest, pest, test, cent, lent, sent, tent, went, end, bend, lend, send, spend.

Rhyme riddle: What would you call a bird's nest that is better than the rest? (best nest)

Spelling: best, nest, rest.

Writing: Students compose a booklet or write a piece about the things they like best: best books, foods, games, etc.

Short-e Unit Review. On the chalkboard or an overhead, write the short-*e* vowel pattern words presented in this unit. Mix the patterns so students aren't simply using the first word as a clue to the other words in that column. Words listed in the sorting exercises can be used for this purpose. If students are not able to read 90% of the words, continue to review them until they are able to do so.

Concentration: Pairs of students play concentration with short-*e* words.

Secret message: Write the words on the lines and read the secret message.

1. Take **P** from **Pets** and add **V.** ___ ___ ___ ___
2. Take **s** from **helps.** ___ ___ ___ ___
3. Take **s** from **set** and put in **p.** Then add **s.** ___ ___ ___ ___
4. Take **n** from **net** and put in **g.** ___ ___ ___
5. Take **b** from **bell** and add **w.** ___ ___ ___ ___

_____ _____ _____ _____ _____.

➤➤SHORT-*i* PATTERNS

-it Pattern; is, this, if

Pattern words: it, bit, fit, hit,* sit, little; is, this, if.

Mixed practice: it, at, bit, bat, hit, hat, sit, sat.

Scrambled sentence: Does this mitt fit?

Reading: "Is This a Rat?" fold-and-read book. Text-walk: Have students turn to p. 6. Explain that they will be reading about a rat that can hop like a kangaroo. Have them find the phrase "hop like a kangaroo." Have students read the selection to find out about a bat and about a rat that can hop like a kangaroo. After students have read the selection silently, discuss it with them and have them read sentences orally that tell about the animals. For additional reading, have students create a pattern book that shows what can be little: "Little." A kitten can be little. A puppy can be little. A bug can be little. A bird can be little. A fish can be little.

Shared Singing: "If You're Happy and You Know It."

Sorting: it, bit, fit, hit, sit, bet, let, met, net, pet, best, nest, rest, pest, test.

Riddle: If the ball is hit, I catch it. My name rhymes with *hit,* but there are two *t*'s at the end of my name. What am I? (a mitt)

Spelling: it, sit, little, is, this.

Writing: Students write about places where they like to sit.

-in Pattern

Pattern words: in, pin,* tin, win, chin, skin, thin.

Mixed practice: it, in, pin, pan, tin, ten, thin, wet, win.

Scrambled sentence: Did you win that pin?

Song: "Go in and out the Window."

Reading: Wolcott, P. (1975). *My shadow and I.* Reading, MA: Addison-Wesley.

Sorting: in, pin, tin, win, chin, skin, thin, it, bit, fit, hit, sit, best, nest, rest, pest, test.

Rhyme riddle: What do you call a pin that is not fat? (a thin pin)

Spelling: in, win, skin.

Writing: Have students make a list of fun things that they can do when they have to stay in the house.

-ill Pattern

Pattern words: bill, fill, hill,* will, spill, still.

Mixed practice: bill, bit, fill, fit, hill, hit, set, still.

Scrambled sentence: Jack and Jill went up the hill.

Rhymes: "Jack and Jill"; "There Was an Old Woman"

Sorting: bill, fill, hill, will, spill, still, in, pin, tin, win, thin, it, bit, fit, hit, sit.

Making words: Distribute the letters: *i, p, l, l, s.*

- ➤ Use three letters to make *ill* as in I am ill.
- ➤ Add a letter to make *sill* as in window sill.
- ➤ Change a letter to make the word *pill.*
- ➤ Use three letters to make the word *lip.*
- ➤ Change a letter to make the word *sip* as in I will sip my soda.
- ➤ Add a letter to make the word *slip*
- ➤ Using all the letters, make a word. (*spill*)

Riddle: What goes up and comes down but stays in the same place? (a hill)

Spelling: will, hill.

Writing: Students write about something that they will do today.

-id Pattern

Pattern words: did, hid, kid, lid,* rid, slid.

Mixed practice: lid, led, rid, red, hid, slid, sled.

Scrambled sentence: Did you get rid of the old tin cans?

Reading: Wang, M. L. (1989). *The ant and the dove.* Chicago: Children's Press.

Shared singing: "Did You Ever See a Lassie?"

Sorting: did, hid, kid, lid, rid, slid, in, pin, tin, win, thin, bill, fill, hill, will, spill, still.

Bingo: with -am, -at, and -an words.

Spelling: did, hid, kid.

Writing: Students draw a picture and write a story about something they did that was fun.

Rhyme riddle: What do you call a hat for a little girl or boy? (kid lid)

-ig Pattern

Pattern words: big, wig, dig, pig.*

Mixed practice: big, bill, pig, pill, wig, will.

Scrambled sentence: The big pigs are in the pen.

Shared reading: "Three Little Pigs."

Reading: "Pigs Can Dig" fold-and-read book. Text-walk: Have students read the story and find out and discuss some of the things that pigs can do. Using strategies already taught, students should be able to read all of the words, but provide helpful prompts as needed.

Sorting: big, wig, dig, pig, did, hid, kid, lid, bill, fill, hill, will, spill, still.

Rhyme riddle: What do you call a large hog? (big pig)

Spelling: big, pig, dig.

Writing: Students write about some things they would like to do when they get big.

-ing Pattern

Pattern words: king, ring,* sing, wing, bring, spring, thing.

Mixed practice: rat, ring, sat, sing, tin, thing, when, wing sing, spring.

Scrambled sentence: The king can sing.

Reading: "Hummingbird" fold-and-read book. Text-walk: Tell students that they will be reading about a little hummingbird. Have them find the words *hummingbird* and *little* on p. 1. Tell them that a hummingbird can make its wings go fast. Have them find the word *fast* on p. 3. Have them read the book to find out what the hummingbird can do with its big bill. Have students orally reread sentences that tell how big the bee hummingbird is and what it can do with its big bill.

Greydanus, R. (1968). *Let's get a pet.* Mahwah, NJ: Troll.

Rhyme: "Happy Thoughts."

Sorting: king, ring, sing, wing, bring, big, wig, dig, pig, did, hid, kid, lid, rid, slid.

Making words: Distribute the letters: *g, i, n, p, r, s.*

> ➤ Use four letters to make the word *sing.*
> ➤ Change a letter to make *ring.*
> ➤ Change a letter to make the word *ping* as in Ping-Pong.
> ➤ Using all the letters, make a word. (*spring*)

Riddle: A bell can do this. And you can put this on. It rhymes with *sing.* What is it? (a ring)

Spelling: ring, sing, thing, bring.

Writing: Students write a piece telling what they would do if they were a king or a queen.

-ip Pattern

Pattern words: lip, tip, drip, ship,* skip, slip, trip.

Mixed practice: tip, tap, trip, sat, ship, sled, slip.

Scrambled sentence: Did you take a trip on a ship?

Reading: Share-read a version of "The Three Billy Goats Gruff" that ends with the lines: "Trip, trap, trip. This tale's told out."

Sorting: lip, tip, drip, ship, skip, slip, trip, king, ring, sing, wing, bring, big, wig, dig, pig.

Riddle: You need two of these to kiss. (lips)

Spelling: ship, trip, slip.

Writing: Students write about a trip they might like to take on a ship.

-ick Pattern

Pattern words: chick, kick, lick, pick, sick, stick,* trick.

Mixed practice: lick, let, pick, pet, sick, set, tap, trick.

Scrambled sentence: I will pick up the stick.

Reading: Meister, C. (1999). *When Tiny was tiny.* New York: Puffin.

"Big bug" fold-and-read book. Text-walk: Tell students that they will be reading about bugs. Have them find the words *bugs* and *spot* on p. 1. Tell them they will be reading about two big bugs. One of the big bugs is called a walking stick. Have them find the words *walking stick.* Have them read to find out about the two big bugs.

Rhyme: "Jack Be Nimble."

Song: "A Tisket, a Tasket."

Sorting: kick, lick, pick, sick, stick, trick, lip, tip, drip, ship, skip, king, ring, sing, wing, bring, spring, thing.

Rhyme riddle: What do you call a hen that is not well? (sick chick)

Making words: Distribute the letters: *c, i, k, s, t.*

> ➤ Use three letters to make the word *sit.*
> ➤ Change a letter to make the word *kit.*
> ➤ Use four letters to make the word *sick.*
> ➤ Change a letter to make the word *tick.*
> ➤ Using all the letters, make a word. (*stick*)

Spelling: pick, sick, trick.

Writing: Have students make a list of things that make them feel sick.

-ish Pattern

Pattern words: dish, fish,* wish.

Mixed practice: dish, den, fish, fit, wish, we.

Scrambled sentence: Did you wish for a fish?

Rhyme: "Star Light, Star Bright."

Reading: Cox, M. (1997). *Big egg.* New York: Random.

Sorting: dish, fish, wish, kick, lick, pick, sick, stick, trick, lip, tip, drip, ship, skip, slip, trip.

Riddle: I can be in the sea, or I can be on a dish. I rhyme with *wish.* What am I? (fish)

Spelling: dish, fish, wish.

Writing: Students write about some things that they might wish for. Compose a class booklet of student wishes and place it in the class library.

Short-i Unit Review.   On the chalkboard or an overhead, write the short-*i* vowel pattern words presented in this unit. Mix the patterns so students aren't simply using the first word as a clue to the other words in that column. Words listed in the sorting exercises can be used for this purpose. If students are not able to read 90% of the words, continue to review them until they are able to do so.

Concentration: Pairs of students play concentration with short-*i* words.

Secret message: Write the words on the lines and read the secret message.

1. Take **D** off **Dig** and put on **B.** ___ ___ ___
2. Add **s** to **bird.** ___ ___ ___ ___ ___
3. Take **m** from **man** and put on **c.** ___ ___ ___
4. Keep **have** as it is. ___ ___ ___ ___
5. Add **tle** to **lit.** ___ ___ ___ ___ ___ ___
6. Take **th** from **things** and put in **w.** ___ ___ ___ ___ ___.

_____ _____ _____ _____ _____ _____.

➤➤SHORT-o PATTERNS

-op Pattern

Pattern words: hop, mop,* pop, top, shop.

Mixed practice: hop, hid, mop, map, pop, pill, top, tin.

Scrambled sentence: Can pop hop?

Rhyme: "Mix a Pancake."

Reading: Foster, A., & Erickson, B. (1991). *A mop for pop.* New York: Barron.

Shared reading: Geisel, T. S. (Dr. Seuss). (1963). *Hop on pop.* New York: Random House.

Sorting: hop, mop, pop, top, shop, dish, fish, wish, chick, kick, lick, pick, sick, stick, trick.

Rhyme riddle: What do you call the best dad? (top pop)

Spelling: hop, top, shop.

Writing: Students write about some animals that like to hop.

-ot Pattern

Pattern words: dot, hot, lot, not, pot,* spot.

Mixed practice: hot, hop, mop, not, pot, pop, dot, got.

Scrambled sentence: The pot is not hot.

Reading: "Lady Bug" fold-and-read book. Text-walk: Have students turn to p. 2. Have them guess what kind of bug is shown. Have them turn to p. 3 and find the words "lady bug." Have students read the story to find out about lady bugs. After students have read the selection silently, discuss what they learned and have them read sentences that give interesting information about lady bugs.

Rhyme: "Hippity Hop to the Barber Shop."

Reading: McKissack, P. C. (1983). *Who is who?* Chicago: Children's Press.

Sorting: dot, hot, lot, not, pot, spot, hop, mop, pop, top, shop, dish, fish, wish.

Making words: Distribute the letters: *o, p, s, t.*

> ➤ Use three letters to make the word *top.*
> ➤ Use the same three letters to make the word *pot.*
> ➤ Add a letter to make the word *stop.*
> ➤ Using all the letters, make a word. (*spot*)

Rhyme riddle: What do you call a very warm place? (hot spot)

Spelling: lot, hot, not, spot.

Writing: Students write about some things that they like to do on a hot day.

-ock Pattern

Pattern words: lock,* rock, sock, block, clock.

Mixed practice: lock, lot, clock, so, sock, red, rock.

Scrambled sentence: We will lock up the gold rocks.

Rhyme: "Hickory, Dickory, Dock."

Sorting: lock, rock, sock, block, clock, dot, hot, lot, not, pot, spot, hop, mop, pop, top, shop.

Bingo: with -op, -ot, and -ock words.

Riddle: How can you make time fly? (throw a clock high in the sky)

Spelling: block, clock.

Writing: Students tell what they are doing at certain times of the day: 9 o'clock (morning), 12 o'clock (noon), 3 o'clock (afternoon), 6 o'clock (evening), 12 o'clock (midnight).

Short-o Unit Review. On the chalkboard or an overhead, write the short-*o* vowel pattern words presented in this unit. Mix the patterns so students aren't simply using the first word as a clue to the other words in that column. Words listed in the sorting exercises can be used for this purpose. If students are not able to read 90% of the words, continue to review them until they are able to do so.

Concentration: Pairs of students play concentration with short-*e* words.

Secret message: Write the words on the lines and read the secret message.

1. Add **s** to **Elephant.** ___ ___ ___ ___ ___ ___ ___ ___ ___
2. Take **r** away from **ran** and put in **c.** ___ ___ ___
3. Take **h** away from **hot** and put in **n.** ___ ___ ___
4. Take **t** away from **top** and put in **h.** ___ ___ ___

_____ _____ _____ _____.

➤➤SHORT -*u* PATTERNS

-*ug Pattern*

Pattern words: bug,* dug, hug, mug, rug.

Mixed practice: bug, bag, dug, den, hug, hen, mug, man, rug, ran.

Scrambled sentence: A bug ran on the rug.

Rhyme: "Three Little Bugs."

Reading: McKissack, P., & McKissack, F. (1988). *Bugs!* Children's Press.

Sorting: bug, dug, hug, mug, rug, dot, hot, lot, not, pot, spot, lock, rock, sock, block, clock.

Riddle: Bugs run on me. Cats and dogs run on me. And you run on me. I rhyme with *hug.* What am I? (a rug)

Spelling: bug, rug, hug.

Writing: Students draw a picture of a bug and then write a story about the bug.

-*un Pattern*

Pattern words: fun, gun, run, sun.*

Mixed practice: fun, fat, gun, got, run, ran, sat, sun.

Scrambled sentence: We had fun in the sun.

Reading: "What Is Fun?" fold-and-read book. Text-walk: Discuss some things that are fun. Have students tell what the children are doing on p. 1. Have them find the word *singing.* Discuss the -*ing* on the end of *singing.* Have students tell what the boy and girl are doing on p. 2. Have them find the word *running* and note the -*ing* at the end of *running.* Have students read the rest of the story and find out about some other things that are fun. After students have read the story silently, discuss some things that were fun and some things that they think are fun. Students might read orally the page that shows something that they think is fun. Students might also read orally the list of fun things that the teacher in the story has put on the board.

Hawkins, C., & Hawkins, J. (1988). *Zug the bug.* New York: Putnam.

Rhyme: "Hot Cross Buns."

Sorting: fun, gun, run, sun, bug, dug, hug, mug, rug, dot, hot, lot, not, pot, spot.

Riddle: I get up before you get up. And I get up before hens and pigs get up. I am not a son. But I sound just like *son.* What am I? (the sun)

Spelling: fun, run, sun.

Writing: Students draw a picture of something that is fun to do and write a story about it.

-ut Pattern

Pattern words: but, cut, nut,* shut.

Mixed practice: bat, but, cut, cat, nut, not, shot, shut.

Scrambled sentence: He has a cut on his hand.

Sorting: but, cut, nut, shut, fun, gun, run, sun, bug,* dug, hug, mug, rug.

Bingo: with -ub, -un, and -ut words.

Rhyme riddle: What do you call a cut that has closed up? (shut cut)

Spelling: but, cut, shut.

Writing: Students write about a time they were sad but got happy.

-up Pattern

Pattern words: up, cup,* pup.

Mixed practice: us, up, cup, cap, pup, pet.

Scrambled sentence: Do not pick up the pup.

Song: "Lazy Mary."

Reading: Hawkins, C., & Hawkins, J. (1988). *Zug the bug.* New York: Putnam.

Functional reading: pudding cup.

Shared reading: Dr. Seuss. (1974). *Great day for up.* New York: Random House.

Sorting: up, cup, pup, but, cut, nut, shut, fun, gun, run, sun.

Rhyme riddle: What do you call a puppy that is not down? (an up pup)

Spelling: up, cup, puppy.

Writing: Students draw a picture of a puppy that they now have, had in the past, or might like to have. Then they write a story telling about the puppy.

-ub Pattern

Pattern words: cub, rub, tub.*

Mixed practice: cub, cut, ran, rub, tub, ten.

Scrambled sentence: A cub is in the bath tub.

Rhyme: "Rub-a-Dub-Dub."

Sorting: cub, rub, tub, up, cup, pup, shut, fun, gun, run, sun.

Spelling: cub, rub, tub.

Rhyme riddle: What do you call a bath tub for baby bears? (cub tub)

-ump Pattern

Pattern words: bump, dump, jump,* lump.

Mixed practice: bump, but, den, dump, jet, jump, let, lump.

Scrambled sentence: Can you jump over the bump?

Shared reading: "Jack, Be Nimble."

Reading: Compose a pattern book. One possibility is: "I Can." I can run. I can jump. I can jump over a lump. I can jump over a bump. Can you jump?"

Sorting: bump, dump, jump, lump, cub, rub, tub, bug, dug, hug, mug, rug.

Spelling: bump, jump, dump.

-unk Pattern

Pattern words: bunk, junk, skunk,* trunk.

Mixed practice: bunk, but, jump, junk, skunk, sun, trunk, tent.

Scrambled sentence: A skunk hid in the trunk.

Reading: "Baby Elephants Learn to Use Their Trunks" fold-and-read book. Text-walk: Have students look at the illustration on p. 1. Explain that baby elephants must learn to use their trunks. Have students point to the words *baby, elephants, learn, their,* and *use.* Have students read to find out about some of the mistakes that baby elephants make with their trunks and some of the things that they have to learn. After students have read the selection silently, have them tell about some of the mistakes that baby elephants make with their trunks. They might also read orally the sentences that tell about these mistakes. Discuss some of the things that baby elephants must learn to do with their trunks. Have them read aloud the sentence that tells who helps the baby elephants learn to use their trunks.

Sorting: bunk, junk, skunk, trunk, bump, dump, jump, lump, cub, rub, tub.

Rhyme riddle: What do you call a trunk that is full of old broken things? (junk trunk)

Making words: Distribute the letters: *k, n, r, t, s, u.*

- ➤ Use three letters to make the word *run.*
- ➤ Change a letter to make *sun.*
- ➤ Add a letter to make the word *sunk.*
- ➤ Using all the letters, make a word. (trunks)

Spelling: junk, skunk, trunk.

Writing: Students make a list of things they might pack in a trunk if they were taking a long trip.

-us(s), -ust, -uck Patterns

Pattern words: bus,* us, dust; just, must; duck,* luck, truck.

Mixed practice: bus, but, luck, fun, fuss, us, up, just, luck, must, truck.

Scrambled sentence: The bus is taking us up the hill.

Reading: "School Bus" fold-and-read book. Text-walk: Ask students how many take the bus to school. Have them turn to p. 2 and find the words *takes* and *school.* Have them turn to p. 5 and find the words *taking* and *show.* Have them note the *-ing* ending on *taking.* Have students read the story silently to find out what Bob does once he gets to school. After students have read the story, discuss what Bob does. Have them read orally passages that tell about Bob and his puppy. Have them read the passage that tells why Bob brought his puppy to school.

  Lewison, W. C. (1992). *"Buzz," said the bee.* New York: Scholastic.

Sorting: bus, fuss, us, just, must, dust, bunk, junk, skunk, trunk.

Riddle: I cannot walk or run, but I can take you places. I rhyme with *us.* What am I? (a bus)

Spelling: us, bus, must, just, truck.

Writing: Students write a piece about a bus trip they have taken or might like to take.

Short-u Unit Review. On the chalkboard or an overhead, write the short-*u* vowel pattern words presented in this unit. Mix the patterns so students aren't simply using the first word as a clue to the other words in that column. Words listed in the sorting exercises can be used for this purpose. If students are not able to read 90% of the words, continue to review them until they are able to do so.

Concentration: Pairs of students play concentration with short-*u* words.

Secret message: Write the words on the lines and read the secret message.

1. Take **n** away from **An.** ___
2. Put **p** before **up** and add **py.** ___ ___ ___ ___
3. Take **b** away from **bikes** and put in **l.** ___ ___ ___ ___ ___
4. Take **d** away from **do** and put in **t.** ___ ___
5. Take **f** away from **fun** and put in **r.** ___ ___ ___

___ ___ ___ ___ ___ .

➤➤LONG-*a* PATTERNS

-*ake Pattern*

Pattern words: bake, cake,* lake, take, wake, shake, snake.

Mixed practice: back, bake, cake, cat, let, lake, win, wake, snack, snake.

Scrambled sentence: We will bake a cake.

Reading: Robart, R. (1986). *The cake that Mack ate.* Boston: Little, Brown.

Functional reading: cake mix, baked beans.

Rhyme: "Pat-a-Cake."

Sorting: bake, cake, lake, take, wake, shake, snake, back, tack, pack, Jack, cap, map, nap, tap, snap, trap.

Riddle: I have no legs, so I cannot run. But I can go fast on land or in water. I rhyme with *cake.* What am I? (a snake)

Spelling: cake, take, wake, lake, shake, snake.

Writing: Students draw a picture and write about something that they would like to make.

-*ame Pattern*

Pattern words: came, game, same, tame, name.*

Mixed practice: came, cake, Sam, same, tame, take.

Scrambled sentence: What is the name of that game?

Reading: Oppenheim, J. (1990). *Wake up, baby!* New York: Bantam.

Shared singing: "Bingo."

Reading: Hall, K. (1995). *A bad, bad day.* New York: Scholastic.

Sorting: came, game, same, tame, name, bake, cake, lake, take, wake, shake, snake, back, pack, sack, tack, track.

Riddle: You write me on your paper, but other boys and girls write their own. I rhyme with *game.* What am I? (a name)

Spelling: came, name, same, game.

Writing: Students write about games that they like to play.

-*ate, -ait Patterns*

Pattern words: ate, date, gate,* hate, late, plate, skate, wait.

Mixed practice: at, ate, den, date, hate, hat, lake, late, pat, plate.

Scrambled sentence: I hate to be late.

Rhyme: "Garden Gate."

Sorting: ate, date, gate, hate, late, plate, skate, came, game, same, tame, name, bake, cake, lake, take, wake, shake, snake.

Bingo: with -ame, -ate, and -ake words.

Riddle: I can swing back and forth, but I cannot swing up and down. I rhyme with *late*. What am I? (a gate)

Spelling: ate, date, late, hate, wait.

Writing: Students draw a picture and write about a plate containing the foods that they like best.

-ave Pattern

Pattern words: cave, gave, save, wave,* brave.

Mixed practice: cake, cave, gate, gave, save, sat, wake, wave, bake, brave.

Scrambled sentence: We gave Dave a cake for being brave.

Sorting: cave, gave, save, wave, brave, ate, date, gate, hate, late, plate, skate, came, game, same, tame, name.

Riddle: Flags do this. And boys and girls do it when they want to say, "Hi" or "Good-bye." It rhymes with *brave*. What is it? (wave)

Writing: Students write about a time when they or someone they know was brave.

Spelling: gave, save, wave, brave.

-ade, -aid Patterns

Pattern words: made,* wade, grade, shade; paid.*

Mixed practice: gate, gave, made, wade, wave, late, brave.

Scrambled sentence: The second grade made puppets.

Sorting: made, wade, grade, shade, paid, raid, cave, gave, save, wave, brave.

Riddle: Trees make this. But they only make it when the sun is out. It rhymes with *made*. (shade)

Spelling: made, grade, paid.

Writing: Have students draw a picture of and/or write about something they made or something that someone they know made. Model the assignment for students by drawing a picture of a time when you made something and then writing about the picture.

-ace Pattern

Pattern words: face, race,* place.

Mixed practice: face, fast, rat, race, paid, place.

Scrambled sentence: She came in first place in the race.

Sorting: face, race, place, made, wade, grade, shade, paid, raid.

Riddle: I have eyes to see, a nose to smell, and a mouth for talking. I rhyme with *race*. What am I? (a face)

Spelling: face, race, place.

Writing: Have students draw a picture of and/or write about the place where they live. Model the assignment for students by drawing a picture of the place where you live and then writing about the picture.

-age Pattern

Pattern words: age, page, cage,* stage.

Mixed practice: page, place, rain, race, cage, face.

Scrambled sentence: This page shows three cats in a cage.

Sorting: age, page, cage, stage, face, race, place, cake, lake, take, wake, shake, snake.

Riddle: I have words but I cannot say anything. I am in a book. I rhyme with *cage.* What am I? (a page)

Spelling: age, page, cage.

Writing: Have students bring in photos or draw pictures of themselves at various ages and write captions for the photos. The captions should include ages. Model the assignment for students.

-ale, -ail Patterns

Pattern words: whale*; nail,* mail, sail, tail, trail.

Mixed practice: whale, page, tail, face, mail, race, sail.

Scrambled sentence: The big whale has a big tail.

Rhymes: "If You Ever"; "I've Got a Dog."

Song: "I Saw Three Ships."

Reading: Stadler, J. (1985). *Snail saves the day.* New York: Thomas Y. Crowell.

Sorting: whale, nail, mail, sail, tail, trail, age, page, cage, stage, face, race, place.

Making words: Distribute the letters: *a, i, l, r, s, t.*

> ➤ Use four letters to make the word *sail.*
> ➤ Change a letter to make the word *tail.*
> ➤ Change a letter to make the word *rail.*
> ➤ Using all the letters, make a word. (*trails*)

Rhyme riddle: What is a story about a whale called? (a whale tale)

Spelling: whale, tail, sail, mail.

Writing: Students draw a picture of a place to which they would like to sail and then write a story that tells about the picture.

-ain, -ane Patterns

Pattern words: rain, train,* pain, chain; cane, Jane, plane.*

Mixed practice: train, tail, chain, cane, pain, pail, rain, whale.

Scrambled sentence: A plane is faster than a train.

Reading: "Rain" fold-and-read book. Text-walk: Explain that this book is made up of rhymes. Have students read the title of the first rhyme and predict what it might be about. Have them find the name *Raymond* and read to find out what Raymond wants to do. After students have read the rhyme, have them tell what Raymond wants to do. Students might also read the rhyme aloud. For the second verse, "Bees," have students read the title and look at the illustration and note that the sun is shining and it is a fine day. Have students find the word *fine.* Have students predict where the bees might be going. Have the students read the rhyme to find out why bees might stay at home some days. After students have read the rhyme, discuss why the bees might stay at home. Discuss, too, how insects and animals might help us to predict what the weather might be like. For the rhyme, "If You Ever," help students read the title. Ask them to find the words *ever, never,* and *touch* in the rhyme. Have students predict what the rhyme might be telling readers. After students have read the rhyme, discuss what you should never do and why. Students might enjoy reading the rhyme orally.

Rhyme: "Rain, Rain, Go Away."

Sorting: rain, train, pain, chain; cane, Jane, plane, whale, nail, mail, sail, tail, trail.

Riddle: I fly high in the sky, but I am not a bird. I rhyme with *rain*. What am I? (a plane)

Spelling: rain, train, plane.

Writing: Students write about a train or plane trip they have taken or would like to take. To help students prepare for this assignment, discuss some train or plane trips that they have taken or might like to take.

-ay Pattern

Pattern words: hay,* day, may, say, stay, gray, play.

Mixed practice: may, mail, play, whale, way, stay, sail, trail, nail, gray.

Scrambled sentence: Play a game with me.

Reading: "Ostrich" fold-and-read book. Text-walk: Have students tell what kind of bird is shown on p. 1. Have them find the words *ostrich, bird,* and *eggs.* Have students read the story to find out about ostriches and their eggs. Encourage students to use picture clues, context, and word parts to figure out any hard words that they run into. After students have read the selection silently, have them tell what they found out about ostriches and their eggs. Have students read orally sentences that tell how many eggs the ostrich hen lays, how big the eggs are, and who sits on the eggs.

Rhyme: "Bees."

Sorting: hay, day, may, say, stay, gray, play, rain, train, pain, chain, cane, Jane, plane, mail, nail, pail, sail, tail (sort by rhyme only, not spelling).

Rhyme riddle: What do you call a day when you have a lot of fun? (play day)

Spelling: day, may, say, stay, play.

Writing: Students draw pictures of games they can play and then write captions for the pictures.

Long-a Unit Review.   On the chalkboard or an overhead, write the long-*a* pattern words presented in this unit. Mix the patterns so students aren't simply using the first word as a clue to the other words in that column. Words listed in the sorting exercises can be used for this purpose. If students are not able to read 90% of the words, continue to review them until they are able to do so.

Concentration: Pairs of students play concentration with long-*a* words.
Secret message: Write the words on the lines and read the secret message.

1. Take **n** away from **An.** ___
2. Put **g** before **ray.** ___ ___ ___ ___
3. Take away **eel** from **wheel** and put in **ale.** Then add **'s.**

   ___ ___ ___ ___ ___
4. Take **m** away from **mail** and put in **t** ___ ___ ___ ___
5. Take **b** away from **books** and put in **l.** ___ ___ ___ ___ ___
6. Take **n** away from **an.** ___
7. Take **t** away from **tail** and add **s.** ___ ___ ___ ___

   _____ _____ _____ _____ _____ _____ _____.

▶▶LONG -e PATTERNS

-e, -ee, -ea, -ey Patterns

Pattern words: he, me, she, bee,* see, free, three, tree; sea, peas, tea,* key*.

Mixed practice: bee, brave, see, save, trap, tree, three.

Scrambled sentence: The bees are in the tree.

Reading: Vinje, M. (1992). *I don't like peas.* Grand Haven, MI: School Zone.

Functional reading: frozen peas, boxes of tea bags.

Rhymes: "A Sailor Went to Sea"; "Rain"; "Lock and Key."

Sorting: bee, see, free, three, tree, hay, day, may, say, stay, gray, play, rain, train, pain, chain.

Riddle: I sound just like *tea,* but I am not something to drink and I am not spelled *t-e-a.* I hold up a football or a golf ball. What am I? (a tee)

Spelling: he, me, she, see, free, tree, three.

Writing: Have students make a list of the three things that they like to do most in their free time.

-eep Pattern

Pattern words: jeep, deep, beep, keep, sleep, sheep.*

Mixed practice: bee, beep, see, sleep, she, sheep.

Scrambled sentence: Sheep sleep at night.

Reading: Gregorick, B. (1984). *Beep, beep.* Grand Haven, MI: School Zone.

Rhyme: "Little Bo-Peep."

Rhyme riddle: What kind of a sleep do fish who are at the bottom of the sea have? (deep sleep)

Sorting: jeep, deep, beep, keep, sleep, sheep, bee, see, free, three, tree, hay, day, may, say, stay, gray, play.

Spelling: keep, sleep, jeep, sheep.

Writing: Have students tell what they would keep if they had to leave their homes and they could only keep three things. Encourage them to explain their choices.

-een, -ean Patterns

Pattern words: queen,* green, seen; bean,* lean, mean, clean.

Mixed practice: bean, beep, sleep, seen, sheep.

Scrambled sentence: Have you seen the can of beans?

Reading: Simon, S. (1985). *Benny's baby brother.* Grand Haven, MI: School Zone.

Rhymes: "Rain"; "Jack Sprat."

Functional reading: green beans, baked beans.

Sorting: queen, green, seen; bean, lean, mean, clean, jeep, deep, beep, keep, sleep, sheep, he, she, me, see, tree, sea (sort by rhyme only, not spelling).

Riddle: I sound like a name. But I am something that you put on. I rhyme with *beans.* What am I? (jeans)

Spelling: green, seen, mean, clean.

Writing: Students make a list of things that they like that are green, or make a "What-Is-Green?" booklet in which they tell about things that are green.

-eet, eat Patterns

Pattern words: feet,* meet, sweet, street; seat,* eat, beat, heat, meat, neat.

Mixed practice: bean, beat, seen, seat, keep, meat, mean.

Scrambled sentence: Did you eat the meat?

Reading: Tripp, V. (1987). *Baby koala finds a home.* Chicago: Children's Press.

   Ziefert, H. (1995). *The little red hen.* New York: Puffin.

Writing: Students write about some sweet foods that they like.

Rhyme: "Little Puppy Dog."

Song: "She'll Be Comin' 'Round the Mountain."

Sorting: feet, meet, sweet; seat, beat, heat, meat, neat, queen, green, seen.

Bingo: with -ean, -eep, -eet words.

Making words: Distribute the letters: *a, e, m, t*.

> ➤ Use two letters to make the word *me*.
> ➤ Add a letter to make the word *met*.
> ➤ Change a letter to make the word *mat*.
> ➤ Using all the letters, make a word. (*meat*)

Riddle: I rhyme with *sweet*. And I am something to eat. What am I? (meat)

Spelling: feet, meet, sweet, heat.

Writing: Students make a list of things that they like that are sweet.

eal, -eel Patterns

Pattern words: seal,* meal, real, steal; wheel,* feel, heel, peel.

Mixed practice: feel, feet, heel, heat, meet, meal, seal, seat.

Scrambled sentence: I saw a real seal.

Song: "Wheels on the Bus."

Reading: Bonsall, C. (1974). *And I mean it, Stanley*. New York: Harper Collins.

Sorting: seal, meal, real, steal; wheel, feel, heel, peel, feet, meet, sweet; seat, beat, heat, meat, neat, deep, jeep, peep, weep (sort by rhyme only, not spelling).

Rhyme riddle: What do you call fish that are given to a seal to eat? (seal meal)

Spelling: feel, meal, real.

Writing: Students write about things that make them feel happy. Model the process of selecting and developing a topic by talking over some of the things that make you feel happy.

-ead, -eed Patterns

Pattern words: read, bead,* lead (v); seed,* feed, need, weed.

Mixed practice: real, read, wheel, weed, feel, feet, seed, seal.

Scrambled sentence: Feed the seeds to the birds.

Sorting: read, bead, lead (v); seed, feed, need, weed, seal, meal, real, steal; wheel, feel, heel, peel, feet, meet, sweet; seat, beat, heat, meat, neat (sort by rhyme only, not spelling).

Rhyme riddle: Where do weeds come from? (weed seeds)

Spelling: read, need, feed.

Writing: Have students talk and then write about the kinds of books that they like to read. You might also want to create a bulletin board featuring the drawings and written pieces about students' favorite books.

-eam Pattern

Pattern words: team, cream, dream,* scream, stream.

Mixed practice: team, tame, cake, cream, dream, drag, seem, scream, stream.

Functional reading: ice cream, cream cheese, whipped cream.

Reading: "Ice Cream" fold-and-read book. Text-walk: Students should be able to read the rhymes independently. If they do have difficulty, help them apply appropriate word analysis strategies. After students have read the rhymes silently, discuss them and invite them to read their favorites orally.

Rhyme: "Ice Cream Rhyme."

Song: "Row the Boat."

Sorting: team, cream, dream, scream, stream, read, bead, lead (v); seed, feed, need, weed.

Making words: Distribute the letters: *a, e, m, r, s, t.*

- ➤ Use two letters to make the word *me.*
- ➤ Use three letters to make the word *tea.*
- ➤ Add a letter to make the word *team.*
- ➤ Add a letter to make the word *steam.*
- ➤ Use four letters to make the word *meat.*
- ➤ Using all the letters, make a word. (*stream*)

Rhyme riddle: What do you call it when you yell during a dream? (dream scream)

Spelling: dream, cream, stream.

Writing: Have students talk and write about their dreams for the future.

Long -e Unit Review.   On the chalkboard or an overhead, write the long-*e* words presented in this unit. Mix the patterns so students aren't simply using the first word as a clue to the other words in that column. Words listed in the sorting exercises can be used for this purpose. If students are not able to read 90% of the words, continue to review them until they are able to do so.

Concentration: Pairs of students play concentration with long-*e* words.

Secret message: Write the words on the lines and read the secret message.

1. Change the **W** in **Wish** to **F.** ___ ___ ___ ___
2. Change the **t** in **steep** to l. ___ ___ ___ ___ ___
3. Change the **j** in **jeep** to **d.** ___ ___ ___ ___
4. Take the **f** from **fin.** ___ ___
5. Keep **the** just as it is. ___ ___ ___
6. Change the **t** in **tea** to **s.** ___ ___ ___

_____ _____ _____ _____ _____ _____ .

➤➤LONG *-i* PATTERNS

-ie, -igh Patterns

Pattern words: pie, lie, tie,* die; high,* sigh.

Mixed practice: pie, tea, see, sigh, he, high.

Scrambled sentence: We ate the pie.

Shared reading: "Little Jack Horner."

Functional reading: pie.

Sorting: pie, lie, tie, die; high, sigh, team, cream, dream, scream, stream, seed, feed, need, weed (sort by rhyme only, not spelling).

Riddle: I am round and am good to eat. I rhyme with *tie.* What am I? (a pie)

Spelling: pie, lie, high.

Writing: Students draw a picture of a pie that they like and write a piece that tells about it.

-ight Pattern

Pattern words: night,* fight, light, might, right, sight, tight.

Mixed practice: tie, tight, light, lie, sigh, sight.

Scrambled sentence: I see a bright light.

Reading: Shebar, S. (1979). *Night monsters.* Provo, UT: Aro Publishing.

Ziefert, H. (1984). *Sleepy dog.* New York: Random.

"Bear Cat" fold-and-read story. Text-walk: Have students look at the first page and tell what animal is shown. Have them point to the word *bear.* Tell them that the bear cat has long hair. Have them point to the words "long hair." Have students read the rest of the selection to find out where bear cats live and what they eat. After students have read the selection silently, have them tell where bear cats live and what they eat. Have them read sentences orally that support their answers.

Rhymes: "Fright and Bright"; "Star Light, Star Bright."

Sorting: night, fight, light, might, right, sight, tight, pie, lie, tie, die; high, sigh, cream, dream, scream, stream (sort by rhyme only, not spelling).

Rhyme riddle: What do you call something that is easy to see and rhymes with *night?* (bright sight)

Spelling: night, light, might, right.

Writing: Students make a list of things that they like to do at night.

-ike Pattern

Pattern words: bike,* hike, like, Mike, strike.

Mixed practice: bike, bake, hike, hate, like, late, strike, slip.

Scrambled sentence: I like my bike.

Rhyme: "Three Little Bugs."

Reading: Greydanus, R. (1980). *Mike's new bike.* Mahtawah, NJ: Troll.

Sorting: bike, hike, like, Mike, strike, night, fight, light, might, right, sight, tight, pie, lie, tie, die; high, sigh.

Rhyme riddle: What do you call a long trip on a bike? (bike hike)

Spelling: bike, like, hike.

Writing: Students make a list of things that they like to do during the day.

-ide Pattern

Pattern words: ride,* hide, side, slide, wide.

Mixed practice: hide, hike, ride, rake, side, sight, wide, wake.

Scrambled sentence: Do not ride side by side.

Rhyme: "Little Old Man."

Song: "The Bear Went over the Mountain."

Reading: Gordh, B. (1999). *Hop right on.* Golden Books.

Ziefert, H. (1987). *Jason's bus ride.* New York: Puffin.

Making words: Distribute the letters: *d, e, i, l, s.*

➤ Use three letters to make the word *lie.*
➤ Change a letter to make *lid.*
➤ Add a letter to make the word *slid.*
➤ Use four letters to make the word *side.*
➤ Using all the letters, make a word. (*slide*)

Sorting: ride, hide, side, slide, wide, night, fight, light, might, right, sight, tight, bike, hike, like, Mike, strike.

Rhyme riddle: What do you call a slide that a whale might use? (a wide slide)

Spelling: hide, ride, side, wide.

Writing: Students make a list of things that they like to ride.

-ime, -yme Patterns

Pattern words: time, dime,* lime; rhyme.*

Mixed practice: dime, den, time, Tim, like, lime.

Scrambled sentence: Mike paid five dimes for a lime.

Functional reading: lime Jello or other labels that contain the word *lime*.

Sorting: time, dime, lime, rhyme, ride, hide, side, slide, wide, fight, light, might, right, sight, tight (sort by rhyme only, not spelling).

Riddle: Some people say that I fly, but I have no wings. I go by every day, but no one sees me. I rhyme with *dime*. What am I? (time)

Spelling: time, dime, lime.

Writing: Students draw a picture about the time of day that they like best and then write a piece about their pictures. To stimulate students' writing, model the assignment by drawing a picture of your favorite time of day and writing a short piece about it.

-ine Pattern

Pattern words: nine,* line, mine, pine, vine, shine.

Mixed practice: line, lime, main, mine, pain, pine, vine, van, shop, shine.

Scrambled sentence: We got in line at nine.

Reading: Allen, J. (1987). *My first job.* Provo, UT: Aro Publishing.

Sorting: nine, line, mine, pine, vine, shine, ride, hide, side, slide, wide, night, fight, light, might, right, sight, tight.

Bingo: with -ine, -ide, -ike words.

Reading: "Come on In" fold-and-read book.

Rhymes: "One, Two, Three, Four, Five"; "Come on In."

Riddle: I have no hands or feet, but I can climb up a tree or a wall. My name rhymes with *nine*. What am I? (a vine)

Spelling: nine, line, mine, shine.

Writing: Students list the nine best times in their lives or nine things that they like best.

-ice Pattern

Pattern words: mice, ice, nice, rice, twice.

Mixed practice: mice, mine, nine, nice, rice, rain, twice.

Scrambled sentence: Mice like rice.

Rhyme: "What Are Little Boys Made Of?"

Reading: Hoff, S. (1988). *Mrs. Brice's mice.* New York: Harper Collins.

Functional reading: labels containing the word *rice:* uncooked rice, rice pudding, rice cakes, Rice Krispies.

Sorting: mice, ice, nice, rice, twice, nine, line, mine, pine, vine, shine, time, dime, lime.

Riddle: I am a word. I have *ice* in me. I mean "two times." What word am I? (*twice*)

Spelling: ice, nice, rice, twice.

Writing: Students make a list of things that they think are nice.

-ile, -ife Patterns

Pattern words: mile, pile, smile,* while, life, wife, knife.*

Mixed practice: mice, mile, pill, pile, slide, smile, wide, while.

Scrambled sentence: He smiles while he is singing.

Rhymes: "Three Blind Mice"; "Little Tommy Tucker."

Song: "Five Miles from Home."

Functional reading: replica of a traffic sign containing the word *miles*.

Sorting: mile, pile, smile, while, life, wife, knife, mice, ice, nice, rice, twice.

Riddle: I have a *mile* in me, but I am not long. When you see me, you can tell that someone is happy. What word am I? (a *smile*)

Spelling: ice, nice, rice, twice.

Writing: Encourage students to make a list of things that make them smile. Model the process of developing a topic by talking over some of the things that make you smile.

-ite Pattern

Pattern words: bite, kite,* quite, white.

Mixed practice: bite, bright, night, kite, quit, quite, white, while.

Scrambled sentence: The moon was quite bright.

Rhyme: "One, Two, Three, Four, Five."

Sorting: bite, kite, quite, white, mile, pile, smile, nice, rice, twice.

Rhyme riddle: I am not a bird or a plane, but I can fly high in the sky. I rhyme with *white*. What am I? (a kite)

Spelling: bite, quite, white.

Writing: Students make a list of things that are white: clouds, snow, sheep.

-y Pattern

Pattern words: cry,* by, my, fly, dry, sky, why.

Mixed Practice: mile, my, sky, smile, wide, why, while.

Scrambled sentence: Jets fly in the sky.

Rhymes: "I Asked My Mother for Fifteen Cents"; "There Were Two Black-birds."

Reading: "Flying Car" fold-and-read book. Text-walk: Have students turn to p. 1. Explain that this story is about a car that can be a plane. Have them find the word *plane*. Have students read the story to find out how this car is able to fly and also able to ride on streets and roads. After students have read the selection, have them explain how it flies. Encourage them to read orally sentences that tell how the plane flies.

Sorting: cry, by, my, fly, dry, sky, why, mile, pile, smile, while, bite, kite, quite, white.

Rhyme riddle: What do you call a sky that has no rain? (dry sky)

Spelling: my, cry, sky, why, fly.

Writing: Students draw a picture of a bird flying high in the sky and write a piece about their drawings.

Long -i Unit Review. On the chalkboard or an overhead, write the long-*i* words presented in this unit. Mix the patterns so students aren't simply using the first word as a clue to the other words in that column.

Concentration: Pairs of students play concentration with long-*e* words.

Secret message: Write the words on the lines and read the secret message.

1. Add **B** to **right.** ___ ___ ___ ___ ___ ___
2. Add **s** to **miles.** ___ ___ ___ ___ ___ ___
3. Change the **t** in **tight** to **l.** ___ ___ ___ ___ ___.
4. Take the **c** from **cup.** ___ ___
5. Add **s** to **face.** ___ ___ ___ ___ ___

_____ _____ _____ _____.

➤➤LONG -*o* PATTERNS

-*o*, -*oe* Patterns

Pattern words: go, no,* so; Joe, toe.

Mixed practice: he, Joe, me, go, we, so, see, no, she, toe.

Scrambled sentence: I see Joe.

Shared reading: Issacesen, B., & Holland, M. (1986). *No, no, Joan!*

Sorting: go, no, so, Joe, toe, cry, by, my, fly, dry, sky, why.

Riddle: What do you call when you have a bad toe? (a toe truck)

Spelling: no, go, so.

Writing: Students tell about things they like to go to see: I like to go to see

_____.

-*ow* Pattern

Pattern words: crow,* row, low, grow, show, slow, know.

Mixed Practice: crow, cry, low, lie, row, show, shy, slow, sky.

Scrambled sentence: Row the boat slowly.

Reading: Cobb, A. (1996). *Wheels.* New York: Random House.

Greene, C. (1982). *Snow Joe.* Chicago: Children's Press.

O'Connor, J. (1986). *The teeny tiny woman.* New York: Random. (especially appropriate for older students.)

"If You're Happy" fold-and-read book. Text-walk: Briefly review potentially hard words. Read the title, "If You're Happy and You Know It," to students. Have students point to the words *happy* and *know.* Explain that "Row the Boat" tells about rowing a boat gently and merrily. Have students find the words *gently* and *merrily.* Also discuss how a boat might be rowed *gently* and *merrily.* Read the title, "One for the Money," to students and have them point to the word *money.* Tell them that the rhyme tells about making ready. Have them find the word *ready* and discuss what "Make ready" might mean. Read the title, "Jumping Joan," and explain that sometimes nobody is with Jumping Joan. Have students point to the word *nobody.* Have students read the selections to see which one they like best. After students have read the selections, discuss their favorites and have them read their favorites out loud. Discuss, too, why Jumping Joan is a funny rhyme.

Rhymes: "One for the Money"; "Clouds"

Song: "If You're Happy and You Know It."

Rhyme riddle: What do you call it when you row, but you do not row fast? (slow row)

Sorting: crow, row, low, grow, show, slow, know, go, no, so, Joe, toe.

Spelling: low, grow, show, slow, know.

Writing: Students write about some things that they know now but they didn't know before the school year began. Discuss things that they know and model writing on the topic.

-oat, -ote Patterns
Pattern words: goat,* boat, coat, float; note,* wrote.

Mixed practice: crow, coat, goat, grow, float, boat, belt, no, note, wrote.

Scrambled sentence: A goat jumped into the boat.

Reading: McDermott, G. (1999). *Fox and the stork.* San Diego: Harcourt.

   Milos, Rita. (1989). *The hungry billy goat.* Chicago: Children's Press.

Song: "The Mocking Bird."

Sorting: goat, boat, coat, float; note, wrote, crow, row, low, grow, show, slow, know.

Making words: Distribute the letters: *h, o, r, t, w.*

➤ Use three letters to make the word *row.*
➤ Change a letter to make the word *tow.*
➤ Using all the letters, make a word. (*throw*)

Rhyme riddle: What do you call a ship that has a lot of goats? (goat boat)

Spelling: goat, boat, coat, note, wrote.

Writing: Students write about a boat trip they have taken or a boat trip that they might like to take.

-oad Pattern
Pattern words: toad, load, road.*

Mixed practice: low, load, tow, toad, row, road.

Scrambled sentence: There is a toad in the road.

Song: "I've Been Working on the Railroad."

Reading: Schade, S., & Buller, J. (1992). *Toad on the road.* New York: Random House.

Sorting: toad, load, road, goat, boat, coat, float; note, wrote.

Rhyme riddle: What do you call a road that toads use? (toad road)

Spelling: toad, load, road.

Writing: Students draw a picture or a map showing the road on which they live. They then write a piece that tells about the picture or map.

-ole, -oll Patterns
Pattern words: mole,* hole, pole, stole; roll,* toll.

Mixed practice: roll, road, hole, hot, pole, mole, meet.

Scrambled sentence: The ball rolled into the hole.

Song: "Merrily We Roll Along."

Reading: Armstrong, J. (1996). *The snowball.* New York: Random.

   Gregorich, B. (1991). *Nicole digs a hole.* Grand Haven, MI: School Zone.

Functional reading: labels for rolls.

Sorting: mole, hole, pole, stole; roll, toll, toad, load, road, goat, boat, coat, float, note, wrote (sort by rhyme only, not spelling).

Riddle: This word means "all of it" but it has a *hole* in it. It rhymes with *mole*. What is it? (*whole*)

Spelling: hole, pole, roll.

Writing: Discuss moles and have students write a sentence that tells about moles.

-old Pattern

Pattern words: old, gold,* cold, fold, hold, sold, told.

Mixed practice: hold, hole, so, sold, go, gold, toe, told.

Scrambled sentence: She told us an old story.

Rhyme: "Old King Cole."

Reading: Ziefert, H. (1988). *Strike four!* New York: Penguin.

Functional reading: replica of a "sold" sign.

Sorting: old, gold, cold, fold, hold, sold, told, mole, hole, pole, stole; roll, toll, toad, load, road (sort by rhyme only, not spelling).

Riddle: I am yellow and rhyme with *sold*. You can buy things with me. What am I? (gold)

Spelling: old, gold, cold, fold, hold, sold, told.

Writing: Students draw a picture of themselves and then write a sentence telling how old they are.

-oak, -oke Patterns

Pattern words: oak,* soak; woke, joke, broke, spoke, smoke.*

Mixed practice: poke, sold, soak, cold, choke, bold, broke.

Scrambled sentence: Soak the dirt around the oak tree.

Rhyme: "Owl."

Sorting: oak, soak; woke, joke, broke, spoke, smoke, old, gold, cold, fold, hold, sold, told, bowl, hole, mole, roll, whole (sort by rhyme only, not spelling).

Bingo: with -old, -ow, -oke words.

Rhyme riddle: What do you call a funny story about an oak tree? (oak joke)

Spelling: woke, joke, broke, spoke.

Writing: Students write a favorite joke or riddle that they have heard or read or make one up.

-ose Pattern

Pattern words: hose, nose,* rose, chose, close, those.

Mixed practice: hose, hole, nose, note, those, throw.

Scrambled sentence: She chose a red rose.

Reading: "Adult Elephant's Trunk" fold-and-read book. Text-walk: Direct students' attention to p. 1. Explain that this is a story about an animal that has a big nose. Have them find the word *animal*. Have students read the story to find out which animal has the biggest nose and how it uses that nose. After students have read the story, discuss how the elephant uses its nose. Have students read sentences that support their responses orally.

Rhyme: "Little Girl, Little Girl, Where Have You Been?"

Sorting: hose, nose, rose, chose, close, those, oak, soak; woke, joke, broke, spoke, smoke, old, gold, cold, fold, hold, sold, told (sort by rhyme only, not spelling).

Riddle: I am right on the front of your face. Others can see me, but you cannot. I rhyme with *rose*, but I am not a flower. What am I? (your nose)

Spelling: nose, rose, chose, close, those.

Writing: Students discuss and make a list of things that their noses like to smell: cookies baking, supper cooking, mom's perfume.

-one Pattern

Pattern words: bone, alone, phone.*

Mixed practice: boat, bone, alone, float, phone.

Scrambled sentence: She sat alone by the phone. (Discuss different ways in which this sentence can be reassembled.)

Rhymes: "Little Bo-Peep"; "Jumping Joan."

Functional reading: replica of a phone sign.

Sorting: bone, alone, phone, hose, nose, rose, chose, close, those, woke, joke, broke, spoke, smoke.

Rhyme riddle: You talk into me but not to me. I rhyme with *bone*. What am I? (a phone)

Spelling: bone, alone, phone.

Writing: Students make a list of things they like to do when they are alone.

Long-o Unit Review. On the chalkboard or an overhead, write the long-*o* words presented in this unit. Mix the patterns so students aren't simply using the first word as a clue to the other words in that column. Words listed in the sorting exercises can be used for this purpose. If students are not able to read 90% of the words, continue to review them until they are able to do so.

Concentration: Pairs of students play concentration with long-*o* words.

Secret message: Write the words on the lines and read the secret message.

1. Take the **h** from **hold.** ___ ___ ___
2. Change the **g** in **goat** to **b.** Add **s.** ___ ___ ___ ___ ___
3. Add **c** to **an.** ___ ___ ___
4. Take an **e** from **bee.** ___ ___
5. Add **s** to **home.** ___ ___ ___ ___ ___

_____ _____ _____ _____ _____.

Rhymes: "Fooba Wooba John"; "The Goat."

▶▶LONG-*u* PATTERNS

-ule, -use, -uge, -ute, -ew (few) Patterns

Pattern words: mule,* use, huge, cute, few.

Mixed practice: use, us, hug, huge, fake, few, cut, cute.

Scrambled sentence: The farmer has a few mules.

Sorting: cup, bus, bug, jump, run, trunk, mule, use, huge, cute (sort by vowel sound).

Spelling: use, huge, few.

Riddle: My dad is a donkey, and my mom is a horse. I have very long ears. I am not cute, but I work very hard. What am I? (a mule)

Writing: Have students make a list of animals that are huge.

Secret message: Write the words on the lines and read the secret message.

1. Drop the **n** from **An.** ___
2. Change the **y** in **yule** to **m.** ___ ___ ___ ___
3. Add **c** to **an.** ___ ___ ___
4. Change the **m** in **marry** to **c.** ___ ___ ___ ___ ___
5. Add an **e** to **hug.** ___ ___ ___ ___
6. Change the **t** in **toad** to **l.** ___ ___ ___ ___

——— ——— ——— ——— ——— ———.

➤➤R-VOWEL PATTERNS

-ar Pattern

Pattern words: car, far, jar, tar, star.*

Mixed practice: car, cat, far, fed, tar, tea, star, stop.

Scrambled sentence: The jars are in the car.

Rhymes: "Twinkle, Twinkle, Little Star"; "Star Light, Star Bright"; "Help! Murder! Police!"

Reading: Ziefert, H. (1990). *Stitches.* New York: Puffin Books.

Sorting: car, far, jar, tar, star, bone, alone, phone, hose, nose, rose, chose, those.

Rhyme riddle: What do you call a star that is way up in the sky? (far star)

Spelling: car, far, jar, star.

Writing: Have students tell about a time when they went far away or a place that is far away that they would like to visit.

-ark Pattern

Pattern words: park, bark, dark, mark, shark.*

Mixed practice: car, bark, far, mark, dark, jar, park.

Scrambled sentence: The park closes at dark.

Rhyme: "Bedtime."

Reading: Cole, J. (1986). *Hungry, hungry sharks.* New York: Random House.

Functional reading: Display a replica of a sign for a park.

Sorting: park, bark, dark, mark, shark, car, far, jar, tar, star, bone, alone, phone.

Rhyme riddle: What do you call a place where sharks play? (shark park)

Spelling: park, bark, dark, mark.

Writing: Have students draw a picture of the kind of park in which they would like to play and then write a piece telling about the park.

-arm Pattern

Pattern words: arm,* farm, harm.
Mixed practice: are, arm, farm, feed, harm, heel.
Scrambled sentence: Rain will not harm the farm.
Functional reading: replica of a sign for a farm or a label that uses the word *farm.*
Sorting: arm, farm, harm, park, bark, dark, mark, shark, car, far, jar, tar, star.
Riddle: Hands need me. If hands did not have me, they could not do anything. My name rhymes with *farms.* What am I? (arms)
Spelling: arm, farm, harm.
Writing: Have students write a piece telling how they use their arms. Alter the assignment if any of the students is unable to use his or her arms.

-art, -eart Patterns

Pattern words: art, cart,* chart, part, smart, start; heart.*

Mixed practice: are, art, car, cart, star, start.

Scrambled sentence: Art sat in the cart.

Making words: Distribute the letters: *a, r, s, t, t.*

➤ Use three letters to make the word *art.*
➤ Use the same three letters to make the word *tar.*
➤ Add a letter to make the word *star.*
➤ Using all the letters, make a word. (*start*)

Sorting: art, cart, part, smart, start; heart, arm, farm, harm (sort by spelling).

Bingo: with *-ark, -ar, -art* words.

Riddle: I can carry people and things. *Car* is part of my name, but I am not a car. I rhyme with *start.* What am I? (a cart)

Spelling: arm, farm, harm.

Writing: Have students write about the smartest animal they know or about a smart deed that an animal they know has done.

-air, -are, -ere, -ear Patterns

Pattern words: air, hair, pair, chair*; care, share, scare, square,* where,* there, bear,* wear, pear.

Mixed practice: care, cart, hair, harm, chair, chart, share, scare.

Scrambled sentence: A pair of bears scared me.

Rhymes: "Pussy-cat, Pussy-cat"; "Simple Simon"; "Old Chairs to Mend."

Reading: Arnold, M. (1996). *Quick, quack, quick!* New York: Random House.

Blocksma, M. (1984). *The best dressed bear.* Chicago: Children's Press.

Functional reading: pears.

Sorting: air, hair, pair, chair; care, share, scare, where, there (sort by spelling).

Rhyme riddle: What do you call a bear that likes to sit? (chair bear)

Spelling: air, hair, pair, chair; care, share, scare, where, there.

Writing: Have students draw a picture of and write a piece about a chair that they like best. Encourage them to describe the chair and tell why they like it. Students might also create a homophone book in which they depict word pairs such as *hair, hare; pair, pear, stair, stare; where, wear.*

-or, -ore, -oor, -ore, -our Patterns

Pattern words: or, for; more, sore, tore, wore, store*; door,* poor, floor, four,* pour.

Mixed practice: for, far, mark, more, tar, tore, poor, part, pour.

Scrambled sentence: Open the door to the store.

Rhymes: "It's Raining, It's Pouring"; "The North Wind Doth Blow"; "It Ain't Going to Rain No More."

Reading: Ziefert, H. (1997). *The magic porridge pot.* New York: Puffin.

Functional reading: replica of a sign containing the word *store.*

Sorting: or, for; more, sore, tore, wore, score, store; door, poor, floor (sort by spelling).

Rhyme riddle: What do you call a place that sells doors? (a door store)

Spelling: for; more, tore, wore, score, store; door, poor, floor.

Writing: Have students draw a picture of and write a piece about a store that they like to go to. Encourage them to tell what they like about the store. Have students enter *for—four; poor—pour* into the homophone sections of their notebooks, with sentences or drawings to illustrate the meanings of the words.

-orn Pattern

Pattern words: born, corn, horn,* torn; warn.

Mixed practice: born, boat, corn, coat, tore, torn, warn.

Scrambled sentence: My coat is torn.

Rhymes: "The Donkey"; "Little Boy Blue"; "Red Sky."

Reading: Gelman, R. G. (1977). *More spaghetti I say.* New York: Scholastic.

Functional reading: corn, corn flakes.

Sorting: born, corn, horn, torn; more, sore, tore, wore, score, store; door, poor, floor, air, hair, pair, bear, pear, where, there whole (sort by rhyme only, not spelling).

Riddle: I have ears but I cannot hear. I rhyme with *horn*. What am I? (corn)

Spelling: born, corn, horn, torn.

Writing: Have students write a sentence telling when and where they were born.

-ir, -ur, -urse, -er Patterns

Pattern words: sir, stir,* fur, nurse,* purse, her.

Mixed practice: sir, sore, store, stir, born, bird.

Scrambled sentence: Her kittens were not in their box.

Rhymes: "I'll Sing You a Song"; "Burnie Bee."

Sorting: sir, stir, fur, nurse, purse, born, corn, horn, torn (sort by rhyme only, not spelling).

Making words: Distribute the letters: *e, o, r, s, t.*

➤ Use four letters to make the word *sore.*
➤ Change one letter to make the word *tore.*
➤ Change one letter and make the word *rest.*
➤ Using all the letters, make a word. (*store*)

Riddle: I have fur. And I can purr. I like to run after birds and rats. My name rhymes with *hat*. What am I? (a cat)

Spelling: sir, stir, fur, nurse, her.

Writing: Have students tell what they would do if they had a magical purse that never ran out of money.

-urn, -earn, -ire Patterns

Pattern words: burn, turn*; earn, learn*; fire, tire,* wire.

Mixed practice: sir, sore, store, stir, tir, turn, tore, wire.

Scrambled sentence: We learned how to spell *earn.*

Rhyme: "Fire! Fire!"

Sorting: burn, turn, earn, learn; fire, tire, wire, sir, stir, fur (sort by rhyme only, not spelling).

Riddle: I am not a wheel, but I go round and round. I rhyme with *wire*. What am I? (a tire)

Spelling: burn, turn; earn, learn.

Writing: Students discuss and write about some important or interesting things that they have learned during the past week.

-ird, -eard, -ord, -erd Patterns

Pattern words: bird,* third; word*; herd,* heard.*

Mixed practice: bird, born, third, torn, were, word, her, herd, heard.

Scrambled sentence: I don't know the third word.

Rhyme: "The Mocking Bird."

Sorting: bird, third; word; herd, heard, burn, turn; earn, learn, sir, stir, fur, nurse, purse (sort by rhyme only, not spelling).

Rhyme riddle: If birds could talk, what would their words be called? (bird words)

Spelling: bird, third, word, heard.

Writing: Have students draw a picture of and write a piece about their favorite birds. If possible, have bird books available so that students can have models for their drawings and a source of material for ideas.

-ear, -eer Patterns

Pattern words: ear,* dear, fear, hear, near; deer,* steer.

Mixed practice: fear, for, deer, door, hear, heart, steer, store, stir, turn, tore.

Scrambled sentence: The deer came near us.

Rhyme: "Up, Dear Children"; "Fears and Tears."

Reading: Hoffman, J. (1992). *The last game.* Grand Haven, MI: School Zone.

   Ziefert, H. (1989). *Dr. Cat.* New York: Penguin.

Sorting: ear, dear, fear, hear, near; deer, steer, bird, third; word; herd, burn, turn; earn, learn (sort by rhyme only, not spelling).

Riddle: What kind of deer is found in letters? (a d-e-a-r dear, as in "Dear Jan")

Spelling: ear, dear, fear, hear, near.

Writing: Have students close their eyes and use only their ears. Ask them to notice what they hear. Then have them open their eyes and list all the things they heard.

R-Vowel Unit Review.   On the chalkboard or an overhead, write the *r*-vowel pattern words presented in this unit. Mix the patterns so students aren't simply using the first word as a clue to the other words in that column. Words listed in the sorting exercises can be used for this purpose. If students are not able to read 90% of the words, continue to review them until they are able to do so.

Concentration: Pairs of students play concentration with *r*-vowel words.

Secret message: Write the words on the lines and read the secret message.

1. Take away the **p** from **Parks** and put in **Sh.** ___ ___ ___ ___ ___ ___
2. Add **c** to **an.** ___ ___ ___
3. Add **s** to **care.** ___ ___ ___ ___ ___
4. Add **d** to the end **an** ___ ___ ___
5. Add **h** to **arm.** ___ ___ ___ ___
6. Take **b** away from **bus.** ___ ___

_____ _____ _____ _____ _____ _____.

Rhyme: "Wishes."

➤➤/aw/ PATTERNS

In some dialects, *caught* and some other words included here with /aw/ patterns may be pronounced with a short-*o* sound, so that *caught* rhymes with *hot*. Make adjustments so that instruction fits your students' dialect.

-all Pattern

Pattern words: all, ball,* call, fall, hall, tall, wall, small.

Mixed practice: fall, fear, hear, hall, small, smear.

Scrambled sentence: Throw the small ball.

Rhymes: "Jack Hall"; "Go to Bed Late."

Sorting: all, ball, call, fall, hall, tall, wall, small, ear, dear, fear, hear, near; deer, bird, third; word; herd, heard (sort by rhyme only, not spelling).

Rhyme riddle: What do you call a high wall? (tall wall)

Spelling: all, ball, call, fall, tall, small.

Writing: Have students draw a picture about a game in which a ball is used. Then have them write about the picture they drew.

-aw Pattern

Pattern words: saw,* paw, law, claw, draw.

Mixed practice: saw, small, call, claw, law, lead, draw, drop.

Scrambled sentence: Cats' paws have sharp claws.

Reading: Mann, P. Z.(1999). *Meet my monster.* Pleasantville, NY: Reader's Digest.

Rhyme: "I Saw Esau."

Making Words: Distribute the letters: *a, c, l, s, w.*

➤ Use three letters make the word *saw.*
➤ Change a letter to make *law.*
➤ Change a letter to make *caw* as in "The crows caw."
➤ Using all the letters, make a word. (*claws*)

Sorting: saw, paw, law, claw, draw, all, ball, call, fall, hall, tall, wall, small, ear, dear, fear, hear.

Rhyme riddle: I have teeth, but I can't eat. But I can cut a piece of wood in two. I rhyme with *paw.* What am I? (a saw)

Spelling: all, ball, call, fall, tall, small.

Writing: Have students draw a picture of something interesting or special that they saw today or this week. It could be something that was funny or just interesting.

-alk Pattern

Pattern words: walk,* talk, chalk.

Mixed practice: talk, tall, wall, walk, claw, chalk; hawk.

Scrambled sentence: We will talk while we walk home.

Reading: Brenner, B. (1989). *Annie's pet.* New York: Bantam.

Sorting: walk, talk, chalk, saw, paw, law, claw, draw, all, ball, call, fall, hall, tall, wall, small.

Riddle: I fly high in the sky, but I am not a plane. I rhyme with *walk.* What am I? (hawk)

Spelling: walk, talk, chalk.

Writing: Have students write about the person they most like to talk to.

-aught, -ought, -ost Patterns

Pattern words: caught,* taught; ought, bought,* brought; cost, lost*.

Mixed practice: bought, ball, brought, call, caught, talk, taught.

Scrambled sentence: We brought the lost dog to its owner.

Rhyme: "Two Cats of Kilkenny."

Song: "Skip to My Lou."

Sorting: caught, taught; ought, bought, brought; cost, lost, walk, talk, chalk (sort by rhyme only, not spelling).

Spelling: caught, taught; ought, bought, brought; cost, lost.

Riddle: Boys and girls mix me up with *bought*. But *bought* means "buy" in time that has passed. I mean "bring" in time that has passed. I also have one more sound than *bought* does. What word am I? (*brought*)

Writing: Have students draw a picture of something that they lost either recently or a long time ago. Have them write a piece that tells about the lost item. Model the assignment by drawing a picture of something you lost and writing a brief piece about it.

-ong Pattern

Pattern words: long, song,* strong, wrong.

Mixed practice: long, lost, wrong, saw, song, strong.

Scrambled sentence: The birds sang a long song.

Reading: Rylant, C. (1989). *Henry and Mudge get the cold shivers*. New York: Bradbury Press.

Song: "Oh Where, Oh Where Has My Little Dog Gone?"

Sorting: long, song, strong, wrong, caught, taught; ought, bought, brought; walk, talk, chalk (sort by rhyme only, not spelling).

Riddle: I am a word that you do not like to hear. I rhyme with *song*. I am not right, so I must be _____. (wrong)

Spelling: caught, taught; ought, bought, brought; cost, lost.

Writing: Students discuss some interesting or funny things that happened to them a long time ago. Model the process by discussing and writing about some things that happened to you a long time ago.

/aw/ Pattern Unit Review.   On the chalkboard or an overhead, write the /aw/ pattern words presented in this unit. Mix the patterns so students aren't simply using the first word as a clue to the other words in that column. Words listed in the sorting exercises can be used for this purpose. If students are not able to read 90% of the words, continue to review them until they are able to do so. Most important, have students read books that contain /aw/ pattern words.

Concentration: Pairs of students play concentration with /aw/ vowel words.

Secret message: Write the words on the lines and read the secret message.

1. Take away the **M** from **Me** and put in **W**. ___ ___
2. Take away the **b** from **bought**. ___ ___ ___ ___ ___
3. Take an **o** from **too**. ___ ___
4. Take away the **s** from **snow** and put in **k**. ___ ___ ___ ___
5. Take away the **b** from **bright**. ___ ___ ___ ___ ___
6. Take away the **s** from **song** and put in **wr**. ___ ___ ___ ___ ___

_____ _____ _____ _____ _____ _____.

➤➤LONG-/oo/ PATTERNS

-oo, -oon, -une Patterns

Pattern words: zoo,* too, boo, moo, moon,* noon, soon, spoon, tune,* prune.

Mixed practice: moo, moon, zoo, soon, spoon, too, noon.

Scrambled sentence: The zoo opens at noon.

Rhyme: "Hey Diddle, Diddle"; "The Balloon."

Reading: Blocksma, M. (1992). *Yoo hoo, moon.* New York: Bantam.

Functional reading: prunes label.

Sorting: zoo, too, boo, moo, moon, noon, soon, spoon, tune, prune, long, song, strong, wrong (sort by rhyme only, not spelling).

Rhyme riddle: What would you call a zoo for cows? (a moo zoo)

Spelling: zoo, too, moon, noon, soon.

Writing: Students draw a picture of the moon and write a sentence about the moon.

ew, -ue Patterns

Pattern words: new,* chew, flew, grew; blue,* true, Sue.

Mixed practice: new, noon, Sue, soon, blue, boo.

Scrambled sentence: The blue plane flew up into the sky.

Rhymes: "Little Betty Blue"; "The Old Man of Peru."

Reading: Ziefert, H. (1997). *The ugly duckling.* New York: Puffin.

Functional reading: beef stew.

Sorting: new, chew, flew, grew; blue, true, Sue, moon, noon, soon, spoon, tune, prune, long, song, strong, wrong (sort by rhyme only, not spelling).

Riddle: I rhyme with *blue.* I am not a lie, so I must be _____. (true)

Spelling: new, flew, grew; blue, true.

Writing: Have students draw a picture of something new that they have or something new that they would like to have. Then have them write a piece that tells about their picture.

oot, -uit Patterns

Pattern words: boot,* hoot, toot, shoot; fruit,* suit.

Mixed practice: boot, blue, too, toot, suit, Sue, shoot.

Scrambled sentence: The roots of the fruit tree grew deep.

Song: "Take Me out to the Ball Game."

Reading: Gregorich, B. (1984). *Sue likes blue.* Grand Haven, MI: School Zone.

    Witty, B. (1991). *The raccoon on the moon.* Grand Haven, MI: School Zone.

Functional reading: fruit juice, fruit cocktail.

Sorting: boot, hoot, toot, shoot; fruit, suit, new, chew, flew, grew; blue, true, Sue, moon, noon, soon, spoon, tune, prune (sort by rhyme only, not spelling).

Making words: Distribute the letters: *h, o, o, s, t.*

➤ Use two letters to make *to,* as in "Go to school."
➤ Use three letters to make *too,* as in "I ate too much candy."
➤ Use four letters to make the word *hoot.*
➤ Using all the letters, make a word. (*shoot*)

Riddle: I can be a banana, a peach, or an apple. I can be a bunch of grapes or a lime. But I cannot be green beans or peas. What am I? (fruit)

Spelling: boot, shoot, fruit, suit.

Writing: Students draw a picture of their favorite fruits and write a sentence as a caption.

-ool, -ule Patterns

Pattern words: cool, fool, pool, tool, school*; rule.*

Mixed practice: fool, fruit, toot, tool, school, rule, suit.

Scrambled sentence: The new school has a swimming pool.

Rhymes: "This Is the Way We Go to School"; "Mary Had a Little Lamb."

Reading: Platt, K. (1977). *Big Max in the mystery of the missing moose.* New York: Harper Collins.

"Hey Diddle, Diddle" fold-and-read book.

Sorting: cool, fool, pool, tool, school, boot, hoot, toot, shoot; fruit, suit, new, chew, flew, grew; blue, true, Sue (sort by rhyme only, not spelling).

Rhyme riddle: What do you call a pool that is full of cold water? (cool pool)

Spelling: cool, fool, pool, tool, school.

Writing: Have students write a piece that tells about their school.

-oom; -oup Patterns

Pattern words: boom, broom, room, bloom, zoom; soup, group.

Mixed practice: boom, boot, bloom, room, root, zoom.

Scrambled sentence: He swept the room with a new broom.

Rhyme: "Old Woman, Old Woman."

Reading: Dussling, J. (1996). *Stars.* New York: Grosset & Dunlap.

Silverman, M. (1991). *My tooth is loose.* New York: Viking.

Functional reading: names of soups.

Sorting: boom, broom, room, bloom, zoom, cool, fool, pool, tool, school, boot, hoot, toot, shoot; fruit, suit (sort by rhyme only, not spelling).

Bingo: with -oom, -ew, and -oot words.

Rhyme riddle: What do you call a broom that sweeps very fast? (zoom broom)

Spelling: boom, broom, room, bloom.

Writing: Students draw a picture of the room in their homes that they like best and write a description of the room and tell why it is their favorite.

Long-/oo/ Unit Review. On the chalkboard or an overhead, write the long-*oo* vowel pattern words presented in this unit. Mix the patterns so students aren't simply using the first word as a clue to the other words in that column. Words listed in the sorting exercises can be used for this purpose. If students are not able to read 90% of the words, continue to review them until they are able to do so. Most important, have students read books that contain long-*oo* pattern words.

Concentration: Pairs of students play concentration with long-*oo* vowel words.

Secret message: Write the words on the lines and read the secret message.

1. Keep **The** just as it is. ___ ___ ___
2. Take away the **s** from **suit** and add **fr.** ___ ___ ___ ___ ___
3. Add **s** to **tree.** ___ ___ ___ ___ ___

4. Take away the **n** from **new** and add **gr.** ___ ___ ___ ___
5. Take away the **f** from **fall** and put in **t.** ___ ___ ___ ___

_____ _____ _____ _____ _____.

Rhyme: "What Animals Say."

►►SHORT-/oo/ PATTERNS

-ook Pattern

Pattern words: book, cook, look, took, shook.

Mixed practice: cool, cook, broom, book, shook, school, tool, took.

Scrambled sentence: Look at the book.

Rhymes: "Fishy-fishy"; "Little Bird."

Reading: Averill, E. (1960). *The fire cat.* New York: Harper & Row.

Sorting: book, cook, look, took, shook, boom, broom, room, bloom, zoom, cool, fool, pool, tool, school.

Riddle: I have many words. And I have stories. But I cannot talk. I rhyme with *look.* What am I? (a book)

Spelling: book, cook, look, took, shook.

Writing: Have students make a list of some good books that they have read.

-ood, -ould Patterns

Pattern words: wood,* good, hood, stood; could,* would, should.

Mixed practice: could, cook, should, shook, stood, hood, hook.

Scrambled sentence: Look at the book.

Rhyme: "Woodchuck."

Reading: Brenner, B. (1989). *Lion and lamb.* New York: Bantam.

Sorting: wood, good, hood, stood; could, would, should.

     book, cook, look, took, shook, boom, broom, room, bloom, zoom (sort by rhyme only, not spelling).

Riddle: I rhyme with *should* and sound just like *would* spelled w-o-u-l-d, but I am not *would* spelled w-o-u-l-d. You can knock on me and make things out of me. What am I? (wood)

Spelling: wood, good, could, would, should.

Writing: Students draw a picture of something they might make if they had a lot of wood. Students then write a brief piece about their drawings.

-ull, -ush Patterns

Pattern words: pull, full, bull; push, bush.

Mixed practice: pull, push, full, bush, wool.

Scrambled sentence: The bag is full of wool.

Rhyme: "Baa, Baa, Black Sheep."

Sorting: pull, full, bull; push, bush, wood, good, hood, stood; could, would, should (sort by rhyme only, not spelling).

Rhyme riddle: What do you call a bull that has had a lot to eat? (full bull)

Spelling: pull, full, push, bush.

Writing: Have students tell what they would do if they had a bag full of money. Also have students add *wood* and *would* to their homophone books.

Short-/oo/ Unit Review.   On the chalkboard or an overhead, write the short-*oo* vowel pattern words presented in this unit. Mix the patterns so students aren't simply using the first word as a clue to the other words in that column. Words listed in the sorting exercises can be used for this purpose. If students are not able to read 90% of the words, continue to review them until they are able to do so. Most important, have students read books that contain short-*oo* pattern words.

Concentration: Pairs of students play concentration with short-*oo* vowel words.

Secret message: Write the words on the lines and read the secret message.

1. Keep **You** just as it is. ___ ___ ___
2. Take away the **w** from **would** and add **sh.** ___ ___ ___ ___ ___ ___
3. Add **t** to **no.** ___ ___ ___
4. Take away the **b** from **bush** and add **p.** ___ ___ ___ ___
5. Take the **f** from **for.** ___ ___
6. Take away the **b** from **bull** and put in **p.** ___ ___ ___ ___

————— ————— ————— ————— ————— —————.

➤➤/ow/ PATTERNS

-ow (cow) Pattern

Pattern words: cow, how, now, wow.

Mixed practice: cow, call, hood, how, would, wow.

Scrambled sentence: The bag is full of wool.

Rhyme: "Bow, Wow, Wow."

Reading: Oppenheim, J. (1989). *"Not now!" said the cow.* New York: Bantam.

Sorting: cow, how, now, wow, pull, full, bull, wood, good, hood, stood.

Riddle: I am not later or sooner. I rhyme with *cow* and I am right _____. (now)

Spelling: cow, how, now, wow.

Writing: Explain to students that people say, "Wow!" when they want to show that they are happy or surprised. Have them draw a picture of a time when they said, "Wow!" and then write a piece that tells about the picture.

-own (town) Pattern

Pattern words: down, town, brown, crown,* clown.

Mixed practice: cow, clown, crown, now, not, boat, brown.

Scrambled sentence: Take the brown cow to town.

Rhymes: "Jack and Jill"; "Dickery, Dickery, Dare"; "Wee Willie Winkie."

Making words: Distribute the letters: *c, n, o, r, w.*

➤ Use two letters to make the word *ow.*
➤ Add a letter to make *cow.*
➤ Add a letter to make *now*
➤ Using all the letters, make a word. (*crown*)

Sorting: down, town, brown, crown, clown, cow, how, now, wow, wood, good, hood, stood.

Riddle: I rhyme with *clown.* I am not up, so I must be _____. (down)

Spelling: down, town, brown, clown.

Writing: Have students draw a picture of a clown and then write a piece that tells about their pictures.

-ound Pattern

Pattern words: found, sound, round, pound, ground.

Mixed practice: round, grow, ground, cow, clown, pound.

Scrambled sentence: She found her brown hat.

Rhyme: "Wheels on the Bus"; "Teddy Bear, Teddy Bear."

Reading: Raffi. (1988). *Wheels on the bus.* New York: Crown.

Functional reading: a lost-and-found sign.

Sorting: found, sound, round, pound, ground, down, town, brown, crown, clown, cow, how, now, wow.

Bingo: with *-ow, -own,* and *-ound* patterns.

Riddle: You cannot see me, but you can hear me. I rhyme with *found.* What am I? (sound)

Spelling: found, sound, round, pound, ground.

Writing: Have students write a list of the sounds that they like best.

-oud, owd Patterns

Pattern words: loud, cloud,* proud, crowd.

Mixed practice: low, loud, cloud, clown, cow, crowd, proud.

Scrambled sentence: The crowd was loud.

Rhyme: "Windy Nights."

Reading: Lobel, A. (1975). *Owl at home.* New York: Harper Collins.

Rylant, C. (1987). *Henry and Mudge under the yellow moon.* New York: Bradbury Press.

Sorting: loud, cloud, proud, crowd, found, sound, round, pound, ground, down, town, brown, crown, clown (sort by rhyme only, not spelling).

Riddle: I can be a lot of boys and girls. And I can be a lot of big people, too. I can also be loud. I rhyme with *proud,* but I have a *w* where *proud* has a *u.* and I begin with a *c* instead of a *p.* What am I? (a crowd)

Spelling: loud, cloud, proud, crowd.

Writing: Have students write a piece telling about something that they are proud of.

-out, -outh, -our, -ouse Patterns

Pattern words: out,* shout, mouth, south,* our, hour,* flour, house,* mouse.

Mixed practice: out, our, mouth, mouse, south, shout, hour, house.

Scrambled sentence: "Go south!" shouted Joe.

Rhymes: "There Was a Crooked Man"; "I'm a Little Teapot"; "Way Down South Where Bananas Grow"; "The Boy in the Barn"; "A Sunshiny Shower."

Reading: Everett, L. (1988). *Bubble gum in the sky.* Mahtawah, NJ: Troll.

Hayward, L. (1988). *Hello, house.* New York: Random House.

Vinje, M. (1992). *Hanna's butterfly.* Grand Haven, MI: School Zone.

Sorting: out, shout, mouth, south, our, hour, flour.

Riddle: What do you call a mouse that lives in someone's house? (house mouse)

Spelling: out, shout, south, our, house, mouse.

Writing: Have students draw a picture of and write a description of their dream houses: houses where they might like to live if they could have any house they wanted.

/ow/ Pattern Unit Review.   On the chalkboard or an overhead, write the /ow / pattern words presented in this unit. Mix the patterns so students aren't simply using the first word as a clue to the other words in that column. Words listed in the sorting exercises can be used for this purpose. If students are not able to read 90% of the words, continue to review them until they are able to do so. Most important, have students read books that contain /ow/ pattern words.

Concentration: Pairs of students play concentration with /ow/ pattern words.

Secret message: Write the words on the lines and read the secret message.

1. Take the **D** from **dog** and put in **F.** ___ ___ ___
2. Take the **h** from **his.** ___ ___
3. Take the **n** from **an.** ___
4. Add **c** to **loud.** ___ ___ ___ ___ ___
5. Keep **close** just as it is. ___ ___ ___ ___ ___
6. Take **d** from **do** and put in a **t.** ___ ___
7. Keep **the** just as it is. ___ ___ ___
8. Add **g** to **round.** ___ ___ ___ ___ ___ ___

_____ _____ _____ _____ _____ _____ _____ _____.

➤➤/oy/ PATTERNS

-oy Pattern

Pattern words: boy, toy, joy.

Mixed practice: boy, ball, toy, tall, jay, joy.

Scrambled sentence: The boy has a new toy.

Rhyme: "The Gingerbread Man."

Sorting: boy, toy, joy, out, shout, loud, cloud, proud, crowd (sort by rhyme only, not spelling).

Riddle: You can have fun with me. I can be a ball or a doll. I can be a game or a very small truck. My name rhymes with joy. What am I? (a toy)

Spelling: boy, toy, joy.

Writing: Have students draw a picture of the toy that they like best and write a piece telling about the toy.

-oil, -oin, -oice, -oise Patterns

Pattern words: oil, boil, join, voice, noise.

Mixed practice: oil, our, boy, boil, joy, join, noise.

Scrambled sentence: The boiling water was making a noise.

Rhyme: "Tom, Tom, the Piper's Son"; "Hot Boiled Beans."

Reading: Witty, B. (1991). *Noises in the night.* Grand Haven, MI: School Zone.

Sorting: oil, boil, boy, toy, joy, shout, mouth, south.

Rhyme riddle: What do you call noise that a crowd of boys make? (boys' noise)

Spelling: oil, join, voice, noise.

Writing: Have students make a list of noises that bother them.

/oy/ Patterns Unit Review.   On the chalkboard or an overhead, write the /oy/ pattern words presented in this unit. Mix the patterns so students aren't simply using the first word as a clue to the other words in that column. Words listed in the sorting exercises can be used for this purpose. If students are not able to read 90%

of the words, continue to review them until they are able to do so. Most important, have students read books that contain /oy/ pattern words.

Secret message: Write the words on the lines and read the secret message.

1. Add **th** to **at** ___ ___ ___ ___
2. Take **b** from **box** and put in **t.** ___ ___ ___
3. Add **s** to **make.** ___ ___ ___ ___ ___
4. Take **c** from **cloud.** ___ ___ ___ ___
5. Add **s** to **noise.** ___ ___ ___ ___ ___ ___

_____ _____ _____ _____ _____.

Short -*a* Illustrations

Short -*e* Illustrations

Short -*i* Illustrations

Short -*o* and Short -*u* Illustrations

Long -*a* and Long -*e* Illustrations

Long *e*, *i*, and *o* Illustrations

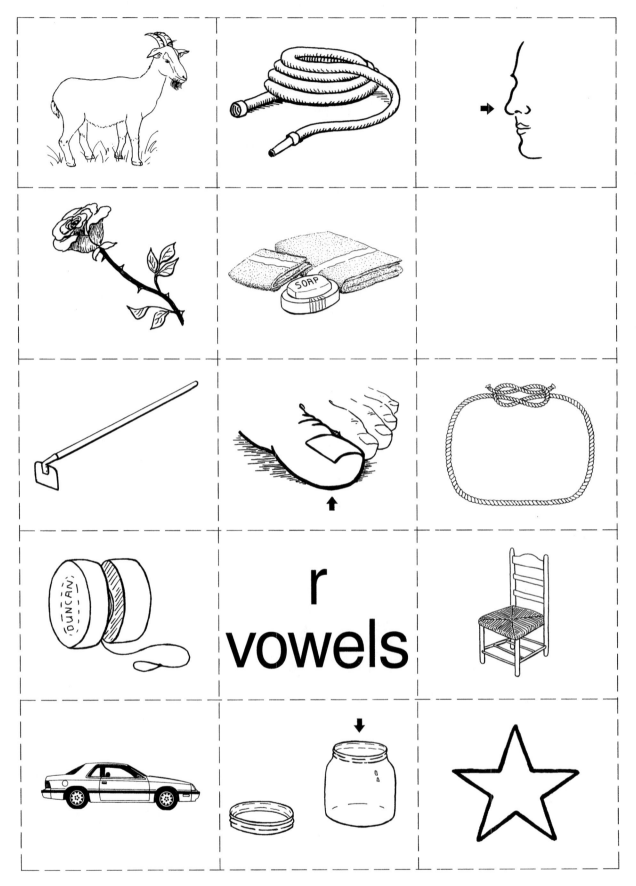

Long -*o* and Long -*r* Vowel Illustrations

R-Vowel and Other-Vowel Illustrations

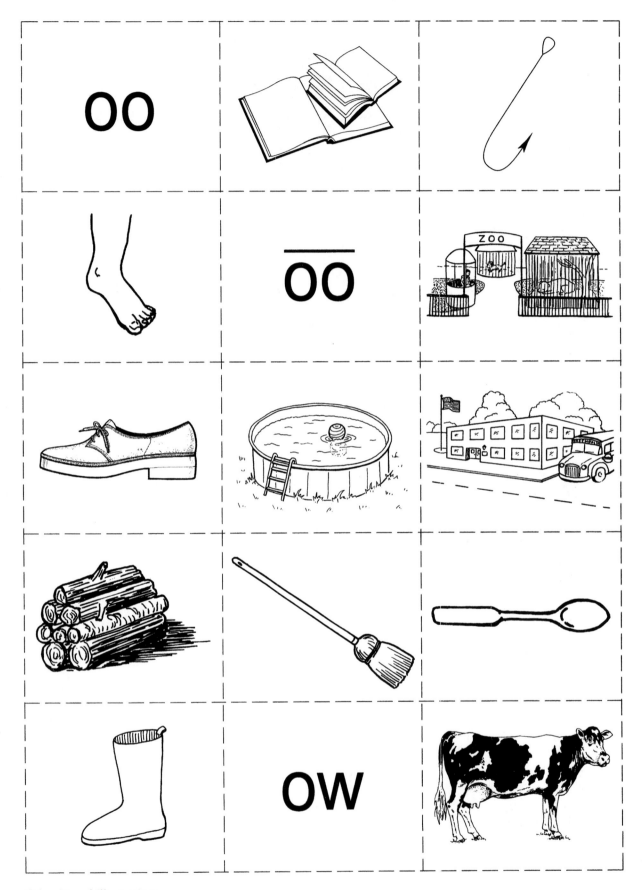

Other-Vowel Illustrations

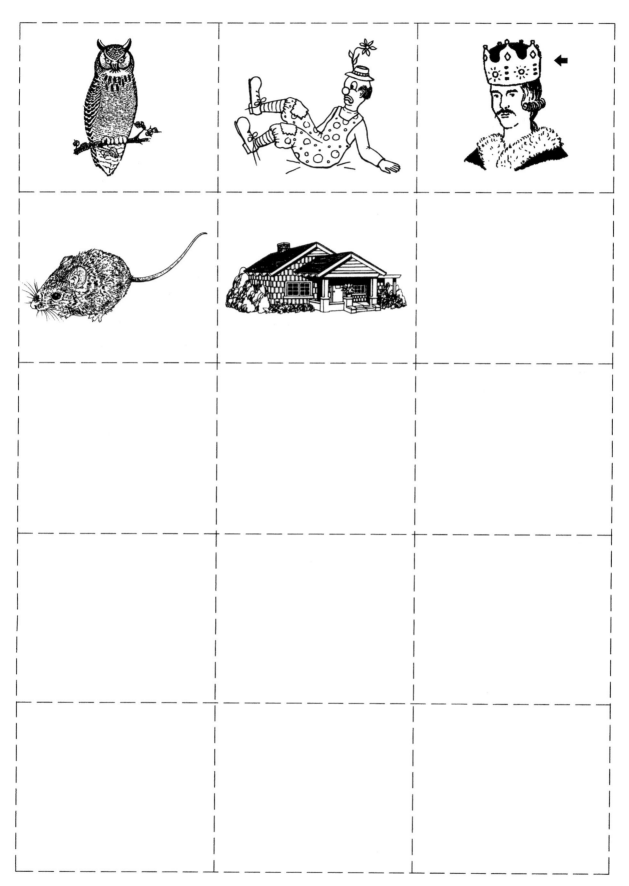

Other-Vowel Illustrations

cat	ran	dad	trap	red
hat	van	had	back	sled
rat	am	mad	pack	led
bat	ham	sad	tack	bell
sat	jam	cap	black	fell
pan	Pam	map	snack	sell
can	Sam	nap	bed	tell
man	bad	snap	fed	yell

Short-*a* and Short-*e* Pattern Words

hen	net	nest	hill
men	pet	rest	will
pen	lent	pest	spill
ten	sent	test	still
when	tent	did	him
get	went	kid	swim
let	spent	lid	in
met	best	rid	pin

Additional column (short-i pattern): slid, big, pig, dig, fig, wig, twig, bill

dot	trick	tick	thing	win
got	hop	lick	lip	chin
hot	mop	quick	tip	twin
lot	pop	trick	drip	king
not	top	thick	ship	ring
pot	drop	pick	trip	sing
shot	shop	sick	kick	wing
spot	stop	stick	pick	bring

Short-i and Short-o Pattern Words

dump	shut	up	gum	lock
jump	duck	cup	hum	rock
junk	luck	pup	drum	block
skunk	truck	us	plum	clock
trunk	lunch	bus	fun	bug
dust	munch	plus	run	dug
just	crunch	but	sun	hug
must	bump	cut	spun	rug

➤➤➤Chapter Five

ORGANIZING AND IMPLEMENTING A PROGRAM FOR BUILDING PHONOLOGICAL AWARENESS AND PHONICS SKILLS AND STRATEGIES

Phonological Awareness and Primary Phonics can be implemented in a number of ways. It can be used with all students or just those students who need more intensive instruction or additional practice. It can be used as the core phonological and phonics skills program or as a supplementary program to complement a basal or children's book approach. It can be used with the whole class, with a small group, or for one-on-one instruction. *Phonological Awareness and Primary Phonics* is highly effective when used as the core phonological awareness and phonics program. All students benefit from a systematic program in phonological awareness and phonics. However, the program should not be used in isolation. Skills taught should be related to the literacy activities in which students are engaged. Rhyming might be related to a study of nursery rhymes. Phonics elements that have been introduced should be applied in stories that students read and write. As a rule of thumb, skills instruction should be limited to 10 or 15 minutes a day. Most of the instructional time should be devoted to application of skills.

➤➤SETTING OBJECTIVES

The starting point of a phonological skills program should be the setting of goals and objectives. What is it that you want your students to be able to do as a result of instruction in phonological awareness and phonics? Possible objectives are listed below but should be adapted to meet the unique requirements of your teaching situation.

Objective 1: Develop Basic Phonological Awareness
Given a series of sets of three illustrations, students can select those whose names rhyme and also illustrations whose names begin with the same sound with 80% accuracy. Given oral presentation of words, students can identify the number of phonemes in the words with 80% accuracy.

Assessment:
➤ Rhyme Survey
➤ Beginning Sounds Survey
➤ Segmentation Survey
➤ Assessment Survey (Observation)
➤ Observations of students' attempts to learn phonological awareness and phonics and to read and write

Objective 2: Achieve a Grasp of Basic Phonics Skills and Strategies

Given the elements in isolation or a series of words containing the basic elements in question, students can pronounce them with 80% accuracy. (Elements include consonants, digraphs, clusters, short-vowel, long-vowel, *r*-vowel, and other-vowel patterns).

Assessment:
➤ Student Decoding Interview
➤ Word Pattern Survey
➤ Assessment Survey (Observations)
➤ Quiz in which 10 to 20 target items are presented
➤ Observations of students' reading of material in which the target element appears

Objective 3: Use Appropriate Strategies to Decode Difficult Words

Students attempt to use the appropriate strategy 80% of the time. (The success rate of decoding the word correctly will usually be somewhat lower than the rate of attempting the strategy. The important point is that students apply strategies. Strategies include pronounceable word part, analogy, sound by sound, picture clue, context.)

Assessment:
➤ Student Decoding Interview
➤ Observations of students' reading
➤ Performance on reading material

Objective 4: Learn to Spell Key Phonic Elements and High-Frequency Words

Assessment:
➤ Performance on periodic quizzes on words taught
➤ Analysis of written work

Although the focus of *Phonemic Awareness and Primary Phonics* is on developing phonological awareness and phonics, the following objectives should be part of a balanced program of literacy instruction. The ultimate goal of word analysis instruction is to develop students' abilities to read and write and to foster a love of reading.

Objective 5: Read a Variety of Materials Incorporating the Phonics Analysis Taught as Evidenced by the Following:

➤ Reading at least 20 minutes a day in school
➤ Reading at least 20 minutes a day out of school

Assessment:
➤ Record of books and other materials read in class
➤ Record of books read at home
➤ Log of time spent reading
➤ Observations of students

Objective 6: Demonstrate Overall Growth in Reading

Assessment:
➤ Ability to read increasingly more difficult books with at least 95% word recognition and 75% comprehension
➤ Performance in class
➤ Performance on benchmark books

➤➤AS AN INTERVENTION PROGRAM

Although *Phonological Awareness and Primary Phonics* is an effective classroom program and has the potential for preventing most reading and writing problems, it is especially effective when used to help struggling readers and writers. Instruction is explicit and systematic and geared to students' literacy levels and stages of development. It is also grounded in the foundational skill of phonological development, an area in which most struggling readers are weak. Struggling readers and writers also need extended opportunities to practice and apply skills and strategies. *Phonological Awareness and Primary Phonics* provides suggestions for a variety of practice activities and lists a number of books and other materials at each level, so students have many opportunities to implement skills and strategies through real reading, which is the most effective practice of all.

Intervention can be conducted by the classroom teacher or by a specialist or, ideally by the classroom teacher and specialist working together. If conducted by a specialist, it can be a pull-out or within-the-class program or a combination of the two. If possible, intervention should be conducted within the classroom. Regardless of where it is conducted, intervention should be carefully coordinated with the classroom program.

➤➤SELECTING STUDENTS

Select students with the greatest needs in reading and writing or those who seem to be at the highest risk of failure. However, when first implementing the program, also select those students most likely to benefit from it. You may want to focus on students whose attendance is dependable and who are cooperative. Once you have experience with the program, you can then work with the more challenging students.

➤➤SIZE OF GROUP

One-on-one instruction is most effective. However, in many situations, one-on-one instruction is not practical. If because of time and staffing constraints it is necessary to work with groups of students, keep the groups to a reasonable size. A group of five or six is the maximum that can be taught effectively. However, the more serious the difficulties, the smaller the group should be.

➤➤SCHEDULING INSTRUCTION

Intervention instruction is most beneficial when is given in addition to the instruction already being provided. Students who are behind or at risk for failure need more instructional time if they can be expected to catch up or keep up. Before school, after school, and summer programs are recommended. However, if this is not practical, arrange intervention sessions when they would best fit into the daily schedule. You might hold intervention sessions when the rest of the class is engaged in sustained reading, working at learning centers, taking part in literature circles, or working on individual or group projects. Students who are not being provided with intervention assistance need to know that you are busy at that time and so they should work independently and hold questions until later. If other professionals are working in the room with you, you might want to work out an arrangement in which the other professionals spend time with the rest of the class while you work with the intervention group.

Intervention groups should be scheduled every day, if possible, but not less than three times a week. Sessions can last from 20 to 45 minutes, with 40 minutes being the recommended duration. Including both regular classroom and intervention instruction, students in grades 1–3 should have a total of at least 90 minutes of literacy instruction each day. Students in grades 4 and 5 should have at least 60 minutes.

The pacing of instruction should be brisk. Emphasis should be placed on the skills and strategies that have the highest payoff and on activities that provide the best practice with these skills and strategies.

➤➤PARTS OF AN INTERVENTION LESSON

An intervention lesson should include certain key elements. As a minimum, there should be a review of past material, an introduction or extension of a new skill or strategy, and opportunity to apply that skill or strategy. The parts of a daily lesson are described below.

Review (2 to 5 minutes). Review previous pattern. Read or reread a verse, song, poem, riddle, or other brief selection that incorporates a pattern presented previously. Also discuss the take-home selection read the previous night.

Introduction or Extension of New Pattern or Strategy (5 to 10 minutes). Introduce a new pattern or extend a pattern presented previously. Build the pattern as explained in the sample lessons. If time allows, provide guided practice by having students sort pattern words, unscramble a sentence, or read a rhyme or other brief selection that contains the pattern.

Reading a New Selection Containing the Pattern (6 to 15 minutes). For younger students or older students reading on a very low level, use a text walk. For other older students, use a less structured procedure such as guided reading. The selection should be on the students' instructional level (95% of the words are known) and should incorporate the new pattern.

Spelling/Writing (5 to 10 minutes). Introduce or review spelling words related to the new pattern and/or compose a sentence or brief selection using one or more of the new pattern words. The sentence or brief selection is dictated by the group and scribed by the teacher. For sentences, students copy each word on a 3" by 5" card, mix the cards up, and place them in an envelope. As a home assignment, students reassemble the scrambled sentence. As students become more proficient and have mastered short vowel patterns, phase out this activity. Instead, as time allows, have the students write a piece on a topic of their choosing. The piece might be developed over a number of sessions. In addition to the time spent on writing during their lessons, students need a full program of writing development in which they write letters, narratives, and various kinds of expository pieces.

Conclusion of Session (2 to 5 minutes). The session ends with a riddle or a gamelike activity, such as a mystery word, that incorporates the new pattern. Students also choose or are given a take-home selection to read. The take-home selection can be a children's book, a booklet that you or the students have made, one of the fold-and-read books, an experience story, or a periodical.

➤➤MANAGING THE LESSON

One-on-one sessions work well because instruction can be geared to the specific needs of the learner. When groups of students are taught, needs are more diverse. Insofar as possible, select students who have common needs. Since the focus of the program is on developing phonological awareness and phonics skills and strategies, use students' decoding skills as a basis for grouping. Place all the students who have difficulty with short vowels, for instance, in the same group. It isn't necessary that all have exactly the same level of knowledge. For students who have very limited knowledge of short vowels, the lessons will be an introduction to new skills. For those who have some knowledge of short vowels, the lessons will be an extension or review.

If necessary, adjust the demands of the reinforcement activities. Rhymes, riddles, songs, and other practice activities should be at the appropriate level of difficulty. However, if they are a bit too hard for just one or two members of a group, share-read them with the whole group. Similarly, if you are using multiple copies of a book for application reading, use a text-walk to give students a thorough preparation for the reading of the book. Or you might provide each student with a book written on his or her level. A sample lesson in which the -eal, -eel patterns are presented to a group of five students of somewhat varying abilities is presented next.

▶▶SAMPLE LESSON 5.1:
TEACHING THE -EEL, -EAL PATTERNS

Review (2 to 5 minutes).   Review the -eet, -eat patterns, which were introduced in a previous lesson. The class share-reads "Little Puppy Dog." The pattern words *meat* and *street* are emphasized. Students briefly discuss the selection they read the night before.

Introduction or Extension of New Pattern or Strategy (5 to 10 minutes).   The -eal, -eel patterns are introduced. Students sort words into -eal, -eel, and -eet patterns.

Reading a New Selection Containing the Pattern (6 to 15 minutes).   Using a text-walk, the teacher introduces *And I Mean It, Stanley* (Bonsall, 1974). Students are invited to read the title and to predict what the story might be about. The teacher then walks students through the story picture by picture. Have students turn to the first page of the story. Explain that the girl is talking to Stanley, who is behind the fence. Have them point to the word *fence,* which may be an unfamiliar word. Have them turn to pp. 8–9. Tell them that the girl seems angry and is saying, "I don't care, Stanley. I don't want to play with you." Have them point to the word *care,* which is an unfamiliar word. Turning to pp. 10–11, explain that the girl is telling Stanley, "I can play by myself, Stanley." Have students point to the word *myself,* which is unfamiliar. Turning to pp. 12–13, explain that the girl is saying that she is having a lot of fun and, on pp. 14–15, she is saying that she is making a really, truly great thing. Have them tell what was added to *real,* a word in their lesson, to make the word *really.* Also have them point to each word in the phrase, "A really, truly great thing," as you read it. Have students predict what the really, truly great thing is and who Stanley might be. Since the words and concepts in the rest of the story are familiar, have the students read the book on their own and see how their predictions come out.

After reading the whole selection silently, the students discuss their predictions and talk over the rest of the story. Students reread orally passages which verify, clarify, or amplify their responses. Each student might also be asked to read aloud his or her favorite part.

Spelling/Writing (5 to 10 minutes).   Students are introduced to the spelling words: *feel, meal, real.* If time allows, the group writes about things that make them feel happy. Model the process of selecting and developing a topic by talking over some of the things that make you feel happy.

Conclusion of Session (2 to 5 minutes).   Students take home a copy of *And I Mean It, Stanley* (Bosnall, 1974) to reread or *Wheels on the Bus* (Raffi, 1988), or another text that reinforces the *-eel* or *-eal* pattern. Students conclude the session by singing "Wheels on the Bus" as the teacher points to each word of the song, which has been written on the chalkboard or is displayed on a transparency.

➤➤COORDINATED PROGRAM

The intervention program should be closely coordinated with the school's program. The school's program should be of high quality. A highly effective literacy program is the best way to prevent literacy learning problems. A high-quality program also builds on the gains that students make in a successful intervention program. Gains made in an intervention program are in danger of being lost unless they are nurtured in a high-quality classroom program.

➤➤STAFFING

The program can be taught by the classroom teacher, by a specialist working in or out of the classroom, or by well-trained and well-supervised paraprofessionals or volunteers. If paraprofessionals or volunteers are used, they need to be carefully supervised. In-service sessions should be held on a regular basis to keep up with the latest developments in the field, to test new ideas, to share ideas, to work out problems, and to discuss new materials. Supervision with feedback or coaching sessions is especially helpful. If outside help is not available, assess your program as objectively as you can. Use the Building Literacy Self-Assessment Checklist (Table 5.1) as a guide for coaching or self-assessment sessions.

TABLE 5.1   Building Literacy Self-Assessment Checklist

	Yes	No	Partially	Plans for Implementation
New pattern is carefully introduced.				
Materials being read incorporate the new pattern.				
Materials are on the appropriate level.				
Reinforcement activities are varied and effective.				
Reinforcement activities include sorting and/or other high-payoff activities.				
Students attempt to apply strategies.				
Students are given appropriate prompts and feedback.				
Students read materials at home that incorporate pattern.				
Patterns are reviewed as necessary.				
Teacher builds on what students know.				

➤➤MONITORING PROGRESS

It is important to monitor progress. Otherwise, students might move into phonics before they have developed adequate phonological awareness or attempt long-vowel patterns before they have mastered short-vowel patterns and therefore become overwhelmed. The best way to assess students' progress is to observe their daily work. Ask such questions as: After reading a selection, is the student able to retell it or answer questions about it? If comprehension is lacking, the selection might be too hard. There may be too many unknown words in the selection. Also ask: How does the student do when new elements are introduced? Does the student seem to be learning the new elements? How successful is the student at sorting? How successful is the student at completing take-home activities?

After discussing take-home selections, have each student read a favorite sentence or passage. Note the accuracy of students' reading and the strategies they use when they encounter difficult words. If students are missing one word out of every ten, the selection is probably too hard. You might want to check further to make sure the student is being given material at the right level. Also note what students do when they encounter a word that fits a pattern that has been taught but that was not included with the words presented. If students are able to decode the word, this suggests that they are applying skills.

Some difficulties are to be expected. Otherwise, the material and activities may not be challenging enough. Some prompting and reteaching may be necessary. However, if nearly every skill needs to be retaught and prompting seems necessary for nearly every response, then the program may be at too high a level. Some adjustments may need to be made. It is important that students be instructed at a level where they are successful most of the time.

While observation provides a wealth of information, it is somewhat subjective. Once students have started working with vowel patterns, assess them on a weekly basis. These assessments might include the following:

➤ Oral quiz on the pattern taught. Test all of the words or a sampling of ten of them. Performance that is less than 80% suggests the need for reteaching and added practice.

➤ Dictated quiz on the week's spelling words. Performance below 90% suggests the need for some reteaching or additional studying.

➤ Sample of students' oral reading. Once every week or every two weeks, have students read a 100-word sample orally. Word recognition should be 95%. Comprehension should be 75%. Count as errors words that have been mispronounced, words that have been skipped, words that you have supplied, and words that have been inserted. Do not count hesitations, repetitions, or misread words that have been corrected by the student.

➤➤PERIODIC EVALUATION

In addition to conducting ongoing assessment activities, you should also evaluate students' progress at key points. This could be at the end of a unit, quarter, semester, or after students have completed a significant block of learning, such as after all the short-vowel patterns have been presented. For this cumulative type of evaluation, the following might be used:

➤ Examine performance on benchmark books. Use actual children's books to serve as benchmarks. Applying the same standards as you do for oral reading passages—95% word recognition and 75% comprehension—have students read selected passages and retell the story or respond to comprehension questions that you compose.

➤ Give the Word Pattern Survey as a post-test.

➤ Assess samples of students' work collected in a portfolio.

➤ Use results of district-wide state-wide, or national performance and/or norm-referenced tests of reading and writing. These tests might not address the specific objectives of this program and/or may not assess strategies in the way they were taught. However, test results should provide general information about students' overall achievement in reading and writing.

See the section on objectives for additional suggestions for evaluation.

Whatever devices are used to monitor and evaluate students' progress, it is important that this information be used to provide assistance as needed and to make necessary adjustments. The first step in the evaluation process is to define objectives. The final step is to use the results of the evaluation to improve the program.

➤➤PARENTAL AND COMMUNITY INVOLVEMENT

Parents can provide valuable support for the school's literacy program. They can foster voluntary reading by encouraging their children to read and by helping them obtain books. They can also help develop a positive attitude toward reading and writing and set aside a time and place for studying. Be sure to explain the program to parents and keep them fully informed about their child's progress. Also provide specific suggestions for ways in which they can help their children. The community can provide volunteers, needed financial resources, and overall support. Some businesses, for instance, give their employees time off to tutor in local schools. And some provide free ice cream, pizza, or other incentives for voluntary reading programs.

➤➤AMPLE OPPORTUNITY TO READ AND WRITE

All readers and writers, but especially those who are struggling, also need lots of opportunities to read and write. This means that they should be provided with a wide variety of books and other reading materials at an appropriate level and lots of meaningful writing activities that are challenging but not overwhelming.

➤➤CHECKLIST FOR EVALUATING YOUR LITERACY PROGRAM

A strong program in word analysis, such as that presented in *Phonological Awareness and Primary Phonics*, should be complemented by an equally strong program in comprehension, writing, and reading the finest in children's literature. Students should have the opportunity to make full use of and extend the decoding and spelling skills presented in *Phonological Awareness and Primary Phonics*. How does your literacy program shape up? Table 5.2 is a checklist designed to help you evaluate the effectiveness of your literacy program and identify areas of strength as well as areas of weakness so that you might make plans for improvement.

TABLE 5.2   Building Literacy Evaluation Checklist

	Yes	No	Somewhat	Plans for Improvement
Objectives are clearly stated.				
Focus is on high-payoff skills and strategies.				
Program builds on what students know.				
Direct, systematic instruction is provided.				
Pacing is brisk.				
Ample time is provided for reading and writing.				
Reading, writing, and spelling are related.				
Progress is continuously monitored.				
Intervention program is coordinated with class program.				
Students are placed at appropriate levels.				
Materials on appropriate levels are available.				
Parents and community are involved.				

➤➤➤References

Adams, M. J. (1990). *Beginning to read: Thinking and learning about print.* Cambridge, MA: MIT Press.

Adams, M. J. (1994). Modeling the connections between word recognition and reading. In R. B. Ruddell, M. R. Ruddell, & H. Singer (Eds.), *Theoretical models and processes of reading* (4th ed.) (pp. 838–863). Newark, DE: International Reading Association.

Bear, D., & Barone, D. (1989). The elementary spelling inventory (with error guide). *Reading Psychology, 10,* 275–292.

Bear, D., Invernizzi, M, Johnston, F., & Templeton, S. (1996). *Words their way: Word study for phonics, spelling, and vocabulary development.* Upper Saddle River, NJ: Merrill.

Bonsall, C. (1974). *And I mean it, Stanley.* New York: HarperCollins.

Cunningham, P. M., & Allington, R. L. (1999). *Classrooms that work: They can all read and write (2nd ed.).* New York: Longwood.

Cunningham, P. M., & Cunningham, J. W. (1992). Making words: Enhancing the invented spelling-decoding connection. *The Reading Teacher, 46,* 106–115.

Education Department of Western Australia. (1994). *Writing resource book.* Melbourne: Longman.

Ehri, L. C. (1994). Development of the ability to read words: Update: In R. B. Ruddell, M. R. Ruddell, & H. Singer (Eds.), *Theoretical models and processes of reading* (4th ed.), (pp. 323–358). Newark, DE: International Reading Association.

Ehri, L. C., & McCormick, S. (1998). Phases of word learning: Implications for instruction with delayed and disabled readers. *Reading and Writing Quarterly: Overcoming Learning Disabilities, 14,* 135–163.

Elkonin, D. B. (1973). Reading in the USSR. In J. Downing (Ed.), *Comparative reading* (pp. 551–579). New York: Macmillan.

Gentry, R. (1997). *My kid can't spell.* Portsmouth, NH: Heinemann.

Greaney, K., Tunmer, W. E, & Chapman, J. W. (1997). The use of rime-based orthographic analogy training as an intervention strategy for reading-disabled children. In B. A. Blachman (Ed.), *Foundations of reading acquisition and dyslexia: Implications for early intervention* (pp. 327–345). Mahwah, NJ: Erlbaum.

Gunning, T. (1975). *A comparison of word attack skills derived from a phonological analysis of frequently used words drawn drom a juvenile corpus and an adult corpus.* Unpublished doctoral dissertation, Temple University, Philadelphia.

Gunning, T. (1988). Decoding behavior of good and poor second grade students. Paper presented at the annual meeting of the International Reading Association, Toronto, May.

Gunning, T. (1995). Word building: A strategic approach to the teaching of phonics. *The Reading Teacher, 48,* 484–488.

Gunning, T. (1999, December). *Word analysis knowledge and processes of second graders.* Paper presented at the annual meeting of the National Reading Conference, Orlando.

Harris, A. J., & Sipay, E. R. (1990). *How to increase reading ability* (9th ed.). New York: Longman.

Hoff, S. (1988). *Mrs. Brice's mice.* New York: HarperCollins.

Iverson, S., & Tunmer, W. E. (1993). Phonological processing skills and the Reading Recovery program. *Journal of Educational Psychology, 85,* 112–126.

Johnston, F. R. (1999). The timing and teaching of word families. *The Reading Teacher, 53,* 64–75.

Juel, C. (1991). Beginning reading. In R. Barr, M. L. Kamil, P. Mosenthal, & P. D. Pearson (Eds.), *Handbook of reading research,* Vol. II (pp. 759–788). New York: Longman.

Liberman, I. Y., & Shankweiler, D. (1991). Phonology and beginning reading: A tutorial. In L. Rieben & C. A. Perfetti (Eds.), *Learning to read: Basic research and its implications* (pp. 3–18). Hillsdale, NJ: Lawrence Erlbaum.

Liberman, I. Y., Shankweiler, D., Fischer, F. W., & Carter, B. (1974). Explicit syllable and phoneme segmentation in the young child. *Journal of Experimental Child Psychology, 18,* 201–212.

Maclean, M., Bryant, P., & Bradley, L. (1987). Rhymes, nursery rhymes, and reading in early childhood. *Merrill Plamer Quarterly, 33,* 255–281.

Metsala, J. L. (1999). Young children's phonological awareness and nonword repetition as a function of vocabulary development. *Journal of Educational Psychology, 91,* 3–19.

Moore, I. (1991). *Six-dinner Sid.* New York: Simon & Schuster.

Morris, D. (1999). *The Howard Street tutoring manual: Teaching at-risk readers in the primary grades.* New York: Guilford Press.

Moustafa, M. (1997). *Beyond traditional phonics: Research discoveries and reading instruction.* Portsmouth, NH: Heinemann.

Nicholson, T. (1999). Literacy in the family and society. In G. B. Thompson & T. Nicholson (Eds.), *Learning to read: Beyond phonics and whole language* (pp. 1–22). Newark, DE: International Reading Association.

Pinnell, G. S., & Fountas, I. C. (1998). *Word matters.* Portsmouth, NH: Heinemann.

Read, C. (1971). Pre-school children's knowledge of English phonology. *Harvard Educational Review, 41,* 1–34.

Raffi (1988). *Wheels on the bus.* New York: Crown.

Robart, R. (1986). *The Cake that Mack ate.* Boston: Little, Brown.

Santa, C., & Høien, T. (1999). An assessment of Early Steps: A program for early intervention. *Reading Research Quarterly, 34,* 54–79.

Savin, H. B. (1972). What the child knows about speech when he starts to learn to read. In J. F. Kavanagh & I. G. Mattingly (Eds.), *Language by ear and by eye* (pp. 319–326). Cambridge, MA: MIT Press.

Sawyer, D. J. (1987). *TALS Test of Awareness of Language Segments.* Rockville, MD: Aspen.

Seuss, Dr. (1974). *There's a wocket in my pocket* New York: Beginner.

Seuss, Dr. (1988). *Green eggs and ham.* New York: Random House.

Snow, C. E., Burns, M. S., & Griffin, P. (1998). *Preventing reading difficulties in young children.* Washington, DC: National Academy Press.

Stahl, S. A., Osborne, J., & Lehr, F. (1990). *Beginning to read: Thinking and learning about print: A summary.* Urbana, IL: Center for the Study of Reading, University of Illinois at Urbana-Champaign.

Stahl, S., Stahl, K. A., & McKenna, M. (1998, December). How do phonological awareness, spelling, and word recognition relate to each other? Paper presented at the annual meeting of the National Reading Conference, Austin, TX.

Temple, C., Nathan, R., Temple, F., & Burris, N. A. (1993). *The beginnings of writing* (3rd ed.). Boston: Allyn & Bacon.

Tremain, R. (1997). Spelling in normal children and dyslexics. In B. A. Blachman (Ed.), *Foundations of reading acquisition and dyslexia: Implications for early intervention* (pp. 191–218). Mahwah, NJ: Erlbaum.

Tunmer, W. E., & Chapman, J. W. (1999). Teaching strategies for word identification. In G. B. Thompson & T. Nicholson (Eds.), *Learning to read: Beyond phonics and whole language* (pp. 74–102). Newark, DE: International Reading Association.

Venezky, R. L. (1965). A study of English spelling-to-sound correspondences on historical principles. Unpublished doctoral dissertation, Stanford University, Stanford, CA.

Watson, A. J. (1984). Cognitive development and units of print in early reading. In J. Downing & R. Valten (Eds.), *Language awareness and learning to read* (pp. 93–118). New York: Springer-Verlag.

Wylie, R. E., & Durrell, D. D. (1970). Teaching vowels through phonograms. *Elementary English, 47,* 787–791.

Yopp, H. K. (1988). The validity and reliability of phonemic awareness tests. *Reading Research Quarterly, 23,* 159–177.

Yopp, H. K. (1995). A test for assessing phonemic awareness in young children. *The Reading Teacher, 49,* 20–29.

REINFORCEMENT RHYMES AND SONGS

The following rhymes, which are arranged alphabetically by title, can be used to reinforce phonological awareness and phonic elements presented in Chapters 1, 3, and 4.

A-Hunting We Will Go
A-hunting we will go,
A-hunting we will go.
We'll catch a fox
And put him in a box.
And then we'll let him go.

Baa, Baa, Black Sheep
Baa, baa, black sheep,
Have you any wool?
Yes, sir, yes, sir,
Three bags full.

One for the master,
One for the dame,
But none for the little boy
Who cries in the lane.

The Balloon
"What is the news of the day, my good
Mr. Gray?
They say the balloon
Has gone up to the moon."

The Bear Went over the Mountain
The bear went over the mountain,
The bear went over the mountain,
The bear went over the mountain,
To see what he could see.

Bedtime
Down with the lambs
    Up with the lark,
Run to bed, children,
    Before it gets dark.

Bees
If bees stay at home,
Rain will soon come.
If they fly away,
Fine will be the day.

Bingo
There was a farm-er who had a dog.
And Bing-o was his name-o.
B-I-N-G-O, B-I-N-G-O, B-I-N-G-O,
And Bing-o was his name-o.

Bow, Wow, Wow,
Bow, wow, wow,
Whose dog art thou?
Little Tom Tinker's dog,
Bow, wow, wow.

The Boy in the Barn
A little boy went into a barn,
And lay down on some hay.
An owl came out, and flew about,
And the little boy ran away.

Burnie Bee
Burnie bee, burnie bee,
Tell me when your wedding be?
If it be tomorrow day,
Take your wings and fly away.

By Mr. Nobody
Tis he who always tears our books,
    Who leaves the door ajar,
He pulls the buttons from our shirts,
    And scatters pins afar.
That squeaking door will always squeak,
    For don't you see,
We leave the oiling to be done
    By Mr. Nobody.
The fingermarks upon the door
    By none of us are made,
We never leave the blinds unclosed,
    To let the curtains fade.
The ink we never spill; the boots
    That lying around you see
Are not our boots—they all belong
    To Mr. Nobody.

Clouds
Christina Rossetti

White sheep, white sheep,
On a blue hill,
When the wind stops
You all stand still.

When the wind blows
You walk away slow.
White sheep, white sheep,
Where do you go?

Come on In
Come on in,
The water's fine.
I'll give you
Till I count nine.
If you're not
In by then,
Guess I'll have to
Count to ten.

Dickery, Dickery, Dare
Dickery, dickery, dare,
The pig flew up in the air;
The man in brown
Soon brought him down,
Dickery, dickery, dare.

Did You Ever See a Lassie?
Did you ever see a lassie, a lassie, a lassie,
Did you ever see a lassie go this way and that,
Go this way and that way and this way and that way?
Did you ever see a lassie go this way and that?

The Donkey
Donkey, donkey, old and gray,
Open your mouth and gently bray;
Lift your ears and blow your horn,
To wake the world this sleepy morn.

Engine, Engine, Number Nine
Engine, Engine, Number Nine,
Running on the Chicago line.
See it sparkle, see it shine,
Engine, Engine, Number Nine.

The Farmer in the Dell
The farm-er in the dell,
The farm-er in the dell,
Heigh-ho the der-ry-o,
The farm-er in the dell.

The farm-er takes a wife.
The farm-er takes a wife.
Heigh-ho the der-ry-o,
The farm-er takes a wife.

Fears and Tears
Tommy's tears and Mary's fears
Will make them old
Before their years.

Fire! Fire!
"Fire! Fire!" said Mrs. McGuire
"Where? Where?" said Mrs. Hare.
"Downtown!" said Mrs. Brown.
"Heaven save us!" said Mrs. Davis

Fishy-fishy
Fishy-fishy in the brook,
Daddy caught him with a hook.
Mama fried him in the pan,
And baby ate him like a man.

Five Little Ducks
Five little ducks went out one day,
Over the hills and far away.
One little duck went
"Quack, quack, quack."
Four little ducks came swimming back.

Four little ducks went out one day,
Over the hills and far away.
One little duck went
"Quack, quack, quack."
Three little ducks came swimming back.

Three little ducks went out one day,
Over the hills and far away.
One little duck went
"Quack, quack, quack."
Two little ducks came swimming back.

Two little ducks went out one day,
Over the hills and far away.
One little duck went
"Quack, quack, quack."
One little duck came swimming back.

Five Miles from Home
(sung to tune of "The Farmer in the Dell")

We're five miles from home.
We're five miles from home.
We sing a-while and talk a-while,
We're four miles from home.

We're four miles from home.
We're four miles from home.
We sing a-while and talk a-while,
We're three miles from home.

We're three miles from home, etc.

We're two miles from home, etc.

We're one mile from home.
We're one mile from home.
We sing a-while and talk a-while,
And now we're at home.

Fooba Wooba John
Saw a flea kick a tree,
Fooba wooba, fooba wooba,
Saw a flea kick a tree,
Fooba wooba, John.
Saw a flea kick a tree
In the middle of the sea,
Fooba wooba, fooba wooba,
Fooba wooba John.

Saw a crow flying low,
Fooba wooba, fooba wooba,
Saw a crow flying low,
Fooba wooba John.
Saw a crow flying low,
Miles and miles beneath the snow,
Fooba wooba, fooba wooba,
Fooba wooba John.

Saw a bug give a shrug . . .
In the middle of the rug . . .

Saw a whale chase a snail . . .
All around a water pail . . .

Saw two geese making cheese . . .
One would hold and the other would squeeze . . .

Saw a mule teaching school . . .
To some bullfrogs in the pool . . .

Saw a bee off to sea . . .
With his fiddle across his knee . . .

Saw a hare chase a deer . . .
Ran it all of seven year . . .

Saw a bear scratch his ear . . .
Wonderin' what we're doin' here.

Fright and Bright
Poor Cat Fright
Ran off with all her might
Because the dog was after her—
Poor Cat Fright!

Poor Dog Bright
Ran off with all his might
Because the cat was after him.
Poor Dog Bright!

Fuzzy Wuzzy
Fuzzy Wuzzy was a bear.
Fuzzy Wuzzy had no hair.
Fuzzy Wuzzy wasn't fuzzy,
Was he?

Garden Gate
Two, four, six, eight.
Meet me at the garden gate.
If I'm late, do not wait.
Two, four, six, eight.

The Gingerbread Man
Smiling girls, rosy boys,
Come and buy my little toys;
Monkeys made of gingerbread,
And sugar horses painted red.

Go and Tell Aunt Nancy
Go and tell Aunt Nancy,
Go and tell Aunt Nancy,
Go and tell Aunt Nancy,
    The old gray goose is dead.

The one that she was saving,
The one that she was saving,
The one that she was saving,
    To make a feather bed.

She died on Friday,
She died on Friday,
She died on Friday,
    Behind the old barn shed.

She left nine little goslings,
She left nine little goslings,
She left nine little goslings,
    To scratch for their own bread.

Go in and out the Window
Go in and out the win-dow,
Go in and out the win-dow,
Go in and out the win-dow,
As we have done be-fore.

Go to Bed Late
Go to bed late,
Stay very small.
Go to bed early,
Grow very tall.

The Goat
There was a man—now please take note—
There was a man who had a goat.
He loved that goat—indeed he did—
He loved that goat just like a kid.

One day that goat felt frisky and fine,
Ate three red shirts from off the line.
The man, he grabbed him by the back,
And tied him to a railroad track.

But when the train drove into sight,
The goat grew pale and green with fright.
He heaved a sigh as if in pain,
Coughed up those shirts, and flagged the train.

Gobble, Gobble
A turkey is a funny bird,
His head goes wobble, wobble,
And he knows just one word,
Gobble, gobble, gobble.

Good, Better, Best
Good, better, best,
Never let it rest,
Till your good is better
And your better best.

Happy Thought
Robert Louis Stevenson

The world is so full,
of a number of things,
I'm sure we should all
be as happy as kings.

Hey Diddle, Diddle
Hey diddle, diddle,
The cat and the fiddle,
The cow jumped over the moon.
The little dog laughed
To see such a sport,
And the dish ran away with the spoon.

Help! Murder! Police!
Help! Murder! Police!
My mother fell in the grease.
I laughed so hard, I fell in the lard.
Help! Murder! Police!

Hiccup, Hiccup
Hiccup, hiccup, go away!
Come again another day.
Hiccup, hiccup, when I bake,
I'll give to you a butter-cake.

Hickory, Dickory, Dock
Hickory, dickory, dock,
The mouse ran up the clock.
The clock struck one,
The mouse ran down!
Hickory, dickory, dock.

Higher than a House
Higher than a house,
Higher than a tree,
Oh! Whatever can that be?

Hippity Hop to the Barber Shop
Hippity hop to the barber shop,
To get a stick of candy,
One for you and one for me,
And one for sister Mandy.

Hot Boiled Beans
Boys and girls come to supper—
Hot boiled beans
And very good butter.

Hot Cross Buns!
Hot cross buns! Hot cross buns!
One a penny, two a penny,
Hot cross buns!

If you have no daughters,
Give them to your sons;
One a penny, two a penny,
Hot cross buns!

I Asked My Mother for Fifteen Cents
I asked my mother for fifteen cents
To see the elephant jump the fence,
He jumped so high he touched the sky
And never came back 'till the Fourth of July.

I Saw Esau
I saw Esau sawing wood,
And Esau saw I saw him;
Though Esau saw I saw him saw,
Still Esau went on sawing.

I Saw Three Ships
I saw three ships come sail-ing by,
Come sail-ing by, come sail-ing by,
I saw three ships come sail-ing by,
On New Year's Day, in the morn-ing.

Ice Cream Rhyme
I scream, you scream,
We all scream for ice cream.

If You Ever
If you ever ever ever ever,
If you ever ever ever ever meet a whale,
You must never never never never never,
You must never never never never never touch
    its tail,
For if you ever ever ever ever ever,
For if you ever ever ever ever ever touch its tail,
You will never never never never never,
You will never never never never never meet
    another whale.

If You Should Meet a Crocodile
If you should meet a crocodile,
Don't take a stick and poke him;
Ignore the welcome in his smile,
Be careful not to stroke him.
For as he sleeps upon the Nile,
He thinner gets and thinner;
And whene'er you meet a crocodile,
He's ready for his dinner.

If You're Happy and You Know It
If you're hap-py and you know it,
Clap your hands.
If you're hap-py and you know it,
Clap your hands.
If you're hap-py and you know it,
And you really want to show it,
If you're hap-py and you know it,
Clap your hands.

I'll Sing You a Song,
I'll sing you a song,
Though not very long,
Yet I think it as pretty as any.

Put your hand in your purse,
You'll never be worse,
And give the poor singer a penny.

I'm a Little Teapot
I'm a little teapot short and stout:
Here is my handle and here is my spout.
When I get all steamed up, I just shout:
    "Just tip me over and pour me out!"

It Ain't Going to Rain No More
It ain't going to rain no more, no more,
It ain't going to rain no more;
How in the heck can I wash my neck
If it ain't going to rain no more?

It's Raining, It's Pouring
It's raining, it's pouring,
The old man is snoring.
He went to bed and bumped his head.
And he wouldn't get up in the morning.

I've Been Working on the Railroad
I've been work-ing on the rail-road,
All the live long day,
I've been work-ing on the rail-road,
Just to pass the time a-way.
Don't you hear the whistle blowing?
Rise up so early in the morn.
Don't you hear the cap-tain shout-ing,
"Di-nah, blow your horn!"
Di-nah, won't you blow,
Di-nah, won't you blow
Di-nah, won't you blow your horn?

Some-one's in the kitch-en with Dinah,
Some-one's in the kitch-en, I know,
Someone's in the kitch-en with Dinah,
Strum-ming on the old ban-jo, and sing-ing:
Fee-fi-fidd-lee-i-o, Fee-fi-fidd-lee-i-o,
Fee-fi-fidd-lee-i-o, Strum-ming on the old ban-jo.

I've Got a Dog
I've got a dog as thin as a rail,
He's got fleas all over his tail;
Every time his tail goes flop,
The fleas on the bottom all hop to the top.

Jack and Jill
Jack and Jill went up the hill,
To fetch a pail of water,
Jack fell down and broke his crown,
And Jill came tumbling after.

Jack, Be Nimble
Jack, be nimble
Jack, be quick,
Jack, jump over the candlestick.

Jump it lively,
Jump it quick,
But don't knock over
The candlestick.

Jack Hall
Jack Hall,
He is so small,
A rat could eat him,
Hat and all.

Jack Sprat
Jack Sprat could eat no fat,
His wife could eat no lean.
And between them both, you see,
They licked the platter clean.

Jumping Joan
Here am I,
Little Jumping Joan;
When nobody's with me
I'm all alone.

Lazy Mary
La-zy Mar-y, will you get up,
Will you get up, will you get up?
La-zy Mar-y, will you get up,
Will you get up to-day?

Oh, no, moth-er, I won't get up,
I won't get up, I won't get up.
Oh, no, moth-er, I won't get up,
I won't get up to-day.

Let's Be Merry
Christina Rossetti

Mother shake the cherry-tree,
    Susan catch a cherry;
Oh how funny that will be,
    Let's be merry!
One for brother, one for sister,
    Two for mother more,
Six for father, hot and tired,
    Knocking at the door.

Little Betty Blue
Little Betty Blue,
Lost her new shoe.
What will poor Betty do?
Why, give her another,
To match the other,
And then she will walk in two.

The Little Bird
Once I saw a little bird
    Come hop, hop, hop;
So I cried, "Little bird,
    Will you stop, stop, stop?"
I was going to the window
    To say, "How do you do?"
But he shook his little tail,
    And far away he flew.

Little Blue Ben
Little Blue Ben, who lives in the glen,
Keeps a blue cat and one blue hen,
Which lays of blue eggs a score and ten;
Where shall I find the little Blue Ben?

Little Bo-Peep
Little Bo-Peep has lost her sheep,
    And can't tell where to find them;
Leave them alone, and they'll come home,
    Wagging their tails behind them.

Little Boy Blue
Little boy blue, come blow your horn;
The sheep's in the meadow, the cow's in the corn.
Where is the little boy who looks after the sheep?
He's under the haystack fast asleep.
Will you wake him? No, not I;
For if I do, he's sure to cry.

Little Girl, Little Girl, Where Have You Been?
Little girl, little girl, where have you been?
Gathering roses to give to the Queen.
Little girl, little girl, what gave she you?
    She gave me a diamond as big as my shoe.

Little Jack Horner
Little Jack Horner
Sat in a corner,
Eating his Christmas pie;
He put in his thumb,
And pulled out a plum,
And said, "What a good boy am I!"

Little Old Man
A little old man came riding by.
Said I, "Old man, your horse will die."
Said he, "If he dies, I'll tan his skin.
    And if he lives, I'll ride him again."

The Little Plant
Kate L. Brown

In the heart of a seed,
Buried down so deep,
A little plant
Lay fast asleep.

"Awake," said the sun,
"Come up through the earth,"
"Awake," said the rain,
"We are giving you birth."

The little plant heard
With a happy sigh,
And pointed its petals
Up to the sky.

Little Puppy Dog
My father owns the butcher shop
My mother cuts the meat,
And I'm the little puppy dog
That runs down the street.

Little Tommy Tucker
Little Tommy Tucker
	Sings for his supper.
What shall we give him?
	White bread and butter.
How shall he cut it
	Without a knife?
How shall he be married
	Without a wife?

Lobby Loo
Here we go lobby loo,
Here we go lobby light.
Here we go lobby loo
All on a Saturday night.

Put your right hand in,
Put your right hand out.
Shake it a little, a little,
And turn yourself about.

Lock and Key
"I am a gold lock."
"I am a gold key."
"I am a silver lock."
"I am a silver key."
"I am a brass lock."
"I am a brass key."
"I am a lead lock."
"I am a lead key."
"I am a don lock."
"I am a don key."

Mary's Lamb
Sara Josepha Hale

Mary had a little lamb,
Its fleece was white as snow,
And everywhere that Mary went
The lamb was sure to go.
It followed her to school one day—
That was against the rule,
It made the children laugh and play
To see a lamb at school.

Merrily We Roll Along
Mer-ri-ly we roll a-long, roll a-long, roll a-long,
Mer-ri-ly we roll a-long, o-ver the deep blue sea.

Mix a Pancake
Christina Rossetti

Mix a pancake,
Stir a pancake,
	Pop it in the pan;
Fry a pancake,
Toss the pancake—
	Catch it if you can.

The Mocking Bird
Hush, little baby, don't say a word,
Papa's going to buy you a mocking bird.

If that mocking bird won't sing,
Papa's going to buy you a diamond ring.
If the diamond ring turns to brass,
Papa's going to buy you a looking-glass.
If the looking-glass gets broke,
Papa's going to buy you a billy goat.
If that billy goat runs away,
Papa's going to buy you another today.

The Mulberry Bush
Here we go round the mulberry bush,
	The mulberry bush,
	The mulberry bush,
Here we go round the mulberry bush,
On a cold and frosty morning.

This is the way we clap our hands,
	Clap our hands,
	Clap our hands,
This is the way we clap our hands,
On a cold and frosty morning.

My Son John
Deedle, deedle, dumpling, my son John,
Went to bed with his stockings on;
One shoe off, and one shoe on,
Deedle, deedle, dumpling, my son John.

The North Wind Doth Blow
The north wind doth blow,
And we shall have snow,
And what will poor Robin do then?
	Poor thing!
He'll sit in a barn,
And keep himself warm,
And hide his head under his wing.
	Poor thing!

Oh Where, Oh Where Has My Little Dog Gone?
Oh where, oh where has my little dog gone?
	Oh where, oh where can he be?
With his ears cut short and his tail cut long
	Oh where, oh where is he?

Old Chairs to Mend

If I'd as much money as I could spend,
I never would cry old chairs to mend;
Old chairs to mend, old chairs to mend;
I never would cry old chairs to mend.

If I'd as much money as I could tell,
I never would cry old clothes to sell;
Old clothes to sell, old clothes to sell;
I never would cry old clothes to sell.

Old King Cole

Old King Cole
Was a merry old soul,
And a merry old soul was he.
He called for his pipe,
And he called for his bowl,
And he called for his fiddlers three.

Old MacDonald

Old MacDonald had a farm, E-I-E-I-O.
And on this farm he had some sheep, E-I-E-I-O.
With a baa-baa here and a baa-baa there,
Here a baa, there a baa, ev-ry-where a baa baa,
Old MacDonald had a farm, E-I-E-I-O.

The Old Man of Peru

There was an old man of Peru,
Who dreamt he was eating his shoe.
He woke in the night
In a terrible fright,
And found it was perfectly true.

Old Woman, Old Woman

There was an old woman tossed in a basket,
Seventeen times as high as the moon;
But where she was going no one could tell,
For under her arm she carried a broom.
"Old woman, old woman, old woman, " said I,
"Where, oh where, oh where so high?"
"To sweep the cobwebs from the sky;
And I'll be with you by and by."

One for the Money

One for the money,
Two for the show,
Three to make ready,
And four to go.

One, Two, Three, Four, Five

One, two, three, four, five
Once I caught a fish alive,
Six, seven, eight, nine, ten,
Then I let it go again.
Why did you let it go?
Because it bit my finger so.
Which finger did it bite?
The little finger on the right.

Our Van

We have a van,
Our van is very, very nice.
But our van squeaks,
Do you think our van has mice?

Out

Out goes the rat,
Out goes the cat,
Out goes the lady
With the big green hat.
Y, O, U spells you;
O, U, T spells out!

Owl

A wise old owl lived in an oak,
The more he heard, the less he spoke.
The less he spoke, the more he heard.
Why aren't we all like that wise old bird?

Pat-a-Cake

Pat-a-cake, pat-a-cake, baker's man,
Bake me a cake just as fast as you can.
Pat it and stick it, and mark it with a B
Put it in the oven for baby and me.

Pease Porridge

Pease porridge hot,
Pease porridge cold,
Pease porridge in the pot nine days old.

Polly, Put the Kettle On

Polly, put the kettle on,
Polly, put the kettle on,
Polly, put the kettle on,
And let's drink tea.

Pussy-cat, Pussy-cat

Pussy-cat, pussy-cat, where have you been?
I've been to London to visit the Queen!
Pussy-cat, pussy-cat, what did you there?
I frightened a little mouse under her chair.

Rain

Rain on the green grass,
And rain on the tree,
Rain on the house-top,
But not on me.

Rain, Rain, Go Away

Rain, rain, go away,
Come again another day;
Little Raymond wants to play

Red Sky

Red sky at night,
Sailor's delight;
Red sky in the morning,
Sailor's warning.

Roll Over

Ten men in the bed, and the lit-tle one said,
"Roll o-ver! Roll o-ver!"
They all rolled o-ver
And one fell out.

Nine men in the bed, and the lit-tle one said,
"Roll o-ver! Roll o-ver!"
They all rolled o-ver
And one fell out.

[Continue until there is just one left.]

One man in the bed, and the lit-tle one said,
"Alone at last!"

Row the Boat

Row, row, row your boat
Gently down the stream,
Merrily, merrily, merrily, merrily,
Life is but a dream.

Rub-a-Dub-Dub

Rub-a-dub-dub,
Three men in a tub,
And who do you think they be?
The butcher, the baker,
The candlestick maker.
Rub-a-dub-dub all three.

A Sailor Went to Sea

A sailor went to sea
To see what he could see,
And all that he could see,
Was the sea, sea, sea.

Sing, Sing

Sing, sing,
    What shall I sing?
The cat's run away
    With the pudding string!
Do, do,
    What shall I do?
The cat's run away with the pudding, too.

She'll Be Comin' 'Round the Mountain

She'll be com-in' 'round the moun-tain when she
    comes,
She'll be com-in' 'round the moun-tain when she
    comes,
She'll be com-in' 'round the moun-tain,
She'll be com-in' 'round the moun-tain,
She'll be com-in' 'round the moun-tain when she
    comes.

She'll be driv-in' six white hor-ses when she comes,
She'll be driv-in' six white hor-ses when she comes,
She'll be driv-in' six white hor-ses,
She'll be driv-in' six white hor-ses,
She'll be driv-in' six white hor-ses when she comes.

Oh, we'll all go out to meet her when she comes,
Yes, we'll all go out to meet her when she comes,
Oh, we'll all go out to meet her,
Yes, we'll all go out to meet her,
We will all go out to meet her when she comes.

Simple Simon

Simple Simon met a pieman
    Going to the fair.
Says Simple Simon to the pieman,
    "Let me taste your ware."
Says the pieman to Simple Simon,
    "Show me first your penny."
Says Simple Simon to the pieman,
    "Indeed I have not any."

Skip to My Lou

Lost my part-ner, what 'll I do?
Lost my part-ner, what 'll I do?
Lost my part-ner, what 'll I do?
Skip to my Lou, my dar-ling.

Star Light, Star Bright

Star light, star bright,
First star I see tonight,
I wish I may, I wish I might
Have the wish I wish tonight.

A Sunshiny Shower

A sunshiny shower
Won't last half an hour.

Swim, Swan, Swim
Swan swam over the sea,
⠀⠀⠀Swim, swan, swim!
Swan swam back again,
⠀⠀⠀Well swum, swan!

Swing, Swing
William Allingham

⠀⠀⠀Swing, swing,
⠀⠀⠀Sing, sing,
Here! my throne and I am a king!
⠀⠀⠀Swing, sing,
⠀⠀⠀Swing, sing,
Farewell, earth, for I'm on the wing.

⠀⠀⠀Low, high,
⠀⠀⠀Here I fly,
Like a bird through sunny sky!
⠀⠀⠀Free, free,
⠀⠀⠀Over the lea,
Over the mountain, over the sea!

⠀⠀⠀Soon, soon,
⠀⠀⠀Afternoon,
Over the sunset, over the moon!
⠀⠀⠀Far, far,
⠀⠀⠀Over all bar,
Sweeping on from star to star!

⠀⠀⠀No, no,
⠀⠀⠀Low, low.
Sweeping daisies with my toe!
⠀⠀⠀Slow, slow,
⠀⠀⠀To and fro,
Slow—
slow—
slow—
slow!

Take Me out to the Ball Game
Take me out to the ball game,
Take me out to the crowd,
Buy me some peanuts and Crack-er Jacks,
I don't care if I ev-er get back,
And it's root, root, root for the home team,
If they don't win, it's a shame,
For it's one, two, three strikes, "You're out!"
At the old ball game.

Teddy Bear, Teddy Bear
Teddy Bear, Teddy Bear, turn around,
Teddy Bear, Teddy Bear, touch the ground.

Teddy Bear, Teddy Bear, read the news,
Teddy Bear, Teddy Bear, shine your shoes.

There Was a Crooked Man
There was a crooked man,
Who walked a crooked mile,
He found a crooked sixpence
Against a crooked stile;
He bought a crooked cat,
Which caught a crooked mouse.
And they all lived together
In a little crooked house.

The Little Turtle
Vachel Lindsey

There was a little turtle.
He lived in a box.
He swam in a puddle.
He climbed on the rocks

He snapped at a mosquito.
He snapped at a flea.
He snapped at a minnow.
And he snapped at me.

There Was an Old Woman
There was an old woman
Who lived under a hill.
And if she's not gone
She lives there still.

Two Little Blackbirds
Two little blackbirds
Sat upon a hill,
One named Jack,
The other named Jill;
Fly away, Jack,
Fly away, Jill,
Come again, Jack,
Come again, Jill.
Two little blackbirds
Sitting on a hill.

This Is the Way We Go to School
This is the way we go to school.
Go to school, go to school.
This is the way we go to school,
On a cold and frosty morning.

Three Blind Mice
Three blind mice, three blind mice,
See how they run, see how they run.
They all ran after the farmer's wife,
Who cut off their tails with the carving knife.
Did you ever see such a sight in your life,
As three blind mice?

Three Little Bugs
Three little bugs in a basket,
Hardly room for two.
One like Lee, one like Linda,
And one that looks like you.

The Three Little Kittens
Eliza Lee Follen

Three little kittens
Lost their mittens
And they began to cry,
"Oh mother dear,
We sadly fear
Our mittens we have lost."

"Lost your mittens!
You naughty kittens!
Then you shall have no pie!"
"Mee-ow, mee-ow, mee-ow."
"Then, you shall have no pie."

The three little kittens
They found their mittens
And they began to cry,
"Oh mother dear,
See here, see here,
Our mittens we have found."

"Found your mittens,
You good little kittens?
Then you shall have some pie.
Mee-ow, mee-ow,
Then you shall have some pie."

A Tisket, A Tasket
A tis-ket, a tas-ket, a green and yel-low bas-ket,
I wrote a let-ter to my love,
And on the way, I lost it,
I lost it, I lost it,
I lost my yellow basket.

A little laddie picked it up and put it in his pock-et.

Tom, Tom, the Piper's Son
Tom he was a piper's son,
He learned to play when he was young;
But the only tune that he could play was,
"Over the hills and far away."

Now Tom with his pipe made such a noise,
That he pleased all the the girls and boys;
And they stopped to hear him play,
"Over the hills and far away."

Turn to the East
Turn to the east,
And turn to the west,
And turn to the one that you love best.

Twinkle, Twinkle, Little Bat
Lewis Carroll

Twinkle, twinkle, little bat!
How I wonder what you're at!
Up above the world you fly,
Like a tea-tray in the sky.
Twinkle, twinkle—

Twinkle, Twinkle, Little Star
Twinkle, twinkle, little star,
How I wonder what you are!
Up above the world so high,
Like a diamond in the sky.

Two Cats of Kilkenny
There were once two cats of Kilkenny.
Each thought there was one cat too many.
So they fought and they fit,
And they scratched and they bit,
Until, except for their nails,
And the tips of their tails,
Instead of two cats, there weren't any.

Up, Dear Children
Come, my dear children,
Up is the sun,
Birds are all singing,
And morn has begun.
Up from the bed, Miss
Out on the lea;
The horses are waiting
For you and for me!

Way Down South Where Bananas Grow
Way down South where bananas grow,
A grasshopper stepped on an elephant's toe.
The elephant said, with tears in his eyes,
"Pick on somebody your own size!"

Wee Willie Winkie
Wee Willie Winkie runs through the town,
Upstairs and downstairs in his nightgown,
Rapping at the window, crying through the lock,
Are the children all in bed, for now it's eight o'clock?

What Animals Say
Bow-wow, says the dog,
Mew, mew, says the cat,
Grunt, grunt, goes the hog,
And squeak goes the rat.

Tu-whoo, says the owl,
Caw, caw, says the crow,
Quack, quack, says the duck,
What cuckoos say you know.

What Are Little Boys Made of?
What are little boys made of?
    Frogs and snails
    And puppy dogs' tails.
That's what little boys are made of.

What are little girls made of?
    Sugar and spice
    And all things nice.
That's what little girls are made of.

What Birds Say
Some birds say, "Cuckoo! Cuckoo!"
Some birds say, "Caw! Caw!"
What do you say?

Wheels on the Bus
The wheels on the bus
Go round and round,
Round and round, round and round.
The wheels on the bus
Go round and round,
All over town.

Whistle, Daughter
Whistle, daughter, whistle; whistle, daughter dear.
I cannot whistle, mommy; I cannot whistle clear.
Whistle, daughter, whistle; whistle for a pound.
I cannot whistle, mommy; I cannot make a sound.

Windy Nights
Robert Louis Stevenson

Whenever the moon and stars are set,
    Whenever the wind is high,
All night long in the dark and wet,
    A man goes riding by.
Late in the night when the fires are out,
Why does he gallop and gallop about?

Whenever the trees are crying aloud,
    And ships are tossed at sea,
By, on the highway, low and loud,
    By at the gallop goes he.
By at the gallop he goes, and then,
By he comes back at the gallop again.

Wishes
Said the first little chicken
With a queer little squirm,
"I wish I could find a fat little worm."

Said the second little chicken
With an odd little shrug,
"I wish I could find a fat little slug."

Said the third little chicken
With a sharp little squeal,
"I wish I could find
Some nice yellow meal."

"Now see here." said their mother
From the green garden patch.
"If you want any breakfast,
Just come here and SCRATCH!"

Woodchuck
How much wood
Would a woodchuck chuck
If a woodchuck could chuck wood?

The Zigzag Boy and Girl
I know a little zigzag boy
Who goes this way and that.
He never knows just where he put
His coat or shoes or hat.

I know a little zigzag girl
Who flutters here and there.
She never knows just where to find
Her brush to fix her hair.

If you are not a zigzag child
You'll have no cause to say,
That you forgot, for you will know
Where things are put away.

►►►Appendix B

FOLD-AND-READ BOOKS

Tear the page from the book along the perforated line. The perforated page will be narrower than a sheet of paper, therefore, when photocopying, center it side to side in the 8-1/2 by 11 page area.

For six-page books:

1. Fold the page in half vertically so that pages 4, 5, 6, and 1 are facing you.
2. Fold in half once more so that pages 1 and 6 are facing you.
3. Fold a third time so that only page 1 is facing you.

For four-page books:

1. Fold the page in half vertically so that pages 4 and 1 are facing you.
2. Fold again so that only page 1 is facing you.

1

I see a bear.

2

I see a seal.

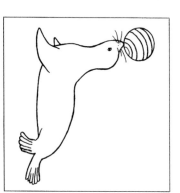

6

I see a monkey.

5

I see a fish.

4

I see a rabbit.

3

I see a goat.

Consonants: *c* = /k/, *d, h, l, t*

1

I see a camel.

6

I see a tiger.

5

I see a lion.

I see a cat.

2

4

I see a horse.

I see a deer.

3

1

I like dogs.

6

I like books.

5

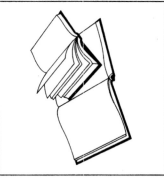

I like wagons.

4

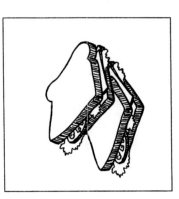

I like sandwiches.

3

I like carrots.

2

I like bikes.

I see a zebra.

1

I see a penguin.

6

I see a giraffe.

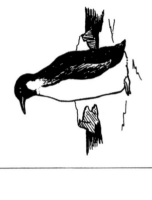

5

I see a pig.

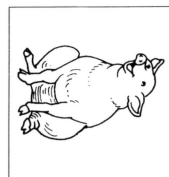

2

I see a kangaroo.

3

I see a wolf.

4

1

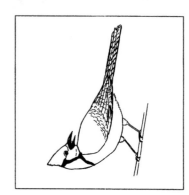

I am a bird.

6

I am a bear.

5

I am a camel.

4

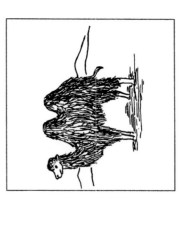

I am a cat.

3

I am a fish.

I am a horse.

2

1

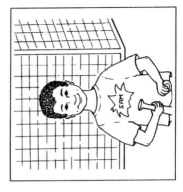

I am Sam.

6

I am 8.

5

I am a girl.

4

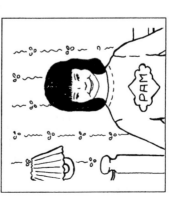

I am Pam.

I am a boy.

2

I am 7.

3

1

The rat ran.

2

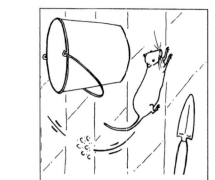

The cat ran.

3

The cat ran after the rat.

4

The dog ran.

5

The dog ran after the cat that ran after the rat.

6

The rat, the cat, and the dog ran.

1

What is red?
A wagon can be red.

6

What is red?
A rose can be red.

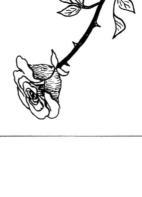

5

What is red?
Tomatoes are red.

4

What is red?
A stop sign is red.

2

What is red?
A ball can be red.

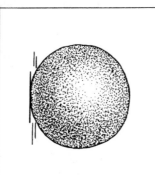

3

What is red? A fire
truck can be red.

1

Is this a rat?

2

This is not a rat.

3

This is a bat.

4

Is this a rat?

5

That is a rat. This is a kangaroo rat.

6

A kangaroo rat can hop like a kangaroo.

Pigs are big. But pigs have little legs.

1

Pigs can dig with their little legs.

2

Pigs can run. But can pigs swim?

3

Pigs can swim.

4

Pigs paddle and kick with their legs.

5

Pigs can swim fast.

6

1

This bird is little. It is a hummingbird.

6

And it drinks from flowers.

5

With its big bill, it can get bugs.

2

This bird is the bee hummingbird.

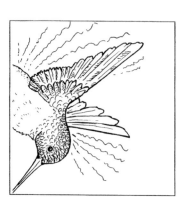

4

This hummingbird has a long bill.

3

A hummingbird can make its wings go fast.

Bugs can be little.
One bug is as little
as this spot.

1

Bugs can be big.
This bug is as big
as you hand.

2

This bug has big
wings. With its big
wings, it can fly.

3

This bug is a
walking stick. It
looks like a stick.

4

The walking stick
has six legs. Can
you see them?

5

Some walking sticks
have wings and
they can fly.

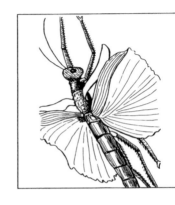

6

Can you see the dot?

1

The dot is red. And it has black spots.

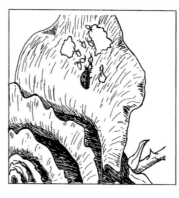

2

The dot is a lady bug. Some lady bugs are yellow.

3

Do not step on lady bugs.

4

Lady bugs are good bugs.

5

Lady bugs eat bad bugs.

6

What is fun?

1

What do you think
is fun?

6

What is fun?
Patting a cat is fun.

5

What is fun?
Running is fun.

2

What is fun?
Hitting a ball is fun.

4

What is fun?
Swimming is fun.

3

Baby elephants must learn how to use their trunks.

1

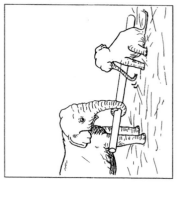

A baby elephant's mother shows it how to use its trunk.

6

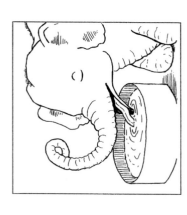

To get water, a baby elephant drinks with its mouth.

5

A baby elephant's trunk gets in its way.

2

Baby elephants step on their trunks.

3

A baby elephant can not drink with its trunk.

4

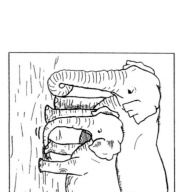

1

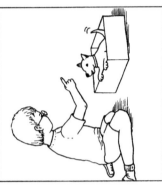

"Get on the bus," says Gus.

6

"Don't fuss," Bob tells his puppy.

5

Bob is taking the puppy to school for show and tell.

2

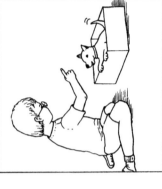

Gus runs the bus that takes us to school.

3

Bob gets on the bus. Bob has a puppy.

4

The puppy is in a box.

Rain, Rain, Go Away

Rain, rain, go away,
Come again another day;
Little Raymond wants to play.

For if you ever ever ever ever ever,
For if you ever ever ever ever ever,
    touch its tail,
You will never never never never never,
You will never never never never never
    meet another whale.

Bees

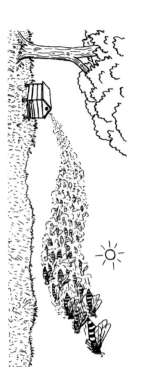

If bees stay at home,
Rain will soon come.
If they fly away,
Fine will be the day.

If You Ever

If you ever ever ever ever ever,
If you ever ever ever ever meet a whale,
You must never never never never never,
You must never never never never never
    touch its tail.

An ostrich is the biggest bird of all. It lays big eggs.

1

An ostrich can lay ten eggs. It lays its eggs in a big nest.

2

An ostrich egg is big. It is almost as big as a soccer ball.

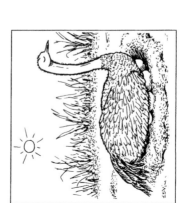

3

The ostrich hen sits on the eggs during the day.

4

The father ostrich sits on the eggs at night.

5

The eggs hatch in five or six weeks. The babies are small.

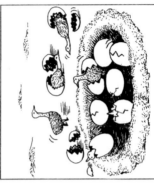

6

Ice Cream

I scream, you scream,
We all scream for ice cream.

1

Little Bo-Peep

Little Bo-Peep has lost her sheep,
And can't tell where to find them;
Leave them alone, and they'll come home
Wagging their tails behind them.

2

Clouds

White sheep, white sheep,
On a blue hill,
When the wind stops
You all stand still
When the wind blows
You walk away slow.
White sheep, white sheep,
Where do you go?

4

Long e̅: -e, -e, -ea, -eam, -eep

Rain

Rain on the green grass,
And the rain on the tree,
Rain on the house-top,
But not on me.

3

The bear cat has long hair and a long tail.

1

This bear cat lives in a tree.

2

The bear cat has a long tail. It can swing from a tree.

3

The bear cat sleeps during day. It comes out at night.

4

Bear cats eat fruit, bugs, and small animals.

5

Bear cats dive into the water. They catch fish and eat them.

6

Can a car be a plane?
This car can.
This car can fly.

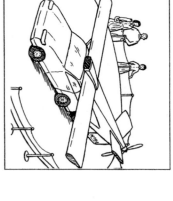
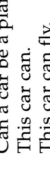

1

This car has wings
and a tail that fit
onto the car.

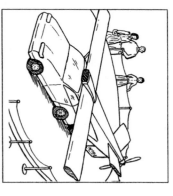

2

When you want to
fly, put the wings
and tail on.

3

When you want to
ride, take the wings
and tail off.

4

The wings fold up.
The wings and tail
have a wheel.

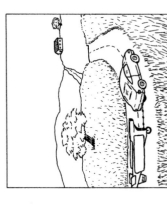

5

Now the car can
ride on streets and
roads.

6

1

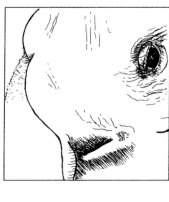

Which animal has
the biggest nose?

6

An elephant can
even give itself a
bath with its trunk.

5

An elephant's trunk
is like a hose. It gets
a drink with its trunk.

4

An elephant's trunk
is like a hand. It can
pick up things.

3

An elephant smells
with its trunk.

2

The elephant does.
The elephant's trunk
is its nose.

If You're Happy and You Know It

If you're hap-py and you know it,
Clap your hands.
If you're hap-py and you know it,
Clap your hands.
If you're hap-py and you know it,
And you really want to show it,
If you're hap-py and you know it,
Clap your hands.

Row the Boat

Row, row, row your boat
Gently down the stream,
Merrily, merrily, merrily, merrily,
Life is but a dream.

One For the Money

One for the money,
Two for the show.
Three to make ready,
And four to go.

Jumping Joan

Here am I,
Little Jumping Joan;
When nobody's with me
I'm all alone.

Long -o-, -oa-, -ow-